ECONOMIC JUSTICE

ECONOMIC JUSTICE: PRIVATE RIGHTS AND PUBLIC RESPONSIBILITIES

An AMINTAPHIL Volume

Edited by

Kenneth Kipnis
University of Hawaii at Manoa

and

Diana T. Meyers
Cornell University

ROWMAN & ALLANHELD
PUBLISHERS

ROWMAN & ALLANHELD

Published in the United States of America in 1985
by Rowman & Allanheld, Publishers
(a division of Littlefield, Adams & Company)
81 Adams Drive, Totowa, New Jersey 07512

Copyright © 1985 by Rowman & Allanheld

Library of Congress Cataloging in Publication Data

Main entry under title:

Economic justice.

   Bibliography: p. 244
   Includes index.
   1. Distributive justice. I. Kipnis, Kenneth.
II. Meyers, Diana T.
HB523.E36   1985   330.1   84-17917
ISBN 0-8476-7384-7
ISBN 0-8476-7385-5 (pbk.)

85 86 87 / 10 9 8 7 6 5 4 3 2 1
Printed in the United States of America

Table of Contents

Part III: Human Needs and the Humane Society

Preface

In 1962 a book appeared entitled *Social Justice.* Edited by Richard B. Brandt, it was an anthology of original articles by Kenneth E. Boulding, Paul A. Freund, William Frankena, Alan Gewirth, and Gregory Vlastos. Taken together, the five essays comprise an historical "snapshot" of the way some of the best scholars of that day understood what justice is in society, in economic systems, and so on. Brandt remarks in his Preface to that volume that, compared to the shower of materials that had been produced on other subjects, philosophy in those decades had produced only "scattered drops" on the topic of justice. Looking back on that collection more than twenty years later, one is struck by the concern for equality that the five authors shared; a concern that had been evident a few years earlier in *Brown* v. *Board of Education* and that was to inform the civil rights struggles that would erupt a few years afterwards.

In the years since, we have seen the War on Poverty, the Great Society, Medicare, affirmative action, and the era of Reaganomics. And in the same period two important and quite different philosophical works appeared that together have recast some of the same problems that were earlier treated in *Social Justice* and which have helped to generate a steady torrent of fresh writings on the subject. The first of these two works was John Rawls's *A Theory of Justice*, published in 1971. In that work Rawls viewed the "basic structure" of society—its political constitution and principal economic and social arrangements—as a human artifact that could be crafted well or badly. His project was to set out and justify a particular set of principles for the assessment of that basic structure. The principles were justified by showing how they could be unanimously agreed to by free and rational persons. Rawls's favored principles required equality in the assignment of basic rights and opportunities but permitted inequality if and only if it could be expected to result in compensating benefits for everyone, particularly the least advantaged. On Rawls's view the question of justice has chiefly to do with how society's institutions should distribute the fruits of social cooperation.

The second work was Robert Nozick's *Anarchy, State, and Utopia*, published in 1974. Nozick began his analysis with the idea that the rights of individuals strictly limit what the state and its officials may do. Of particular importance are property rights—our entitlement to the things we own. Taking issue with Rawls's conception of distributive justice, Nozick stresses that there are no unowned fruits of social cooperation for society to distribute. Rather, people find, make, and freely exchange things and are thus entitled to them. As a result, social *re*distribution of goods violates the rights of those who own the goods that society wishes to redistribute. On Nozick's view, justice has chiefly to do with the initial acquisition of entitlements and with their consensual transfer to others. While it may benefit the poor to transfer to them the holdings of the well-off, Nozick protests that this violates the rights of the well-off.

The essays in *Economic Justice: Private Rights and Public Responsibilities* have been written largely within the intellectual milieu created by Rawls and Nozick. In a variety of ways the papers scrutinize and engage the tensions and relationships between the rights accorded to individuals and the public purposes and responsibilities properly given over to civil government. Most of the papers that follow were among the more than sixty presented at the Ninth Plenary Conference of the American Section of the International Association for Philosophy of Law and Social Philosophy (AMINTAPHIL), held in Gainesville at the University of Florida in January of 1983. But this volume is not the proceedings of that conference. It has not been the editors' purpose to capture the orientation and tone of that particular gathering. Rather, we have tried to convey something of the liveliness of the current debate as well as a sense of the diversity of the topics that now come under the heading of justice. We have tried to create for the present a snapshot comparable to the one Brandt took more than twenty years ago.

One of the essays that follow, the introductory piece entitled "Economic Justice: Concepts and Criteria," was prepared especially for this volume by Alan Gewirth whose "Political Justice" graced the pages of Brandt's collection. The editors are deeply grateful for his contribution to this volume. Gratitude is also owed to Virginia Held, President of AMINTAPHIL, and to Rex Martin, its Executive Director, for the encouragement and support that they gave to us throughout the process of editing this anthology. The editors thank as well the University of Hawaii Foundation and Rex Wade, Dean of the Faculty of Arts and Humanities of the University of Hawaii, for help at crucial stages of the editorial process, and Floris Sakamoto, Dale Fukumoto, Renee Kojima, Nadine Maeda, and Gail Dwight who provided important assistance in the preparation of the manuscript.

Kenneth Kipnis
Diana T. Meyers

Part I
Reason, Unreason, And Economic Justice

Whatever social institutions and policies justice may dictate in diverse historical settings, justice always requires that similar cases be treated similarly. Institutions and policies must be administered consistently and must be guided by principles that license only the invocation of morally relevant distinctions. In other words, just principles require the distribution of social goods according to criteria that would be accepted by a knowledgeable and impartial judge—either an ideal observer who is equally sympathetic to everyone's interests or a participant who takes care not to be swayed by self-interest—and just institutions and policies may not deviate from these standards. A society that meets these standards gives to all its citizens that which is due them. But while few would question the importance of the claim to justice and the abstract characterization of it presented above, humankind has for centuries hotly disputed precisely what this entitlement consists of. The controversy shows no signs of abating.

At least six conceptions of personal desert can be extracted from recent discussions of justice:

1. To each according to his or her virtue
2. To each according to his or her effort
3. To each according to his or her contribution
4. To each according to his or her agreements with others
5. To each according to his or her needs
6. To each according to his or her society's rules

None of these is altogether lacking in appeal.

The criterion of virtue, though somewhat impractical because of the difficulty of gauging it, is nevertheless attractive because it focuses on the undeniable and arguably unparalleled value of human goodness. Likewise, the criterion of effort takes into account a person's good intentions, a part of human goodness to be sure. But this narrower criterion rewards only the willingness to undertake the burdens of cooperative activity, ignoring other, equally worthy virtues. While the criterion of contribution also adverts to the importance of acknowledging social responsibility, this conception of desert stipulates that good intentions must result in valuable achievements. Measurable output is to be rewarded: unproductive virtue and futile effort are negligible. But how is contribution to be measured?

The criterion of agreements-made-with-others finesses this problem by relying on the market for a practical scale of desert. Contributions are worth whatever buyers are willing to give sellers for them. Contrasting sharply with the four earlier proposals, the criterion of need dispenses with any indicator of voluntarily attained worthiness and regards each person's needs as having an equal claim to our attention. Though we may have different needs and thus may deserve different allotments geared to those needs, different accomplishments in the realm of virtue and social contribution do not affect what people deserve. Finally, though the criterion of social rules does not preclude conventions favoring desired qualities or achievements, its primary concern is to prevent the disappointment of expectations conceived on the basis of established social practices. This last criterion resembles the criterion of need inasmuch as it does not itself certify any method of excelling.

The six conceptions of personal desert sketched here fall into two main categories. On the one hand, the criteria of virtue, effort, contribution, and agreements each range recipients differentially along a select dimension. They thereby establish channels for personal gain, and our life prospects are improved or downgraded depending on how successfully we avail ourselves of these opportunities. On the other hand, the criteria of need and social rules each stress that persons are similar in a certain way: We all have needs that may go unsatisfied, and we all can be seriously harmed by changes in social conventions. The first four conceptions of personal desert, then, are liberty-oriented ones, and the last two are equality-oriented. However, few theories of justice are pure expressions of just one of these conceptions. Indeed, the most plausible accounts enhance their appeal by incorporating a number of these maxims. Thus theories of justice typically balance and blend liberty and equality.

But how is one to combine these traditionally opposed desiderata in a single coherent theory of economic justice? In designing and defending an account of why persons are entitled to economic goods (employment opportunities, wealth, income, decision-making authority, and the like), four overarching perspectives and four corresponding modes of argument predominate. A theory of economic justice may start from a list of rights and ask what economic arrangements are necessary to respect them. It may start from an array of compelling needs or desires and ask what economic arrangements would maximize their satisfaction. It may start from an analysis of tyranny and ask what economic arrangements can best prevent it. Or it can start from a conception of a social ideal—possibly an ordered selection of the preceding considerations—and ask what economic arrangements would facilitate its achievement. In specifying the maxims of personal desert to be embodied in its preferred economic structure, a theory of economic justice defines and commends certain forms of liberty and equality.

Yet implementation of sound maxims may not suffice to bring about economic justice, for past injustices or present contextual conditions may distort the impact of the approved principles. To contend with these problems, theories of economic justice must supplement principles of personal desert with principles of rectification and principles of background justice. These supplementary principles may be either principles of individual justice, providing remedies in individual cases, or principles of social justice, addressing problems afflicting whole social classes and even whole societies. To illustrate, an individual rectificatory principle can provide for compensation when someone is injured because another has failed to discharge contractual obligations; a social rectificatory principle can permit rebellion against an oppressive economic class; an individual background principle can forbid gender discrimination in hiring; and a social background principle can require subsidies to schools in economically disadvantaged neighborhoods. Not only do these additional principles further detail and differentiate theories of economic justice, but also they mandate divergent positions regarding social change. Depending on whether and how a society satisfies requisite background conditions and whether and how past injustices stand in need of correction, a theory of economic justice may advocate revolution, reform, stasis, or reversal.

Economic justice requires that equals be treated equally, that a set of principles be observed, and that injustice be corrected. Yet there is widespread disagreement about which maxims to adopt and, consequently, there is little accord about what conditions and acts are unjust and how acknowledged injustices should be remedied. These are critical substantive issues, and the essays in Parts II and III are devoted to various specialized aspects of these problems. Part I focuses mainly on a preliminary metatheoretical question: the role of reason in economic justice.

Since Plato first took up the problem of justice in the *Republic*, philosophers as diverse as Thomas Hobbes and John Stuart Mill have assumed that reason could discern the nature of justice and that implementation should follow. However, this view of the matter has not gone unchallenged. In the *Republic* itself Thrasymachus defines justice as the interest of the stronger, and in the latter half of the nineteenth century Karl Marx launched his scathing attack on the class interests and class exploitation concealed by false consciousness and ideology. In the four essays that follow, Alan Gewirth argues for the rational tractability of the problem of economic justice; Virginia Held maintains that reason alone cannot overcome self-interest in discussions of justice; and Timo Airaksinen describes how poverty can spawn irrationality in matters of economic justice; and June Axinn analyzes the obstacles to establishing a rational and practical criterion for poverty.

In "Economic Justice: Concepts and Criteria," Alan Gewirth defends the claim that "there are certain criteria [of economic justice] whose acceptance is rationally obligatory for all agents because they derive from the generic features of purposive action." He begins his inquiry by mapping out several conceptual distinctions, separating the economics of justice from the justice of economics, formal justice from substantive justice, and antecedentialist criteria of justice from consequentialist ones. For Gewirth, a central problem for moral and political philosophy is how to decide among these assorted conceptions of justice. Gewirth proposes his "dialectically necessary method" as a means of resolving these controversies. This form of argumentation uses two generic features of action—voluntariness and purposiveness—to show that each agent must grant that all agents have rights to freedom and well-being. Though Gewirth insists that the latter right entails that rendering positive aid is sometimes mandatory, he stresses that the primary point of this aid is to enable recipients to achieve self-sufficient agency and that aid of this sort is compatible with freedom.

Virginia Held's essay, "Reason and Economic Justice," exhibits less optimism in regard to our ability to establish through reason a universal theory of economic justice. In Held's view, egoism is a logically consistent code of conduct, even though it authorizes persons to pursue their own self-interest and to disregard others' needs and desires. Moreover, Held doubts that there are generic features of action that all agents are rationally bound to accept. On the contrary, she urges that a perceived advantage may color one's analysis of agency without necessitating a commitment to self-contradictory judgments. As an alternative to Gewirth's reliance on rationality and reason, Held suggests that we appeal instead to the notions of cooperation and trust, that we consider the conditions under which social cooperation can flourish and social trust is not misplaced.

Timo Airaksinen, in "Hegel on Poverty and Violence," begins his examination of the problem of reason and economic justice with Hegel's insights into the nature of poverty. Setting aside the objective and statistical aspects of poverty, Hegel is concerned with how and why the poor (not the "temporarily unsuccessful") are transformed into "a rabble of paupers," an amoral segment of the social system characterized by its exclusion from ordinary social life. For Hegel, morality is socially constituted. Thus those without social roles—the rabble—lack "clear-cut internalized norms and shared values." It is this distinctive alienation that is Hegel's and Airaksinen's central focus. Following Hegel's treatment of the "systematic social causes" of poverty, Airaksinen draws the conclusion that poverty "cannot be prevented because some successful agents profit from it; yet this is morally wrong." Airaksinen notes that, because Hegel's rabble have no hope for a life in civil society, they may rebel against the state. And because the poor regard themselves as victims of "structural violence," their rebellion would have a moral point. Yet Airaksinen warns that the rabble may rebel against affluent victims who are not responsible for structural violence against the poor. But whether the rabble are correct in seeing themselves as the victims of structural violence may make no difference: if the poor feel that the wealthy have failed utterly to consider their well-being, they may pay the rich back in their own coin.

Taking off from Airaksinen's observations, June Axinn's piece, "Explorations of the Definition of Poverty," reminds us that defining poverty is not just a concern for the theorist. In governmental welfare programs since the mid-1960s, the "poverty line" has figured in assessments of the national economic health as well as in official threshold conditions for entry into various types of assistance programs. Reviewing the history of the income level separating those who are officially poor from those who are not, Axinn considers the problems that have been raised in calculating and applying the figure. Are those who live in more expensive areas entitled to a higher "poverty line," or should they be expected to move to cheaper locations? How are "in-kind" transfers (school lunches, medicare and other benefits) to be figured into assessments of income? How should "transitional poverty" (students, female heads of families) be taken into account? Axinn suggests that the object of the exercise should be the measurement of human well-being on a life-cycle basis.

Diana T. Meyers

1
Economic Justice: Concepts and Criteria

Alan Gewirth
Department of Philosophy
University of Chicago

Economic justice is one of the most controversial subjects in the whole range of moral philosophy. As a first approximation, justice may be characterized as being concerned with who should get what, and why. In economic justice the 'what' in question consists in economic goods, and controversy rages especially over the 'why'—the criteria for determining who should get these goods. The controversy is particularly intense because of the great importance of economic goods for human life and well-being and because the distribution of these goods is a crucial mark of the moral status and basic values of any society.

In an obvious way, the disputes over economic justice are normative. But underlying them are further, more conceptual issues: issues about the nature of the economic and of justice, about the very relevance of moral criteria to economic arrangements, about the place of justice among these criteria, and about the methods or principles for determining which of these criteria should apply, and in what order.

In this essay I wish to examine some of the central conceptual and criterial considerations that underlie the issues of economic justice.

1. Two Concepts of the Economic

The concept of the economic has developed in a way parallel to the concept of the political. The traditional meaning of the 'political' has been *institutional*: politics has been viewed as being concerned with the societal institutions of the state, government, and law. But, especially in recent years, the 'political' has also taken on a more general *behavioral* sense. According to this, the political is to be found not only in formal governmental and legal institutions, but in all interpersonal interactions where one person or group exercises or seeks to exercise power, influence, authority, or control over other persons or groups. Hence, 'political science,' in some of its more recent 'behavioral' developments, has been concerned with the informal mechanisms of interpersonal influence and

control even more than with the formal structures of governmental and
legal institutions.[1]

The concept of the economic has undergone a parallel process of
generalization. In its traditional meaning—partly derivative from its ety-
mological connection with the household [*oikos*]—the 'economic' has had
a *material* sense: it has been understood to refer to wealth, income,
property, and the commodities—material goods and services—that can be
bought and sold with these. But more recently the 'economic' has been
defined as a more general *procedural* concept, as being concerned with the
'economizing' methods and behaviors that aim at the maximizing of
satisfactions, especially where means are limited and have alternative
uses. Here, as in the case of the political, what constitutes the economic
behavior or problems studied by 'economic theory' now includes a great
deal more than the pursuit and spending of money for material goods and
services. It involves all the 'economizing' strategies whereby persons seek
to maximize their satisfactions or achieve their goals, regardless of whether these are 'economic' in the narrow material sense of money used for acquiring commodities.[2]

This shift from the material to the procedural concept has not entailed
that the word 'economic' is purely equivocal as between the two
meanings. For the shift has been based on the recognition that the behavioral patterns used in markets for acquiring and increasing one's material
possessions are species of more general modes of procedures and operations that are also manifested in a wide variety of other contexts. Thus
nearly all human relations may come to be viewed as 'economic' or at
least as having an 'economic' dimension, since the concept is now applied
to all goal-oriented behavior where there are scarce means, not only to a
person's pursuit of wealth and income.

The relevance of this conceptual shift to the problems of economic justice may be grasped most directly if we note that it also entails two divergent meanings for the very concept of 'economic justice.' These two
meanings are, first, *the justice of economics*, and second, *the economics of
justice*. In the first meaning (the justice of economics), economic justice is
concerned with certain moral criteria for evaluating the distribution of
economic goods in the material sense of wealth and income, including the
opportunities and social structures that undergird this distribution. But in
the second meaning (the economics of justice), the divergent criteria of
justice are themselves evaluated according to how they bear on the
economic in the procedural sense of the maximizaton of preference
satisfaction.[3] Thus, in the first meaning, justice evaluates economics
(distribution of wealth and income), but in the second meaning, economics (maximization of preferences) evaluates justice.

Although each of these meanings of economic justice can be traced
back to Hume and other founders of modern economic theory, there can
be little doubt that it is the first, material meaning that has been predomi-
nant in traditional and contemporary discussions of economic justice.
Nevertheless, the second, procedural meaning has also exerted a strong

influence, especially in utilitarian and other consequentialist analyses of the ways in which alternative criteria of justice are to be evaluated according to their consequences for the maximizing of utilities or preferences, and hence for 'efficiency'.

Important normative alternatives are posed by these two concepts of economic justice. Since the criteria of distributive justice are distinct from questions about the aggregation of preferences, to focus on the procedural economics of justice in the sense just indicated may serve to blur the independent requirements of economic justice viewed as the justice of economics in the material sense of how wealth and income ought to be distributed. It may indeed turn out that the maximization of preference satisfactions will lead to greater wealth and income for all, including the least affluent members of a society, and even to greater equality. But this is a contingent connection that also requires certain sociopolitical institutions for its implementation. And it still leaves open the distinct question of what is the just distribution of wealth and income, regardless of how these are to be maximized.

2. Two Concepts of Justice

The better to understand these issues, we must note that there are also significant variations in the concept of justice itself. It is sometimes held that the *concept* of justice must be distinguished from *conceptions* of justice, in that the former comprises the general meaning common to all the divergent criteria that are employed to evaluate what arrangements are just. This distinction is parallel to a distinction about the word 'good' that goes back at least to G. E. Moore and was further developed by R. M. Hare.[4] According to this, the *meaning* of 'good' must be differentiated from the question of what things are good and what are the *criteria* for ascertaining this. The meaning of 'good' is constant amid the divergent criteria; thus, when Nietzsche says that the 'superman's' use of power is good, and when Schweitzer says that mercy is good but the 'superman's' use of power is not good, there is a common meaning for 'good,' since otherwise the two statements would not contradict one another.

In a parallel way, the concept of justice is held to comprise the general meaning common to all uses of 'just,' while the conceptions of justice comprise the divergent criteria that are adduced to give variable, even conflicting answers to the question of what transactions or arrangements are just.[5]

This distinction is sound as far as it goes, but it may lead to overlooking certain complexities in the very *concept* of justice. These complexities were recognized already by Aristotle in his distinctions between general and particular justice and, within the latter, between distributive, rectificatory, and commutative justice, with their distinct patterns of "geometrical" and "arithmetical" equality.[6] Without going into the details of these, it is important to recognize another, more general distinction within the very concept of justice that cuts across these other distinctions and is especially pertinent to economic justice. This is the distinction between a *formal or comparative* view of the meaning of 'justice' and a *substantive or noncomparative* view. The formal or comparative concept is found in the traditional definition of justice as *treating similar cases similarly.* The substantive or noncomparative concept is found in the equally traditional definition of justice as *giving to each person his due, or what he has a right to.*[7]

Each of these concepts of justice may be held to be "formal" in a certain obvious respect, for the comparative concept leaves open the question of what is the criterion of relevant similarities, and the substantive concept leaves open the question of what is each person's 'due' or 'right.' Nevertheless, the comparative concept is formal in a further, more specific sense, in that it is relational or structural. For to ascertain what is just, on the comparative view, requires examining the structure of or the relation between the treatments accorded two or more persons. If, for example, a woman is paid only half as much as a man for doing the same work, this relational consideration itself establishes that she is treated unjustly according to the comparative concept. For here one case—a worker—is treated differently from another, relevantly similar case: another worker. In the substantive or noncomparative view, on the other hand, to ascertain what is just requires not the relating or comparing of one person's treatment with another's, but rather the direct consideration of what a given person is entitled to. It is in this concept of justice that the equation of justice with the fulfillment of rights is made central. If, for example, a person is deprived of his right to free speech or to a fair trial, then he is treated unjustly, regardless of how other persons are treated in these matters. In the comparative concept, by contrast, justice is directly identified not with the fulfillment of rights, but rather with arithmetical or proportional equality of treatments as between two or more persons.

Despite this important difference, the word 'justice' is not purely equivocal between the two concepts. For each concept is concerned with the rationally justified, morally obligatory distribution of goods (and, to a lesser extent, of evils). The relational concept focuses on the proportion in which the goods are to be distributed, while the substantive concept focuses on the mandatory content of what is to be distributed, including its relation to the negative duties of other persons not to interfere with the distribution and also, in some contexts, to their positive duties to assist in the distribution. The word 'distribution' or 'distributive,' however, need not refer here to an explicit act or process of carrying out allocations of goods or evils; its central focus in this context is rather on the direct or proportional having of the goods themselves.

Each of the two concepts of justice has a certain kind of inherent rationality that serves to explain why the requirements of justice are so stringent and, indeed, categorical. The comparative concept whereby similar cases ought to be similarly treated is inherently rational in that to violate it is to incur self-contradiction. For if one says that A ought to have X *because* A has the property P (where this "because" is that of sufficient justificatory condition), then one is saying or at least implying that *all* cases that are similar to A in having the property P ought also to have X. Hence, if one goes on to say that it is not the case that B, who has the property P, ought to have X, then one contradicts oneself. Here, the relevant similarity of A and B makes it logically necessary that they ought to be treated in a relevantly similar way, this similarity being determined by their common possession of the justifying property P.

The substantive concept of justice, whereby each person ought to have or be given what he or she has a right to, is also inherently rational in two respects. The more familiar one is based on the idea that every right has a logically implied correlative.[8] Thus in the case of claim-rights, if A has a right to X, then all other persons have a correlative duty at least to refrain from interfering with A's having or doing X; and if the right in question is a positive one (as in the case, for example, of medical care), then some person or group also has the correlative duty to see to it that A has X. To deny these 'oughts' after accepting the initial right is to incur self-contradiction.

There is also a second, less familiar way in which the concept of rights is inherently rational, at least where the rights in question are human, or universal moral, rights. For the objects of these rights are the necessary conditions of purposive *action*.[9] Hence, no *agent* can deny that he has these rights, on pain of rejecting the very conditions that enable him to be an agent. By the same token, every agent logically must admit that all other actual or prospective agents have these rights.

Despite their inherent rationality, each of these concepts of justice may be held in various ways to be prior to the other and to be required by the other in order to obtain a full account of justice. Thus similar persons may be treated with similar undeserved harshness or oppressiveness, so that while the requirement of the relational or comparative concept is satisfied, nevertheless, in an important sense, the treatment is unjust. Hence, what is required in addition, if the treatment is to be just, is that it fulfill or at least not violate the *rights* of each of the persons concerned. On the other hand, it may be contended that it is difficult in practice, at least in certain kinds of cases, to ascertain what rights a person has without considering how other, comparable persons are treated. In academic grading, for example, a student's right to a certain grade is often determined by seeing how other students with similar performances have been graded. In a parallel way, part of the civil-rights movement in the United States was based on the consideration of the *relative* deprivations undergone by blacks in comparison with whites.[10]

This point bears directly on some of the central polemics about the bearing of equality on justice. It is sometimes maintained that equality is a dispensable consideration so far as economic and other kinds of justice are concerned. For if each person has what he has a *right* to, then, so far as concerns *justice*, why should there be any further question of how his holdings compare with those of other persons, including whether his holdings are *equal* to those of other persons? It is thus sometimes maintained that the comparative concern is simply a manifestation of envy or some other unworthy emotion.[11]

There are at least two answers to this attempt to dispose of the comparative concept of justice in favor of exclusive reliance on the substantive concept. One is that, as mentioned, persons often learn what rights they have by comparing their treatment with that of other, more favored persons. The other is that drastic *disparities* of material economic goods may themselves lead to a loss of even those goods to which persons are entitled, to which they have *rights*. Especially in times of scarcity, those who live on a very narrow margin of economic security may find themselves unable to compete for economic goods with persons of greater wealth, so that the disparity (with which the comparative concept is concerned) may result in a reduction below the economic level to which the former group has a right (with which the substantive concept is concerned).

For these and other reasons, an adequate concept of justice should include both the substantive and the comparative concepts. It should involve not only relevant similarity or equality, and not only rights, but relevant similarity or equality of rights. Of course, this still leaves open the questions of why justice as thus conceived ought to be established, what similarities are relevant, and how similarity or equality of rights is related to equality of wealth and income. What exactly is it that persons have a right to, and why must these rights of theirs be similar or, at the extreme, equal? The understanding of these and related questions requires that we explicitly consider the specific criteria of economic justice in the sense of the justice of the distribution of material economic goods.

3. Criteria of Economic Justice

It is in connection with these criteria that the controversial character of economic justice becomes most evident. In her introduction to Part One, Diana T. Meyers notes that in recent discussions of justice six different criteria have been upheld: to each according to his virtue, effort, contribution, agreements, needs, and society's rules.[12] As Meyers also points out, these six criteria have quite different implications for social policy, including the relations between freedom and equality.

Now each of these six criteria may be interpreted either according to the substantive concept of justice as rights or according to the comparative concept of justice as similarity of treatment. Thus virtue, effort, needs, and the rest may be viewed either as bases of rights or as supplying the criteria of similarities that are relevant to the requirement that similar cases must be similarly treated. Conversely, the two general concepts of justice may each be expressed in terms of the formula "to each according to" that figures in all six criteria. Thus the substantive concept says, "To each according to his rights," and the comparative concept says, "To each according to how similar cases are treated."

In addition to the conflicts of criteria posed by the six alternatives, the diversity among the criteria themselves provides a prime example of the dissensus that also characterizes so many other segments of morality. The diversity can be seen to be even greater when we recognize that each of the criteria involves many possible evaluative alternatives. For example, there are many different criteria not only of what constitutes virtue but also of what are a person's contributions and needs. There are also problems of how effort is to be measured, of when agreements are genuinely voluntary, of what are the contents of society's rules, especially in cases of conflict, and so forth.

The better to understand these criteria, it must be noted that they fall into two groups, which I shall call *antecedentalist* and *consequentialist*. The antecedentalist criteria answer the question of economic justice by referring to *antecedents* of the distribution of economic goods; that is, to various background conditions, including human actions of production or exchange, that are temporally prior to the acquisition and distribution of commodities. The consequentialist criteria, on the other hand, refer to the *consequences* of the distribution, including the fulfillment of needs or the achievement of economic equality or some other distributive pattern.[13]

From the above list, effort, contribution, and agreements are antecedentalist criteria, for they answer the question of the just distribution of economic goods by referring to circumstances *prior* to the distribution, including the effort that has been expended in order to produce the goods, or the contribution that has been made to that production or to other relevant conditions, or agreements that have been entered into prior to the actual distribution. On the other hand, the criterion of needs is consequentialist, for it answers the question of just distribution by reference to the alleviation of needs that is to *result from* the distribution. Virtue may be either an antecedentalist or a consequentialist criterion. It is antecedentalist if its use as a criterion is interpreted as requiring that preexisting virtue (or merit) should determine the distribution of economic goods. But it is consequentialist if the point is rather that economic distribution should serve to foster virtue as its end result.

The distinction between antecedentalist and consequentialist criteria is similar to the distinction drawn in theories of criminal punishment between retrospective or backward-looking criteria (such as retribution and restitution) and prospective or forward-looking criteria (such as deterrence and rehabilitation). For in the former theories punishment is to be based on the criminal's actions prior to the infliction of punishment, while in the latter theories it is to be based on what results from that infliction.

Very close to the antecedentalist criterion is the neoclassical economic doctrine that the share of income that each factor of production receives in a free market economy is equal to its "marginal product"; that is, the extra or differential value produced by one incremental unit of that factor. For in this conception distribution is determined by prior contribution in the productive process. This doctrine embodies a conception of economic justice insofar as it holds that such determination is "equitable" or that it reflects the "value to society" of the respective factors.[14]

This neoclassical doctrine of distribution is different from the doctrine of the 'economics of justice.' In both doctrines the question of the just distribution of wealth and income is answered by reference to the productive process, which may be viewed as a species of 'economizing' behavior or procedure in the production of commodities. But whereas the neoclassical doctrine is antecedentalist in basing its criterion of distribution on prior contribution to the productive process, the doctrine of the economics of justice is consequentialist, for it holds that distribution ought to be made with a view to attaining the maximization of satisfactions as its end result.

In Marx, both an antecedentalist and a consequentialist criterion can be found. He says that in the initial communist society that emerges from capitalist society, "the individual producer receives back from society—after the deductions have been made—exactly what he gives to it."[15] Here, as in the ancient Aristotelian formula for distributive justice, distribution is to be determined by antecedent contribution—an antecedentalist criterion. Marx also says, however, that in "the higher phase of communist society" the restriction of distribution by antecedent contribution will be surmounted, and that instead the society will uphold the criterion of "to each according to his needs."[16] This criterion is consequentialist insofar as it involves that distribution should be made with a view to having as its end result the alleviation of needs.

The references to Marx raise the question of the very possibility of the moral assessment of economic distribution. On the one hand, he frequently used what seems to be moral language: thus he talks of "oppressors" and "oppressed," "exploiters" and "exploited," and he characterized the former in each pair as "robbing" their victims.[17] On the other hand, Marx also held a determinist position both about economic distribution and about criteria of justice. He maintained that the distribution of consumption goods "results automatically" from the way in which the conditions of production are themselves distributed.[18] And he held, more generally, that the criteria of justice upheld in any society, far from being results of independent critical moral reflection, are parts of the legal and ideological superstructure that is determined by that society's economic basis. Thus each society has its own criteria of justice in consequence of its dominant mode of production and its resulting property relations, so there is no point in disputing about the "correct" criteria of economic justice.[19]

Without going into the extensive ways in which Marx both buttressed and qualified his thesis of economic determinism, I will simply note that, far from being passive reflections of an independent economic order, criteria of justice, when espoused in certain circumstances, have operated to change and indeed overthrow an antecedently existing economic structure, including the modes of production themselves. Hence, the evaluative discussion of criteria of justice can and should have an intellectual and moral autonomy of its own. Marx's practice in the use of moral language also exhibited this more activist view of moral criticism.

Among the most widely known contemporary conceptions of justice, Robert Nozick's "entitlement" theory is antecedentalist, since it maintains that "justice in holdings is historical" in that it depends upon past voluntary acquisitions and transfers of holdings.[20] Here, distribution of economic goods is to be determined by certain previous choices of persons who produce or transfer the goods. John Rawls's "difference principle," on the other hand, is consequentialist, since it requires that economic goods be distributed in such a way that any inequalities are "to the greatest benefit of the least advantaged."[21] Here, economic justice is characterized in terms of the results of a distribution for certain persons.

Both the antecedentalist and the consequentialist criteria of economic justice are subject to familiar polemical criticisms and controversies. The antecedentalist doctrine that distribution should be determined by prior contribution raises such questions as the following: What of persons who either cannot contribute to the productive process at all or whose contribution is severely limited because of past undeserved handicaps: is it just that they receive either no economic goods at all or only a very slight amount? Moreover, can the differential contribution of one individual or group to the total product be so clearly disentangled from the contributions of other persons or groups? In addition, there is the question whether market or economic considerations of contribution should be the only criteria of distribution, irrespective of the needs or the intrinsic worth of human beings. Similarly, insofar as it is held that distribution should be determined by antecedent voluntary exchanges, what if the starting point of the exchanges—the initial distribution of goods—has itself been unjust because, for example, it has been established by force or fraud and hence is in violation of persons' rights? And can persons who have greater skill and energy in production or exchange or both be said to deserve those profitable characteristics, derived as they are from favorable genetic and environmental backgrounds to which they have not themselves contributed? If they do not deserve them, can they be held to deserve the greater rewards that result from these antecedent circumstances?

The consequentialist criteria are also open to serious challenges. If just distributions are to be determined solely by the consequences of distributing economic goods in one way rather than in another, then it is at least possible that those who contribute most to the productive process will receive little in return, while those who contribute least receive far more. Even if the alleviation of needs is emphasized, and even if 'needs' is given a strict definition in terms of certain basic biological exigencies, there remains the possibility that some persons are required to work for others without receiving any commensurate return for their exertions. The criterion of consequences may also entail that persons receiving economic goods from other persons remain in a condition of passive dependency.

But such a condition is antithetical to human dignity, which requires rational autonomy as against being permanent recipients of the largesse of others.

4. The Dialectically Necessary Method

In view of such controversial diversities and difficulties of the various criteria of economic justice, the question arises: Is there any rational way of choosing among the criteria or ordering them according to rational principles of priority and posteriority? There have indeed been attempts to set forth a plurality of criteria,[22] but the arguments for the resulting theories have not been sufficiently conclusive to show why their rivals are not equally sound or at least plausible. Thus they have not settled the controversies spurred by the oppositions of criteria.

Is there any rational way, then, of achieving such conclusiveness? I now want to suggest that there is. For this purpose, I shall use what I call a *dialectically necessary method*. The method is *dialectical* in that it begins from statements presented as being made or accepted by an agent and it examines what they logically imply. The method is dialectically *necessary* in that the statements logically must be made or accepted by every agent because they derive from the generic features of purposive action.

To see how the dialectically necessary method can achieve the conclusiveness in question, we must note two salient preliminaries—one about the subject matter of conceptions of justice, the other about the modality of the argument.

The subject matter of all conceptions of justice ultimately consists in *actions*. For all conceptions of justice rest explicitly or implicitly on theories of morality, and all moralities are concerned directly or indirectly with how persons ought to *act*, especially toward one another. It may be objected that theories of justice differ from other moral theories in that they are concerned with the structure of *social institutions* rather than with individual agents or actions. But institutions themselves, amid all their varieties, are standardized arrangements for the regulation of various kinds of action and ultimately of the actions of individuals. Hence, it remains that all moralities, including conceptions of justice, are concerned directly or indirectly with how persons ought to act. Thus action is the general context of all moralities, including all conceptions of justice, regardless of their specifically varying contents.

The dialectically necessary method requires that principled moral argument be composed of statements that every agent logically must accept because they derive from the generic features of purposive action. If there are such statements, and if they can be shown to entail a certain conception of economic justice, then that conception also logically must be accepted by every agent on pain of self-contradiction. From this it would follow that the conception in question is conclusively established as right or justified, and any opposed conceptions are thereby shown to be unjustified, since they involve the agent in self-contradiction. In this way the problem of achieving conclusiveness would be resolved. The dialectically necessary method undertakes to achieve this result by tracing what is logically involved in the concept of action.

This brings me to my second preliminary consideration; about the modality of the argument. It may be objected that it is excessively rigorous to demand of a conception of justice that it be logically or rationally necessary in that any agent who denies it incurs self-contradiction. Ever since Aristotle, it has been emphasized that in the "practical sciences" of ethics and politics, only so much precision should be demanded as the subject matter admits of. The subject matter of the practical sciences is human actions and institutions, and these, as Aristotle noted, are susceptible of great variation.[23]

This point, however, does not entail that *normative* theories must be limited by the variabilities of their empirical subject matter. For the purpose of such theories is to impose rational requirements on certain contents; and the requirements may be so inherently rational that their denials are self-contradictory even though the subject matter to which they are applied is less precise. Moreover, there may be aspects of the subject matter itself which share the rational necessity of the normative structures that are applied to them.

5. Morality as Generic Consistency

I shall now try to show this necessity with regard to the subject matter of economic justice, noting that, amid all the criterial diversities and oppositions considered above, there are certain morally relevant aspects of the subject matter on which all protagonists rationally must agree, on pain of self-contradiction. From these rational considerations, a certain moral principle, which I call the *Principle of Generic Consistency*, will be shown to follow, so that it logically must be accepted by every actual or prospective agent.

The argument for the principle falls into two main parts. In the first part, I argue that every agent logically must hold or accept that he has *rights* to the necessary conditions of action and successful action in general. In the second part, I argue that each agent logically must admit that *all other agents* also have the same rights he claims for himself, so that in this way the existence of certain universal moral rights—and with them certain criteria of economic justice—must be accepted within the whole context of action or practice. Since I have presented the argument in considerable detail elsewhere,[24] here I will outline only the main points.

The first part of the argument proceeds as follows. As we have seen, actions are the common objects or subject matter of all moralities, since all moral precepts require, directly or indirectly, that persons act in certain ways. In this regard, as possible objects of moral precepts, all actions have two *generic features*: voluntariness and purposiveness. Actions in the indicated sense are voluntary in that agents control their behavior by their unforced choice while having knowledge of relevant circumstances. The actions are also purposive in that their agents intend to achieve some end or result (which may consist simply in performance of the action itself), which they regard as good or as worth attaining, on whatever criterion of goodness or worth (not necessarily a moral one) enters into their purposes.

The fact that actions are purposive means that agents intend to *succeed* in achieving the ends for which they act. Viewed in this achievemental mode, actions have, as their necessary conditions, *freedom* and *well-being*. These conditions must be regarded by every actual or prospective agent as *necessary goods* for himself, since without them he would not be able to act for any of his purposes either at all or with general chances of success. Freedom is the *procedural* condition of action: it consists, like voluntariness, in controlling one's behavior by one's unforced choice while having knowledge of relevant circumstances. Well-being, as I use the term here, is the *substantive* condition of action and successful action in general: it consists in having the generic abilities and conditions needed in order to act either at all or with general chances of success in achieving the purposes for which one acts. The components of well-being thus fall into a hierarchy of goods, ranging from life and physical integrity to self-respect and education.

Now every agent logically must hold or accept that he has *rights* to freedom and well-being. For, as we have seen, every agent has to accept (1) "I must have freedom and well-being." This 'must' is practical-prescriptive in that it signifies the agent's advocacy of his having the necessary goods of action, which he needs in order to act and to act successfully in general. By virtue of accepting (1), every agent has to accept (2) "I have rights to freedom and well-being." For if he rejects (2), then, because of the correlativity of rights and strict 'oughts,' he also has to reject (3) "All other persons ought at least to refrain from removing or interfering with my freedom and well-being." By rejecting (3), he has to accept (4) "Other persons may (i.e., it is permissible that other persons) remove or interfere with my freedom and well-being." And by accepting (4), he also has to accept (5) "I may not (i.e., it is permissible that I not) have freedom and well-being." But (5) contradicts (1). Since every agent must accept (1), he must reject (5). And since (5) follows from the denial of (2), every agent must reject that denial, so that he must accept (2) "I have rights to freedom and well-being." I shall call them *generic rights* because they are rights to have the generic features of action and successful action characterize one's behavior.

The first part of the argument has thus established that all action is necessarily connected with the essential aspect of the substantive concept of justice, the concept of rights. For every agent logically must hold or accept that he has rights to the necessary conditions of action and successful action in general.

Many questions of course, may, be raised about this argument, and I have dealt with these questions elsewhere. [25]

Now to the second part of the argument. On the basis of his having to accept that he has the generic rights, every agent also logically must accept that all other actual or prospective agents have these rights equally with his own. This generalization is an application of the formal or comparative concept or principle of justice discussed above: that similar cases must be similarly treated. For this principle entails that if any agent A holds that he has the generic rights *because* he is a prospective purposive agent (where the 'because' signifies a sufficient justifying condition), then he also logically must hold that *every* prospective purposive agent has the generic rights.

Suppose, however, that some agent A were to object that the necessary and sufficient justifying condition of his having the generic rights is his having some property R that is more *restrictive* than simply being a prospective purposive agent. Examples of R might include his being a wage earner or an entrepreneur or a banker or a landlord or an American or white or male or being named "Wordsworth Donisthorpe," and so forth. From this it would follow that A would logically have to hold that it is *only* his having R that justifies his having the generic rights, so that if he were to *lack* R, then he would *not* have the generic rights.

But such an agent would contradict himself. For we saw above that, as an agent, he logically must hold that he has the generic rights, since otherwise he would be in the position of accepting that he normatively *need not* have what he normatively *must* have (where the criterion of the "normatively" is the same in each case). Hence, no agent, including A, can consistently hold that he does not have the generic rights, so that he must give up the idea that any R can be the necessary as well as sufficient justifying condition of his having these rights. From this it follows that every agent logically must acknowledge that, simply by virtue of being a prospective purposive agent, he has the generic rights, so he also logically must accept that *all* prospective purposive agents have equal rights to freedom and well-being.

Since this universalized judgment sets a prescriptive requirement for the action of every agent toward all other prospective purposive agents who are or may be the recipients of his action, every agent logically must accept for himself a moral principle that may be formulated as follows: *Act in accord with the generic rights of your recipients as well as of yourself.* I call this the *Principle of Generic Consistency (PGC)* because it combines the formal consideration of logical consistency with the *material* consideration of the generic features and rights of action.

As with the first part of the argument, many questions may be raised about this second part. They include especially questions about the equality of the agents who are asserted to have equal rights. I have also dealt with such questions elsewhere.[26]

The argument for the *PGC*, using the dialectically necessary method, has established as rationally obligatory a moral principle that requires a certain mode of interpersonal action. This principle includes, in its central part, a criterion of justice that embodies both the substantive and the comparative concepts of justice considered above. In requiring of every agent that he act in accord with the generic *rights* of his recipients, the principle embodies the substantive concept. In requiring that he act in accord with the generic rights *of each of his recipients as well as of himself*, the principle embodies the comparative concept, since it says that the agent must treat with similar regard for rights all the persons who are relevantly similar to himself in being actual or prospective purposive agents. In this way, the requirement of generic consistency embodies both these essential components of the general concepts of justice. And it also shows how a substantial moral principle can have the rational conclusiveness that we saw to be lacking in the antecedentalist and consequentialist criteria of justice.

6. Some Questions About the Argument

Two interrelated questions that require special attention in the present context concern the *subjects* and the *objects* of the rights that figure in the argument for the *PGC;* that is, both the agents who claim the rights and to what the rights are claimed. Why must it be *agents in general* who claim rights? Why shouldn't it be, for example, *rich* agents as against *poor* ones, so that the argument would prove that only *rich* agents have certain rights? And why must it be only to the generic features and necessary goods of action that rights are claimed? Why shouldn't it be instead the right to act with the *wealth and other resources* one already has?[27] These questions challenge the egalitarian thrust of the whole foregoing argument.

In addition to the reply made just above to the attempt to impose a more restrictive property R on the criterion for having the generic rights, we must recall here the general point of the dialectically necessary method. This point derives from the fact that, as we saw above, the context of morality in general and economic justice in particular is one of controversial claims and counterclaims about sound criteria, none of them conclusive. The dialectically necessary method undertakes to achieve the required conclusiveness by *restricting* the argument to what logically must be accepted by *every* participant in the dispute. All these participants are involved in the context of *action*. Hence, the dialectically necessary method restricts the argument to what is *necessarily connected* with the context of *action*, which is the general context of all moralities, including economic justice. The point is that in this way the argument achieves rational necessity, as against the seeming arbitrariness and contingency of the initial claims and counterclaims. For *no* agent can rationally deny what is logically connected with action, including its normative implications; but he *can* deny without contradiction any normative practical claims that are not thus logically connected.

If, however, it is contended that only the claims of *rich* agents should be credited, and only their claims to the use of *their own* resources, such a restriction would be arbitrary. For it goes outside what is *necessarily* connected with the context of action. The same point holds if it is maintained that only *rich persons' action* should provide the context of the argument for rights. For this restriction would prematurely take sides on the central issue of economic justice, and it would do so without rational justification in what logically must be accepted by *all* participants in the dispute. Thus any restrictions beyond the ones indicated in the above argument are arbitrary and question-begging, for they go beyond what must be accepted by *every* protagonist in virtue of his involvement in the context of action that is common to all segments of the disputed subject matter.

There are, of course, many different kinds of actions and agents, and the latter make many different and mutually opposed kinds of claims, including those bearing on economic justice. But these diverse claims have a certain kind of arbitrariness in that they derive from variable evaluations based on contingent preferences or choices. These variable claims are not logically necessary, for they are not necessarily connected with the general context of action; hence, agents can deny them without self-contradiction, so they are not conclusive. If, however, certain conceptions of economic justice *are* necessarily connected with the general context of action, then no agent can deny them without self-contradiction, so the requisite conclusiveness is achieved. The claims that are logically connected with the concept of action thus have a kind of rational necessity, by contrast to other claims that are variable and contingent in the ways indicated above.

It may still be contended, however, that this whole procedure involves reinterpreting the concept of an agent in that it is now only an *ideal* agent that figures in the argument, not *real* agents with their varying claims to particular goods. This objection does indeed apply to Rawls's doctrine about agents choosing from behind a "veil of ignorance"[28]; but it does not apply to the argument for the *PGC*. For this argument deals with agents as they really are, acting freely for their respective purposes with knowledge of the proximate circumstances of their actions, including their particular qualities. What has been required of these agents is that they not definitively accept any specific moral principle prior to rational argument, and that they have and use deductive and inductive rationality. Impartiality is morally imposed on these agents not by artificially stripping them of all particular knowledge or inequality, but rather by showing that their actions logically involve them in right-claims and 'ought'-judgments that are such that, to avoid self-contradiction, they must accept that their recipients equally have the same rights. The argument is thus rationally necessary without paying the price of beginning from contrarational assumptions.[29]

7. Implications for Economic Justice: Negative and Positive Rights

If the argument for the *PGC* has been successful, it has established a certain moral principle as rationally conclusive. But although the *PGC* in its central requirements is a principle of justice, there remains the question of its implications for the more specific problems of economic justice. Can these implications achieve the same conclusiveness as the general principle itself?

The *PGC*'s implications for economic justice are not simple: they involve complexities that derive both from the principle itself, including its background in the necessary goods of action, and from the empirical conditions in which it is applied. For present purposes I shall present the *PGC's* criteria of economic justice in a sequence that has two main strands, the second providing pertinent complications of the first.

According to the *PGC*, every prospective purposive agent, and thus every person, has equal rights to freedom and well-being as the necessary conditions of action and successful action in general. The principle thus has two main requirements, bearing on the rights to freedom and to well-being. Each of these requirements serves both to complement and to limit the other.

Let us begin with the right to freedom. Freedom as a necessary condition of action consists in control of one's behavior by one's unforced choice with knowledge of relevant circumstances. Such freedom may be applied by the agent in many different kinds of actions. These actions or series of actions, whether engaged in by oneself alone or, as is far more usual, in combination with other persons, include the production of economic goods or commodities and their voluntary exchange with other persons. Such uses of one's freedom are so far justified by the *PGC*, for they do not involve any violation of the rights of other persons.

These freedoms result in a certain just distribution of economic goods: the goods are justly possessed by the persons who produce them or who acquire them by voluntary exchanges, so they have property rights in those goods. For every person's right to freedom includes the right to engage freely in actions of production and exchange, and it includes also the right to property; that is, to exclusive possession of the commodities that result from these actions. If these implications of the right to freedom were denied, this would entail denial of the right to freedom itself. I shall call this the *freedom criterion* of economic justice or economic rights.

Certain aspects of this right must be stressed. On the one hand, the *freedom* that is here in question is both positive and negative. It is positive in that it involves the agent's power or ability to act as he unforcedly chooses: he controls his behavior by his own unforced choice. But this freedom is also negative in that it involves that his behavior is not controlled by other persons: others do not remove or interfere with his behavior or his control of it.

On the other hand, the *right* to freedom as thus delineated is so far only *negative*. For the duty it requires of other persons (the respondents) is only that they refrain from interfering with the agent's control of his own behavior, including his resulting property. It is not also the positive duty to assist the agent to have or acquire such control.

The criterion of economic justice that emerges from the right to freedom is antecedentalist. It determines that distribution of economic goods is just by reference to conditions prior to and independent of the distribution. Voluntary production and exchange *result in* a certain distribution of goods, but what makes the distribution just is *what it results from*, not *what results from it.*

Thus far, we have the bare rudiments of a classical free market system. But now at least four questions arise about this model—questions that in part were already raised in the general discussion of antecedentalist criteria of economic justice and that serve to cast doubt on the classical model's sufficiency as a criterion of economic justice. First, how clearly can we identify the persons who produce various specific goods amid the enormous complexities of the actual productive processes in modern industrial societies? Second, do persons' abilities to perform their free productive actions derive only from the persons themselves or from a complex prior matrix of inheritance and social nurture, including education? Third, to what extent can persons' participation in the productive process be regarded as 'free' when they are driven by economic necessity to take jobs that are menial, degrading, exhausting, and health-threatening? Fourth, what of those persons who do not participate in the productive process at all, or who do participate, but only to an extent that does not enable them to fulfill their basic needs?

The first three of these questions cast some doubt on the freedom criterion of economic justice insofar as that criterion purports to justify a person's right to *exclusive* possession of the commodities that "result from" his or her "voluntary" actions of production and exchange. But even if further argument may remove some of this doubt, there remains the fourth question, which requires independent scrutiny.

The fourth question bears on the other main segment of the generic rights: the right to well-being. For it is usually because this right is not sufficiently fulfilled for certain persons that they do not participate in the productive process in the ways just indicated. Hence, three points must be considered: first, the components of well-being; second, which lacks of well-being affect persons' participation in the productive process; third, what the right to well-being requires for such persons.

According to the *PGC*, all persons have equal rights to freedom and well-being as the necessary conditions of their action and successful action in general. Omitting for the present the possible varieties of freedom in this actional context, we must note that well-being itself falls into a hierarchy of three kinds of goods that are progressively less necessary for action. *Basic goods* are the essential prerequisites of action; they include life, physical integrity, health, mental equilibrium, and such specific goods as food, clothing, and shelter. *Nonsubstractive goods* are the general abilities and conditions needed for maintaining undiminished one's level of purpose-fulfillment and one's capabilities for particular actions. *Additive goods* are the general abilities and conditions needed for increasing one's level of purpose-fulfillment and one's capabilities for particular actions. Examples of nonsubtractive goods are not being lied to, stolen from, insulted, or threatened with violence. Examples of additive goods are self-esteem, wealth, and education. Persons' generic rights to these three kinds of goods are, respectively, *basic rights*, *nonsubtractive rights*, and *additive rights*.

Now, for persons to participate in the productive process sufficiently to assure themselves a continued supply of basic goods, they must already have the basic goods, and they must also have relevant nonsubtractive and additive goods, including education. But many persons may be unable to participate in this way. They include the very young, the very old, the physically or mentally handicapped, the very ill, the poorly educated. Other persons may suffer productive disabilities that, while less deep, may also threaten their supply of basic goods, because they are unemployed through no fault of their own, or because the prices at which the commodities they produce are bought are not sufficient for their basic needs, or because drought or other natural conditions over which they have no control threaten them with starvation.

All such persons, like all other prospective agents, have *positive rights* to well-being, and especially to basic well-being. The argument for there being such positive rights is parallel to the argument I summarized above for a negative right to both freedom and well-being. I shall now present a summary of the positive-rights argument.

Since well-being is a necessary condition of action and successful action in general, every agent has a general need for its components. Hence, every agent has to accept (1a) "I must have well-being." This "must" is practical-prescriptive in that it signifies the agent's advocacy of his having what he needs in order to act either at all or with general chances of success. Now, by virtue of accepting (1a), the agent also has to accept (2a) "I have a positive right to well-being." For if he rejects (2a), then, because of the correlativity of positive rights and strict positive 'oughts,' he also has to reject (3a) "Other persons ought to assist me to have well-being when I cannot have it by my own efforts." By rejecting (3a), he has to accept (4a) "Other persons may not (i.e., it is permissible that other persons not) assist me to have well-being when I cannot have it by my own efforts." And by accepting (4a), he also has to accept (5a) "I may not (i.e., it is permissible that I not) have well-being." But (5a) contradicts (1a). Since every agent must accept (1a), he must reject (5a). And since (5a) follows from the denial of (2a), every agent must reject that denial, so he must accept (2a) "I have a positive right to well-being."

The further steps of this argument are also parallel to the argument for negative rights. Each agent logically must admit that the sufficient reason or ground on which he claims positive rights for himself is that he is a prospective purposive agent, so he must accept the generalization that *all* prospective purposive agents have positive rights to well-being. Hence, he must also accept that he has positive duties to help other persons attain well-being when they cannot do so by their own efforts and when he can give such help without comparable cost to himself. Such help, however, often requires a context of institutional rules, including the supportive state.

In this way, the duty to act in accord with the positive rights of other persons is rationally justified, so that it is morally right and indeed mandatory to provide help for others when they need this help (and they cannot achieve their well-being by their own efforts), and it can be given without comparable cost to the agent.

In the above argument, unlike the argument given earlier for negative rights to freedom and well-being, there is included the qualification (in 3a and 4a) that the agent cannot attain some aspect of well-being *by his own efforts*. This means that in the 'ought'-judgment (3a) he cannot rationally demand of other persons that they assist him to have well-being unless his own efforts to have it are unavailing. For without this qualification there would not follow (5a) "I may not (i.e., it is permissible that I not) have well-being."

It must also be noted that the above argument applies only to the *necessary* conditions of action and of successful action in general. For without this necessity, the "must" used in step (1a) of the argument would be unfounded. Hence, the argument cannot be used to support a right to dispensable and idiosyncratic objects.

What the argument shows is that, on the basis of the necessity of well-being for action and successful action in general, no agent can rationally deny that he has a positive right to well-being. As rational, he has especially to recognize that there may be times when his life and other aspects of his basic well-being may be threatened so that he may then need the help of others, because he cannot have or maintain his well-being by his own efforts. This point applies even against the kind of rugged individualist whom Sidgwick described as "a man in whom the spirit of independence and the distaste for incurring obligations would be so strong that he would choose to endure any privations rather than receive aid from others."[30] Sidgwick himself presented the qualification that "every one, in the actual moment of distress, must necessarily wish for the assistance of others." There is also a further, more extensive reply to the rugged individualist. It is based on the general conditions of the dialectically necessary method, which I have discussed previously.

8. Positive Rights and Productive Agency

The argument for positive rights to well-being applies especially to persons who cannot participate in the productive process, in accordance with their right to freedom, sufficiently to assure themselves and their dependents a continued supply of basic goods. The rights in question have as their objects not only food, clothing, shelter, and other basic goods; they include also such additive goods as education and also effective opportunities for productive employment.

It may be asked why participation in the productive process should receive such emphasis. Doesn't economic justice require the alleviation of the suffering caused by nonfulfillment of basic needs, regardless of whether the sufferers do or do not produce economic goods that enable them directly or indirectly to support themselves?

The answer to this question must go back to the qualification indicated in the argument for positive rights: that the persons to whom other persons have the duty to supply components of well-being must be unable to obtain those components "by their own efforts." The inability in question may of course be of different sorts (as was indicated); its analysis must include recognition of the vagaries of the market system as they impinge both on employment and on the "tastes" of buyers or consumers. But if the qualification about persons' own efforts is not maintained, then the argument for positive rights to *necessary* goods would not be valid. The result would be an unwarranted infringement of the respondents' own rights to freedom.

There is a further reason for stressing participation in the productive process. It is connected with the *PGC*'s central orientation in the needs of *agency*. The ultimate purpose of the generic rights, whose equal distribution the *PGC* requires, is to secure for each person a certain fundamental moral status: that each person have rational autonomy in the sense of being a self-controlling, self-developing agent who can relate to other persons on a basis of mutual respect and cooperation, in contrast to being a passive, dependent recipient of the agency of others. Even when the rights require positive assistance from other persons, their point is not to reinforce or increase dependence, but rather to give support that enables persons to be agents; that is, to control their own lives and effectively pursue and sustain their own purposes without being subjected to domination and harms from others. In this way, agency is both the metaphysical and the moral basis of human dignity. Now such agency involves, both as end and as means, participation in the productive process. For this reason, an emphasis on such participation is required for economic justice as the rights to freedom and well-being.

It follows from these considerations that the positive rights of the persons who suffer from productive disabilities must be dynamic as well as static. The objects of the rights must include not only sufficient basic goods but also development of the productive abilities and conditions whereby the persons can themselves participate in the productive process at a level sufficient to supply at least their basic needs.

This applies to economic justice on the international as well as the national level. As I have indicated elsewhere,[31] transfers of food and other basic necessities to starving persons in other nations are morally required in cases of emergencies. But apart from emergencies, what is also needed is the development of an international economic order in which the wide disparities between rich and poor nations are removed. Such removal, however, should proceed not by maintaining a relation of recipience and dependence on the part of poor nations, but rather by enabling them to develop and use their own resources, personal and environmental. The point of such a policy, in keeping with the *PGC*'s concern for the conditions of agency, is not to reinforce or increase dependence, but rather to give support that enables persons to maintain these conditions for themselves. On the national level, similarly, welfare assistance must be aimed not only at alleviating the immediate hardships and shortages of poverty and other handicaps but also at helping the poor and other disadvantaged persons to develop for themselves the ability to procure goods and services by their own efforts and thus to improve their capabilities for successful agency. A just economic system will provide for such development and related opportunities.

It is important, then, to reject a purview that assumes a permanent class of welfare dependents (whether domestic or international), with a permanent division between affluent agents and poor, dependent recipients. Instead, the *PGC*'s emphasis on the rights of agency requires that all persons have the necessary conditions of action, including property, and that welfare programs (whether domestic or international) aim at fostering for all persons their acquisition of the conditions and abilities needed for successful agency and hence a cessation of exclusive dependence on others for basic goods.

We thus have a further criterion of economic justice besides the freedom criterion. I shall call it the *need criterion*. It yields a complex positive right to welfare, to well-being in its static and dynamic aspects. This criterion is consequentialist. It determines what distribution of economic goods is just by reference to conditions that result from the distribution: the fulfillment of basic needs and related aspects of well-being.

There is of course an important sense in which freedom is a need of action, just as is well-being. I here confine the "need criterion" to well-being, however, in order to stress its relation to positive rights and duties to fulfill the relevant needs of well-being, in contrast to the negative rights and duties of the freedom criterion.

Who should be the primary respondent of the right to well-being; that is, the agency that has the correlative duty to supply the various static and dynamic components of well-being in the ways just indicated? While voluntary agencies may indeed be helpful for this purpose, the primary duty must rest with the state. The main justification of the state (and hence of political obligation) is indeed that it serves to secure persons' generic rights to both freedom and well-being.

There are three specific reasons why the state should be the primary respondent of persons' positive rights to the components of well-being. First, the goods in question must be securely provided as needed; hence, if they are left to the optional decisions of willing private persons or groups, sufficient funds may not be given. Second, the benefits of these arrangements must be equitably and impartially distributed to the persons who need them, without discrimination based on the variable preferences of potential providers. Third, the duty to contribute to such arrangements through taxes must also be equitably distributed to all persons who have the required economic resources, in proportion to their ability. To leave the fulfillment of this duty solely to voluntary groups would allow many persons to shirk their duty. In this way, the state has a further moral basis as being instrumental to economic justice.

9. Conflicts of Economic Rights

The foregoing discussion has shown, explicitly or implicitly, how the *PGC*'s criteria of economic justice can overcome the objections against both antecedentalist and consequentialist criteria. There remain, however, certain controversial questions about the relation between the consequentialist need criterion's right to well-being and the antecedentalist voluntaristic criterion's right to freedom. Viewed abstractly, the two rights are in conflict with one another. For while the right to freedom involves a right to exclusive possession of one's economic goods, the right to well-being requires that affluent persons give up some of their goods, or the money equivalents thereof, to provide for the well-being of needy persons. As many libertarians have pointed out, this requirement is thus a restriction on the right to freedom, since it imposes on persons a duty they may not want to accept. But why is it justified to infringe the right to freedom of some persons in order to fulfill the right to well-being of other persons? Isn't this to use the former persons as mere means for the latter?

To see how these questions are to be answered, we must recur to the justificatory basis of the generic rights. These rights have as their objects the necessary conditions of human action. From this derives one of the main bases of the resolution of conflicts of rights, which I shall call *the criterion of degrees of necessity for action.* When two rights conflict with one another, that right must take precedence whose object is more necessary for action. This is why, for example, the right not to be lied to is overridden by the right not to be murdered if the latter right can be fulfilled only by infringing on the former. As was noted in connection with the right to well-being, its components of basic, nonsubtractive, and additive rights fall into a hierarchy of progressively less necessary conditions of action.

Now the kinds of freedom also fall into such a hierarchy. 'Freedom' should not be used as a global, undifferentiated concept. There are distinctions between occurrent or particular freedom and dispositional or long-range freedom, and also between different objects of freedom. A temporary interference with a relatively minor freedom, such as a traffic light, is morally less important than a long-range interference with the freedom to perform some highly valued action. Hence, if the affluent are taxed so that a relatively small part of their wealth is removed in order to prevent the destitute from starving, this is a far less significant interference with their freedom than would be the case if they were forced to surrender most of their wealth or were prohibited from supporting political parties, religions, or universities of their choice. Objections that might be raised against this position because of the alleged impossibility of interpersonal comparisons of utilities are readily answerable by the considerations of levels of goods that enter into the argument for the *PGC.* Thus it is not freedom in general that welfare rights restrict. By the same token, the right to freedom in the use of one's surplus property is not absolute; it may be overridden by other rights, such as the rights to life, health, or subsistence, since the objects of the latter rights are more pressing because more necessary for action.

The specific point, then, is that possession of a surplus of economic goods is less necessary for action than are basic well-being and such additive goods as education. This is why property rights in the surplus are overridden by the basic and other rights in cases of conflict.

That property rights may be overridden in certain circumstances does not mean that there are no property rights at all. The empirically based assumption here is that, insofar as some persons cannot fulfill for themselves their essential needs subserved by basic rights, other persons can provide this out of their surplus while still preserving the bulk of their property. None of this, however, amounts to anything like complete expropriation of the providers; the provision is not open-ended, and thus property rights still remain. As we have seen, one of the primary justifications of such rights is that they result from persons' productive work. My position is hence not the same as John Rawls's "difference principle," according to which economic inequalities are unjustified unless they work out to the maximum benefit of the least advantaged.[32] This principle would permit and indeed require constant interference with persons' property in order maximally to benefit the least advantaged, thereby violating the claims of desert as based on voluntary effort and accomplishment. My doctrine, on the other hand, requires only strictly limited redistribution to alleviate basic needs and to enable disadvantaged persons to attain the abilities whereby they can support themselves.

From these considerations, it is apparent that the equality of generic rights prescribed by the *PGC* is an equality of *opportunity* rather than of *outcomes*. What is of central importance here is not that wealth or property itself is to be equalized, but rather that, beyond the minimum required for basic goods, persons have as nearly as possible equal chances for developing and utilizing their own capabilities for successful agency. The main concern must be for each person's equal opportunity to develop and maximize his own capacities for purpose-fulfillment. However, the fostering of such equality requires a certain degree of economic redistribution.

There are of course difficulties in the concept of equality of opportunity. Nevertheless, the main emphasis must be the dynamic one of enabling persons to develop for themselves the means of fulfilling their needs and achieving their goals. These means presuppose the basic goods of life and health, but they also include knowledge and education. It is to the development of these means that equality of opportunity primarily refers, and with it the provision of the required resources. This position is hence not open to Robert Nozick's objection that "no end-state principle or distributional patterned principle of justice can be continuously realized without continuous interference with people's lives."[33] Since the equality that is sought is one of opportunity rather than of outcomes, it is not a global condition bearing on all aspects of the distribution of goods; it is rather a more specific condition bearing only on certain specific distributional aspects. Its achievement would hence leave a wide range of further possibilities that would not be affected by the specific egalitarian requirement and would not require further, let alone "continuous interference with people's lives." It must also be stressed, however, that the unequal outcomes allowed by this conception must not be so extreme that they threaten equality of opportunity itself.

Persons are not treated as mere means—nor is their rationally justifiable freedom violated—when they are taxed in order to help other persons who are suffering from economic privation. For the principle underlying the taxation of the affluent to help others is concerned with protecting equally the rights of all persons, including the affluent. The *PGC*'s requirement that agents act in accord with the generic rights of their recipients entails that all prospective purposive agents must refrain from harming one another (according to the principle's criteria of harm), and that in certain circumstances they must help one another if they can. Hence, limitations on their freedom to abstain from such help are rationally justified. The facts that only some persons may actually be threatened with harm or need help at a particular time, and that only some other persons may be in a position to inflict harm or to give help, do not alter the universality of the *PGC*'s provision for the protection of rights. Such protection is not only occurrent but also dispositional and a matter of principle; it manifests an impartial concern for any and all persons whose rights may need protection. Hence, the *PGC*'s requirement for taxing the affluent involves treating all persons as ends, not merely as means.

What I have tried to show is that, amid the intense controversies over economic justice, there are certain criteria whose acceptance is rationally obligatory for all agents because they derive from the generic features of purposive action. Radical individualists and libertarians may complain that I have gone too far in imposing positive duties on the affluent to alleviate the needs of disadvantaged persons, while radical communitarians and egalitarians may object that I have not gone far enough in upholding the claims of communal cooperation and have accepted too fully an individualist orientation of each agent's pursuits of goods for himself or herself.

Each of these extreme positions, however, has well-recognized dangers. In its requirement that each person respect the equal generic rights of all other persons, the *PGC* goes far toward recognizing the claims of social solidarity on which the communitarian focuses,[34] while at the same time it recognizes the libertarian's valid point that individual freedom is itself a basic good. My argument has tried to show how these conflicting claims can be adjusted to one another through the rights of agency that provide the primary, rationally justified criteria of economic justice.

Notes

1. See Heinz Eulau, *The Behavioral Persuasion in Politics* (New York: Random House, 1963).

2. See Lionel Robbins, *An Essay on the Nature and Significance of Economic Science*, 2d ed. (London: Macmillan, 1952). chap. 1; Gary S. Becker, *The Economic Approach to Human Behavior* (Chicago: University of Chicago Press, 1976).

3. See Richard A. Posner, *The Economics of Justice* (Cambridge, Mass.: Harvard University Press, 1981), pp. 48-115; also Posner, *Economic Analysis of Law*, 2d ed. (Boston: Little, Brown, 1977), chaps. 2, 3, 16, 27, 28.

4. G. E. Moore, *Principia Ethica* (Cambridge: Cambridge University Press, 1903), chap. 1; R. M. Hare, *The Language of Morals* (Oxford: Clarendon Press, 1952), chap. 6.

5. See Ch. Perelman, *The Idea of Justice and the Problem of Argument*, translated by J. Petrie (London: Routledge and Kegan Paul, 1963), pp. 6-29; John Rawls, *A Theory of Justice* (Cambridge, Mass.: Harvard University Press, 1971), pp. 3-4.

6. Aristotle, *Nicomachean Ethics*, vol. 5, chaps. 1-6.

7. I first set forth this distinction in "Political Justice", in R. B. Brandt, ed., *Social Justice* (Englewood Cliffs, N.J.: Prentice-Hall, 1962), pp. 124-25. For a fuller discussion of the distinction but with somewhat different emphases, see Joel Feinberg, "Noncomparative Justice," in *Rights, Justice, and the Bounds of Liberty* (Princeton: Princeton University Press, 1980), pp. 265 ff.

8. See Wesley N. Hohfeld, *Fundamental Legal Conceptions* (New Haven: Yale University Press, 1964), pp. 35 ff.

9. See Alan Gewirth, *Reason and Morality* (Chicago: University of Chicago Press, 1978), pp. 63 ff.; and id., *Human Rights: Essays on Justification and Applications* (Chicago: University of Chicago Press, 1982), pp. 7 ff., 47 ff.

10. Talcott Parsons and Kenneth B. Clark, eds., *The Negro American* (Boston: Beacon Press, 1966), pp. 3 ff. For a general discussion of the concept of relative deprivation, see W. G. Runciman, *Relative Deprivation and Social Justice* (London: Routledge and Kegan Paul, 1966), esp. chaps. 1-3.

11. See F. A. Hayek, *The Constitution of Liberty* (Chicago: University of Chicago Press, 1960), p. 93; Robert Nozick, *Anarchy, State, and Utopia* (New York: Basic Books, 1974), pp. 239-46.

12. For similar (but not identical) lists, see Gregory Vlastos, "Justice and Equality," in R. B. Brandt, ed., *Social Justice*, p. 35; and Nicholas Rescher, *Distributive Justice* (Indianapolis: Bobbs-Merrill, 1966), chap. 4. For summaries of other lists, see J. R. Lucas, *On Justice* (Oxford: Clarendon Press, 1980), pp. 164-65.

13. This distinction between antecedentalist and consequentialist criteria is similar to the distinction drawn by Robert Nozick between "historical" and "end-state" principles of justice (*Anarchy, State, and Utopia*, pp. 150 ff.) But there are also some important differences both in the respective concepts and in the ways in which they are evaluated. Nozick confines just "historical" principles to voluntary procedures ("From each as they choose, to each as they are chosen" [p. 160]). But this ignores the ways in which such a just historical generating principle as merit may reflect an individual's inherited or externally generated endowments, rather than what he has himself chosen or voluntarily acquired. Nozick also seems to hold that all end-state principles involve some overarching "patterns," whose maintenance will require "continuous interference with people's lives" (p. 163). Consequentialist criteria need not, however, require such totalistic patterns; for example, they may provide for equal fulfillment of each person's basic needs while leaving taxpayers free to use their remaining money as they wish.

14. Gunnar Myrdal, *The Political Element in the Development of Economic Theory*, translated by P. Streeten (London: Routledge and Kegan Paul, 1953), p. 10.

15. Karl Marx, *Critique of the Gotha Program* (in R. C. Tucker, ed., *The Marx-Engels Reader*, 2d ed. New York: W. W. Norton, 1972), p. 530.

16. Ibid., p. 531.

17. See, e.g., Marx and Engels, *The Communist Manifesto* in *The Marx-Engels Reader*, p. 474; also Marx, Capital, vol. 1 (New York: Modern Library, n.d.), p. 569.

18. *Critique of the Gotha Program* (in *The Marx-Engels Reader*, p. 531).

19. Ibid., pp. 528, 531. For conflicting interpretations of Marx's views on the status of justice as a moral norm, see the essays collected in M. Cohen, T. Nagel, and T. Scanlon, eds. *Marx, Justice, and History* (Princeton: Princeton University Press, 1980), pt. 1.

20. Nozick, *Anarchy, State and Utopia*, pp. 150 ff.

21. Rawls, *A Theory of Justice*, p. 302.

22. See Rescher, *Distributive Justice*, pp. 81 ff.; David Miller, *Social Justice* (Oxford: Clarendon Press, 1976). pp. 24 ff.; Michael Walzer, *Spheres of Justice* (New York: Basic Books, 1983), pp. 4 ff.

23. Aristotle, *Nicomachean Ethics*, 1. 3. 1094b 12 ff.; 1. 7. 1098a 20 ff.

24. *Reason and Morality*, chap. 2; *Human Rights*, pp. 20 ff., 45-55; "The Epistemology of Human Rights," *Social Philosophy and Policy* 1. 2. (1984): 1-24.

25. See *Reason and Morality*, pp. 82-102; *Human Rights*, pp. 67-76; "Comments on Bond's Article," *Metaphilosophy* 11 (1980): 54-69; "Why Agents Must Claim Rights: A Reply," *Journal of Philosophy* 79 (1982): 403-10; "Replies to My Critics," in E. Regis, Jr., ed., *Gewirth's Ethical Rationalism* (Chicago: University of Chicago Press, 1984), pp. 202-215.

26. In *Reason and Morality*, pp. 112-27; *Human Rights*, pp. 7-8, 76-78; "On Rational Agency as the Basis of Moral Equality: Reply to Ben-Zeev," *Canadian Journal of Philosophy* 12 (1982): 667-72.

27. For these questions, see especially Virginia Held, "Review of Alan Gewirth, *Reason and Morality*," *Social Theory and Practice* 5 (1979): 243-250; also Held's essay in this volume.

28. Rawls, *A Theory of Justice*, pp. 136 ff.

29. See *Reason and Morality*, pp. 357-58; also pp. 96-97.

30. Henry Sidgwick, *The Methods of Ethics*, 7th ed. (London: Macmillan, 1907), p. 389n.

31. "Starvation and Human Rights," in *Human Rights*, pp. 197-217.

32. Rawls, *A Theory of Justice*, pp. 75 ff.

33. Nozick, *Anarchy, State, and Utopia*, p. 163.

34. See Gewirth, *Human Rights*, pp. 18-19.

2

Reason and Economic Justice

Virginia Held
Department of Philosophy
City University of New York

I

How much can reason accomplish? What can we, as philosophers and legal scholars and social scientists with a concern for the moral implications of what we are doing, hope to achieve in the way of progress toward a less unjust world? When we gather to discuss economic justice, do we join together to enjoy our surroundings, with a better excuse than otherwise, while we probably should be demonstrating against Reagan's social policies, or organizing the poor to demand adequate shelter, or working to prevent the further intervention of the CIA in Central America? Can reasoning together eventually achieve the changes in attitude we think necessary?

Let us consider the extent to which economic injustice is vulnerable or invulnerable to the attacks of reason. If we can show those we consider wrong the irrationality of their positions, will they abandon these positions? If we can succeed in clarifying what the practical implications are of the conceptions of justice we both seem to share, will those with whom we disagree come to share our positions? Do people change their views because they become convinced by theoretical arguments about what reason requires, or do they decide on what reason requires in such a way that it will allow them to maintain the practical positions they favor?

What often appears to happen is the following: when people with social privileges come to understand what the practical implications are of the conceptions of justice they think they endorse, they often give up these conceptions of justice. For instance, when the practical implications of a Rawlsian theory of justice were recognized by those with economic power, the search intensified for alternative theories of justice that would allow these people to escape these practical implications with a semblance of theoretical justification. The recent enormous popularity of libertarianism seems to support this view.[1] And the extraordinary influence of neoconservative excuses for *not* moving toward greater equality, and for *not* decreasing the various traditional forms of discrimination and unfair privilege, can perhaps best be explained on similar grounds.[2]

Some of us may be entirely persuaded that the libertarians' own commitment to freedom requires their commitment to the basic preconditions for freedom: assurances of enough food, shelter, health, and employment to be able to be a free person.[3] But do libertarian theorists agree on what freedom here seems to us to require? There is ample evidence that they do not, even when there is little misunderstanding of the rational presuppositions and rational implications of their and our positions. The differences seem to be ones of interest and preference and moral commitment rather than of rational understanding.

The interests that theories are often devised to support may affect description as well as prescription. Consider the conceptual presuppositions for the accurate description of coercion and the moral conclusions affected. Locke understood that one can be coerced by economic necessity. He concluded that "a Man can no more justly make use of another's necessity, to force him to become his Vassal, by withholding that Relief, God requires him to afford to the wants of his Brother, than he that has more strength can seize upon a weaker, master him to his Obedience, and with a Dagger at his Throat offer him Death or Slavery."[4] But how many libertarians agree with Locke rather than with the absurd claim of the libertarians that economic power cannot be coercive? Milton Friedman argues that "since the household always has the alternative of producing directly for itself, it need not enter into any exchange unless it benefits from it."[5] He assumes that even in a contemporary economy with no "commons" that is not covered with asphalt, every economic transaction is voluntary. And Nozick supposes that even if we sell ourselves into slavery in order to eat we do so freely.

To my mind, arguments based on a mythical "state of nature" in which isolated, self-sufficient men acquire exclusive individual rights to property on the grounds that they themselves have "created" it are fanciful: There would be no such men without strong social ties between at least the persons who mothered them and the children they once were, and property rights should reflect the needs of persons in society. Arguments based on Robinson-Crusoe-like myths for Nozickean rights to property appear to me about as persuasive as Filmer's argument that God gave the earth to Adam and that all political title should depend on correct inheritance since. But libertarian conclusions have a strong hold on many people, despite the theoretical weaknesses of their foundations.

If we ask whether intelligent persons can continue indefinitely to maintain positions that cannot be reasonably defended, we can wonder whether the libertarians and neoconservatives of the day are merely last-ditch defenders of foolish positions, the Filmers of our times, whose views will be more or less permanently replaced by their Lockean analogues. I think the answer is: quite possibly. But what can social philosophers contribute to this outcome and to hastening it?

Better theories are necessary even though they are not sufficient for social progress. There could have been no Lockean position without Locke, though Locke had to have followers and the forces of social change on his side to influence history. How can we best contribute to a general recognition of the flaws in and the genuine requirements of the libertarian position, which is to an important degree dominant in the ideologies and institutions of the United States at present, and which contributes substantially to economic injustice? Our abilities in argument may be more developed than our skills in political action. We can try to answer the libertarian position with better arguments. And, eventually, with a great deal of help from nonphilosophers, we can perhaps succeed in narrowing the scope of injustice.

II

Does rationality require a theory of justice that would recognize that the economic rights of the poor to sufficiency must have priority over the economic rights of the rich to a surplus? Libertarians deny that it does. But can we show that their position is irrational? Can we show that reason requires us to acknowledge the rights of the poor to enough for a decent life in a society that can well afford to honor such rights?

It would be helpful to our position if we could show that it is irrational or inconsistent or incoherent to deny the rights to economic justice that we claim. But I am afraid we cannot show this. We might show, at best, that it would be irrational from a Rawlsian or some other original position, but that is a very different matter from showing that it would be irrational from the position that actual human beings are now in. For we would first have to show that it would be irrational for people to be unwilling to put themselves in the position of those behind a veil of ignorance. And it is this, the requirement that persons here and now be willing to take the point of view of an original position, that rationality alone cannot succeed in demanding.

The problem is the problem of egoism. From the class positions they now occupy, it would be contrary to their rational self-interest for the rich and privileged to take the point of view of those in an original position because, were they to do so, they would surely have to give up many actual advantages.[6]

The question we have to address is not whether egoism from an original position is incoherent, but whether egoism from the actual social positions people are already actually in is incoherent. And while it can be shown that egoism from our actual positions is a morally unworthy theory that will have bad consequences for most people, it cannot, in my view, be shown to be irrational.

What "reason" requires is capable of diverse interpretations. The Kantian tradition suggests an answer very different from the tradition that sees it as requiring the rational—meaning efficient—pursuit of self-interest. Ideal theories such as Rawls's, "ideal observer" theories such as Firth's, and "universal prescriber" theories such as Hare's all try to reconcile these positions. But they do so by sacrificing the points of view of actual persons in actual situations. The rational self-interest of persons in actual situations is very different from what the rational self-interest of persons in an ideal situation would be. And persons asking *why* they should choose to live their lives from the point of view of an ideal morality, rather than from the point of view of the actual life they are actually in, will receive no answer from these theories. Instead of heeding what ideal morality would require, such persons may easily cease to pay attention to those who expound ideal morality.

To be rationally self-interested does not rule out being egoistic from the position actual persons find themselves in. Were it to do so, the problem that would have to be addressed would merely have to include the question "Why should I be rational?" along with the question "Why should I be moral?" I will assume for the purposes of the following discussion that we are already committed to being rational, but not that we are already committed to being non-egoistic. What arguments can rationality then provide for the claims of the poor to economic justice?

I agree that rationality requires us, through conceptions of universalizability, to be committed to *some* notion of equal rights. The question is: With what content? Can rationality require people to favor substantive rights to welfare payments or to employment for everyone in need even if rational self-interest indicates that this will be disadvantageous to the people asking this question from the privileged social positions they actually occupy?

The strongest recent argument that has been offered to show that egoism is irrational even from where we are here and now rather than merely in an ideal world has been Alan Gewirth's. He argues that "it is necessarily true of every agent that he regards as good his particular purposes and the freedom and well-being necessary for all his purposive actions; that he hence also holds that he has rights to freedom and well-being," and that he must therefore accept that others also have such rights.[7]

Gewirth thinks rational necessity requires us to accord to everyone, as we demand for ourselves, rights to the generic features of action, that is, to the freedom and well-being necessary for anyone to act, and without which no one can be an agent. Since in acting we claim such rights for ourselves, logical necessity and empirical truth require us to recognize that others have such rights as well.

But it is unclear what it is that, in acting, we claim. The rich person claims the right to act with the resources at his disposal. Rationality requires that he be willing to accord such a right to others, and he can do so. But for the poor person, a right to act with the resources at one's disposal is of little use, since the poor person's difficulty is that she *lacks* resources. It is quite possible that the rich person does *not* claim a right to be provided with resources he does not already have; hence the rich person would not be required by rational necessity to accord such rights to others.

The person who expects to win contests with others can say that in acting in such contests he claims the right to enter them. He can be quite willing to accord this right to others. An agent whose purpose in acting is winning out over others can reason that a logically necessary means to act successfully toward this purpose is to have occasions for such contests. He can agree that everyone ought to have such occasions, and if he is a fanatic supporter of a survival of the fittest approach to life, he can hold this view even if he does not expect to win himself.

The result of such rationality may be a scheme of rights closer to the libertarian one, permitting economic and other contests even if they result in the starvation of the losers, rather than to a scheme of rights assuring basic necessities to all. As R. M. Hare has shown, fanatics can universalize their judgments.[8] Rationality alone has no satisfactory argument against them.

I share the view that there will always be fanatics, and that a requirement to universalize our moral judgments cannot defeat their arguments. What rationality and philosophical clarity may be able to do is to bring it about that only a small number of people are fanatics. Hare remarks that "the true fanatics are relatively few, and would have no power at all to do harm, were it not for their ability to mislead, and thus win the support of large numbers of people who are not themselves fanatics."[9] This is a more optimistic view than may be warranted, but it is at least often accurate. Applying Hare's argument to the libertarian position, one can agree that the only way libertarians have succeeded in being more than a small number of persons has been by confusing and distorting the relevant issues. Some libertarians are fanatics. Most defend theoretical positions that serve their own interests, either directly or through serving the interests of those with whom they identify. But the interests of most people are harmed by the libertarian position.

From a hypothetical original position, people would want to insure themselves against destitution. They would, if they are rational, include rights to enough material resources for a decent life among the rights that ought to be assured by any actual legal system. But from the position of the rich in an existing society, if they accept a scheme providing welfare payments to the poor or publicly funded employment for the unemployed, the rich may bring upon themselves substantial disadvantages over their present position. If they are concerned about the possibility that they too may at some time be poor and unemployed, or if they are concerned about the dangers of social unrest and uncheckably rising crime rates, they may think the insurance provided by such rights to be in their interest also. But if they can calculate the probabilities of their being able to maintain their present class advantages as being comfortably high, they would not agree on grounds of self-interest that they ought to accept a scheme providing welfare payments and public employment. On the contrary, *rational* self-interest from the position of the rich in an existing, stable society would recommend opposition to such a scheme. The rich who vote for Reagan are not all fools.

From a hypothetical original position, rational self-interest would lead one to substantive positions that rights should include the equal rights of everyone who needs them to welfare payments, rights that would turn out to be advantageous to the unfortunate and disadvantageous to the fortunate in an actual society. But from the position of the rich in an actual society, the equal rights one would be led by rationality to recognize would be substantive rights to act and to compete with the resources already possessed, rights that would be advantageous to the rich and of no use to the poor.

Gewirth thinks he can counter such arguments by requiring that it be only the *generic* features of action that are accorded attention, and to which all should be accorded rights. The generic features of action are: sufficient freedom and well-being to be able to be an agent. But his suggestion that we limit our attention to these generic features of action seems arbitrary. It assumes that, in acting, we all claim rights to the same things: these generic features of action. But in acting, the rich may claim something quite different: the right to act with the resources already available to them, or the right to enter competitive contests.

If we require that in acting we are all so similar that we all claim the same thing, then Gewirth's theory is a theory of the ideal agent rather than of real agents, and it suffers from the same problems as the other ideal theories mentioned. It no longer allows Gewirth to make the claim that is central to his argument—and one of the strengths of his approach—that the reasoning process he outlines is one we all *must*, on pain of contradiction, go through. If, on the other hand, Gewirth's theory *is* a theory for actual agents in actual societies, then it is unpersuasive to assert that in acting all agents assert rights to the same things.

Rationality requires that we recognize that each person must be treated equally in certain respects. But what these respects are remains open. Rationality cannot fill in the contents of equal rights in a way that will be damaging to the libertarian position without considerable help from more than rationality.

III

To be able to argue that the rights of everyone to enough resources for a decent life should be recognized by everyone, including the rich and privileged in actual societies, one must, I think, appeal to the notions of cooperation and social trust, rather than merely to rationality and reason.

It can be shown that for societies not to fall apart there must be an adequate level of social trust and cooperation. Trust is a relation between persons that makes cooperation possible. We need to be able to show what would make trust *justifiable*. What sorts of social arrangements would make it *not unreasonable* for persons in an actual society to trust one another?

Societies have not come about because of, and are not built upon, social contracts. Every actual society reflects the results of war, exploitation, imperialism, racism, patriarchy, and everywhere the imposition on the weak of the demands of the strong. For the members of an existing society to be justified in trusting one another, there must be an acceptance of certain fundamental requirements, and an understanding that progress toward more satisfactory arrangements will proceed at an acceptable rate.

Among these requirements is one that no member of a society should be denied the provision of what is essential (within some range of normality) for a decent life and adequate self-development while the society makes it possible for others to have vastly more than they need. Without acceptance of such a requirement, those in danger of being left without the resources adequate for a decent life would be justified in *not* trusting the other members of the society enough to live at peace with them. *They* would have good reasons to refuse to cooperate, and to fail to contribute to the social trust on which societies depend, even though it would be in the rational self-interest of the rich and privileged to try to maintain the social fabric without acknowledging this requirement for social trust.

A first requirement for general trust—not merely trust among the rich or trust among the poor, but general trust—would be a recognition, not yet achieved in the United States, that human beings have basic economic and social rights that are just as important and fundamental as their traditional civil and political rights. These economic and social rights to basic necessities and to adequate self-development ought to be assured by the actual arrangements of the society as adequately as civil and political rights ought to be assured. They ought to be assured as individual rights as well as, where appropriate, as group rights. General policies of promoting economic growth and full employment, even when these are effective, are not enough. There must be assurances that individuals are entitled to actual employment, not merely to equal opportunities to compete for jobs they can never obtain. And welfare payments must be assured as matters of fundamental right, not as public charity that can be withdrawn in times of governmental budget cutting and for which, in accepting, the recipient is expected to surrender such other constitutional rights as the right to the privacy of her home.[10]

Cooperation does not require altruism. But it cannot be based merely on rational self-interest.[11] When individuals and groups all pursue their own interests, even if they do so rationally, the social trust on which cooperation depends cannot develop or it becomes eroded, so that it really is more in the interest of those who can successfully take advantage of others to do so, rather than to contribute, while others freeload, to the creation or maintenance of cooperative arrangements. And when it really is in the rational self-interest of some individuals and groups to take advantage of others, it really is in the interest of those of whom advantage is being taken to resist, to defend themselves, and to refuse to contribute to the social arrangements that allow this to happen. At this point *mistrust* is rational, and societies are in danger of dissolution.[12]

Cooperation refers to a cooperative policy in situations in which interests are partly compatible and partly in conflict. This is the normal situation in actual human affairs. Cooperation may include upholding fair competitive rules instead of breaking them through collusion, or it may include a willingness to change the rules instead of upholding them where the rules are unjustified.

The choice for or against cooperation arises when the pursuit of self-interest at the expense of another's interest will yield a potentially *greater* gain for a given individual than the cooperative pursuit of mutual value. However, if both or all choose the noncooperative, self-interested course of action, the outcome will be *worse* for both or all than if they shared the mutual value—such as the value of trust—of a cooperative policy.

Historically, the poor, the disadvantaged, the weak, and the female, have been taught to be altruistic and trusting. The result has been that others have more easily taken advantage of them. Those of whom advantage has been taken have good reasons to mistrust those who have sought and often won their cooperation while refusing to accord them the respect that would make such trust justifiable. If their mistrust now threatens to engulf an existing society, it is likely that the society as it now exists is not worthy of preservation. Repairing a social fabric that has been worn through by a massive neglect of the basic economic and social rights of many members requires fundamental changes in the institutions and arrangements of a society.

We can distinguish between the rational and the reasonable. It is reasonable to abandon the egoism of rational self-interest and to take a chance on cooperation when others are willing to do so as well. We may never know if others are sincere and actually willing to cooperate, rather than merely deceiving us into being trusting and gullible contributors to their future profit. But it is reasonable to take a chance on cooperation when we lack clear reasons for mistrust.

This imports a normative element into the concept of what "reason" recommends. If reason is understood as requiring us to be reasonable as here described rather then merely rational, then reason can provide grounds for economic justice. But rationality alone, from our actual positions, often cannot.

Can libertarians be persuaded to be reasonable? If libertarians are to be so persuaded, I suspect it will take far more than philosophical discussion. But those in a position to outvote or outmaneuver or occasionally even outspend libertarians may be helped in their endeavors by the arguments philosophers can provide.

Actual societies have long depended on the cooperation of many members whose trust was misplaced. But as those who have been denied the respect they are due as human beings become aware of this denial, they become less and less willing to cooperate in their own disregard. Assurance of the economic resources adequate for a decent life, when assuring this is fully feasible, is a central requirement for social trust to be justifiable. Without such trust, there can be little hope for enough cooperation to keep existing societies satisfactorily afloat in the long run. And the need for social ties that span the globe has become more and more urgent. For enough trust to make it possible for a framework of global cooperation to evolve, progress toward international economic justice is imperative. Understanding what it would be reasonable to demand and to concede from the points of view of the situations we are actually enmeshed in is very difficult, and very important.

Notes

1. The reception given to Robert Nozick's *Anarchy, State and Utopia* (New York: Basic Books, 1974) is an example.

2. See Peter Steinfels, *The Neo-Conservatives: The Men Who Are Changing America's Politics* (New York: Simon & Schuster, 1979).

3. See, for example, Virginia Held, "Men, Women, and Equal Liberty," in *Equality and Social Policy*, W. Feinberg, ed. (Urbana: University of Illinois Press, 1978); and James P. Streba, "Alternative Conceptions of Justice: A Practical Reconciliation," paper for AMIN-TAPHIL Ninth Plenary Conference, January 14-16, 1983.

4. John Locke, *First Treatise*, para. 42. See also Virginia Held, "John Locke on Robert Nozick," *Social Research* 43 (Spring 1976): 169-95.

5. Milton Friedman, *Capitalism and Freedom* (Chicago: University of Chicago Press, 1962), p. 13.

6. See Virginia Held, "On Rawls and Self-Interest," *Midwest Studies in Philosophy* 1 (1976): 57-60.

7. Alan Gewirth, *Reason and Morality* (Chicago: University of Chicago Press, 1978), p. 176.

8. See R. M. Hare, *Freedom and Reason* (New York: Oxford University Press, 1965), chap. 9. In *Moral Thinking: Its Levels, Method, and Point* (Oxford: Clarendon Press, 1981), Hare argues that the fanatic's position must yield to the utilitarianism he now espouses. I do not find the latter arguments persuasive, but I cannot examine them here.

9. Hare, *Freedom and Reason*, p. 185.

10. See *Wyman* v. *James*, 400 U.S. 309 (1971).

11. See, for example David Braybrooke, "The Insoluble Problem of the Social Contract," *Dialogue* 1 (March 1976): 3-37.

12. For further discussion, see Virginia Held, "Rationality and Reasonable Cooperation," *Social Research* 44 (Winter 1977): 708-44, and *Rights and Goods: Justifying Social Action* (New York: Free Press/Macmillan, 1984).

Bibliography

Held, Virginia, ed. *Property, Profits, and Economic Justice.* Belmont, Calif.: Wadsworth, 1980).
———. *Rights and Goods: Justifying Social Action.* New York: Free Press/Macmillan, 1984.
Rawls, John. *A Theory of Justice.* Cambridge, Mass.: Harvard University Press, 1971.
Shue, Henry. *Basic Rights, Subsistence, Affluence, and U.S. Foreign Policy.* Princeton: Princeton University Press, 1980.
Sterba, James P. *The Demands of Justice.* Notre Dame: University of Notre Dame Press, 1980.
Thurow, Lester C. *The Zero-Sum Society.* New York: Penguin Books, 1981.

3

Hegel on Poverty and Violence

Timo Airaksinen
Department of Philosophy
University of Helsinki (Finland)
University of Pittsburgh

In his *Philosophy of Right*, Hegel's comments on poverty and its dysfunctional and immoral social effects are relatively brief.[1] This is hardly surprising, however, since the whole book is in fact a set of published lecture notes. It is accordingly difficult to find a proper theory of poverty and its relation to violence in the book. But we find instead some bold and startling claims concerning the nature of the modern capitalist society, or "civil society," and if we are willing to read between the lines, we can construct some definitions and explanations concerning questions of welfare. All this is potentially interesting. Yet, I think that we should link this historical information closely to a modern analytical account of poverty, its causes and effects. This is exactly what I shall try to achieve: I shall sketch Hegel's original ideas from the point of view of such problems as the meaning of the terms "poverty," "violence," and "social power"; the relationship between coercion and violence; and the alleged immorality of all violent action. And I shall try to utilize Hegel's views and notions to raise questions as to whether poverty is essentially related to violence and whether injustice in social life implies the presence of violence.

Poverty

I cannot present any strict definition of the concept of poverty. (I don't think anybody can.) Instead, I intend to make some basic relevant distinctions: Poverty may be said to be either *absolute* or *relative*, either *objective* or *subjective*, and related either to one's real *needs* or personal *desires*. Then I shall ask what conceptual relations obtain between these six notions.

The first of the distinctions is a standard one, or course. We all recognize that in any actual society it may happen that some people's basic needs are not adequately satisfied so that their physical survival is in real danger. Such people are absolutely poor, and their situation stands in contrast to that of people who have more (even much more; no intrinsic limits can be set to the difference) than the absolutely poor, but still less than, let us say, the average citizen. Some of us are relatively poor. As Nicholas Rescher writes:

> Two quite different things are at issue here: 1. Sufficiency to live at a *minimal* level of *subsistence* . . . , a level of bare survival, calling for the minima of food, shelter, clothing, and medical attention . . . . 2. Sufficiency to live at a *basic* level of *comfort* . . . , a level calling for an adequate share of the "good things in life."[2]

A failure to reach the first level reflects absolute poverty and a failure to reach the second level reflects relative poverty.

Rescher explains the notion of relative poverty by saying that a poor person is "constrained to live in a fashion which is inadequate from a social point of view, lacking the things which people in his environment by and large have."[3] This quotation shows that Rescher applies some kind of *objective criterion* to determine who actually belong to the class of the relatively poor. (Of course, it must be specified before it can be used in policy making, but its basic nature is clear enough.) The criterion in question is simply the availability of typical amenities, understood in statistically measurable terms and used comparatively. Any person who does not possess the things that are needed for what one might call a stereotypically comfortable average life-style is relatively poor. Thus the implicit but basic point is that "relative poverty" can indeed be defined in objective terms. And the same is true of "absolute poverty"; but that is hardly surprising.

However, it is easy to see that "relative poverty" can be understood also in terms of *personal desires*; that is, by saying that any person who is not likely to satisfy his own relevant desires is poor. Personal dissatisfaction is now the key idea. But it is important to notice that a person may not need an extensive array of goods and amenities in order to be satisfied with his own life-style; and therefore no statistical measure of his possessions and privileges will automatically tell whether he is relatively poor or not (in the *subjective* sense). For instance, asceticism is a traditional value in many cultures, and those who subscribe to it may well not be poor. The crucial thing when we discuss relative poverty is what one in fact desires: One's poverty depends on one's desires.

Of course, the subjectivist concept of poverty has its attractive features, but it also tends to make "relative poverty" exceedingly flexible. One may misrepresent one's desires to get a better and better position in life: "Relativity is a game which everyone has an equal right to play."[4] Or one may start thinking that mere manipulation of underprivileged people's explicit understanding of their own needs and desires is sufficient to eliminate their poverty. Therefore, at the level of social policy making, an exclusive emphasis on subjective desires and their satisfaction unduly complicates compensatory allocation procedures. For all these reasons, it seems plausible that both objective and subjective criteria of relative poverty should enter into the conduct of justice-oriented social life. Yet, the objective and subjective measures of poverty may not be combined in any simple way: They are two different things.

My next point is that even if "relative poverty" can be contrasted to "absolute poverty" it is still the case that also the latter notion has a *comparative component.* We can speak sensibly about (absolute) poverty only if it makes sense to say also that *the poor could be doing better than they are doing.* This counterfactual proposition is indeed included in all poverty ascriptions: By calling someone "poor" we imply that some other people are more affluent than he is and, moreover, that he could be better off. "Poverty" implies an open and partially realized better alternative. One cannot say that the cave people were poor, and neither can one say that the native tribes of the Amazon area were poor before they met the white man and adopted some of his values and goals. Since these people could not have been more affluent than they were, their life situation cannot be usefully compared to ours; and because that cannot be done in any sensible way, they cannot be said to be as a whole an absolutely poor group of people, even if they lived in constant danger of starvation (as I suppose). In this sense, "poverty," even in the absolute, seems to be a comparative notion. Furthermore, all social groups who are so severely discriminated against that they are deprived of almost all means of livelihood are absolutely poor. Yet, we may assent to this proposition only if we think that they really could do better; namely, if they were *not* victims of such extreme discrimination. This if-clause is certainly a plausible one, and the basic idea is again that absolutely poor people are poor compared to what they could be. *In sum:* Even "absolute poverty" is a comparative social notion because it implies contrary to fact that the poor could be doing better, like those who actually are better off.

I shall talk about poverty in its two main forms: absolute poverty and relative poverty. (In the case of the latter I shall emphasize its subjective desire-related sense.) "Absolute poverty" is certainly a basic social notion. Although desperate deprivation alone does not imply poverty, persons who are absolutely poor are at or below the crucial subsistence level. Thus absolute poverty implies extreme deprivation. And it is this implication that we are interested in when we restrict our study to modern industrialized societies and their recent history, as we are doing now. If we studied developing countries or primitive social life, our present strategy would be overly simplistic, for we would have to focus on deprivation in general.

But why choose the subjective notion of relative poverty? First, Hegel operates with this type of concept. Second, by leaving aside the objective and statistical notion we are able to understand better some important *motivational* components that influence the decisions and actions of the poor. It is obvious why and how absolute poverty drives the poor to relief-seeking action. But if relative poverty is taken to imply merely that the poor have quantitatively less goods and resources than some other part of the population, it is difficult to see exactly why they feel that poverty is such a personal hardship. Recall my earlier remark about asceticism and think of the Franciscan monks who maintain that (relative) poverty is a highly desirable and valuable religious life-style. They are certainly poor according to any statistical criterion; but if they really are poor, this criterion does not allow us to understand why they do not strive to avoid their alleged poverty. Most of us would do just that, after all.

Only by noticing that from the standpoint of their peculiar personal value commitments they are *not* poor can we see why they do not feel like struggling against their lot: They do not see the point of the poverty-counterfactual that allegedly applies to their economic situation. For them it is senseless to say that they *could* be more affluent; they do not want that. This is the main reason why I suppose that we have to focus on actually unsatisfied but satisfiable subjective desires as the core of relative poverty. Self-induced and freely accepted underprivilege vitiates the objective statistical criterion. (As I shall point out, the statistical criterion is not even a necessary condition of the applicability of the subjective criterion of relative poverty.)

Poverty and Moral Alienation

The following quotation gives us a hint of Hegel's position:

> When the standard of living of a large mass of people fails below a certain subsistence level—a level regulated automatically as the one necessary for the member of the society—and when there is a consequent loss of the sense of right and wrong . . . the result is the creation of a rabble of paupers.[5]

Let us compare this to the corresponding *Addition*:

> The lowest subsistence level, that of a rabble of paupers, is fixed automatically, but the minimum varies considerably in different countries. . . . Poverty in itself does not make men into a rabble; a rabble is created only when there is joined to poverty a disposition of mind.[6]

Both quotations are somewhat ambiguous. In the first one, Hegel's expression "a level . . . necessary for the member of society" does not indicate whether he is talking about one's biological survival or about one's membership in the group. In the second quotation, since the term "rabble of paupers" is used both to *define* the lowest feasible subsistence level (cf. the first quotation) and to describe an independent social *problem* only loosely connected to poverty, it is not clear what factors bring about that notorious "disposition of mind" that is sometimes a characteristic of the poor (if it is *not* the deprivation and underprivilege called "poverty").

The present context can be clarified by noticing that Hegel states explicitly that "It is not simply starvation which is at issue"[7] and that the most crucial problem with poverty is the moral one, the creation of the rebellious rabble of paupers. This is a mass of people who have lost their sense of right and wrong and who consequently form an amoral element in the social system. Absolute poverty and actual starvation are side issues inasmuch as Hegel seems to suppose that the most drastic effects of poverty are always avoidable. Thus relative poverty is the crucial issue. Some people are bound to notice that they have considerably less than others and that they cannot satisfy such needs and desires of theirs as would make them full-fledged members of their society. Relative poverty means to them a more or less permanent exclusion from ordinary social life. From this perspective it is easy to see why Hegel thinks they become destructive and irresponsible. For Hegel, all morality is constituted socially, and thus those who lack a social role are left automatically without any clear-cut internalized norms and shared values. They become morally alienated and suffer from anomie, to use the modern sociological terms.

Now it is necessary to ask what evidence one can produce to justify the claim that "relative poverty" is interpreted in the subjective fashion in the *Philosophy of Right*. Two answers come to mind. First, Hegel's poor are a mass of openly and consciously dissatisfied people; they are irresponsible and destructive; and so, they are active. Their poverty is a motivational condition. Second, civil society is a place in which needs, wants, and desires are created, recognized, redefined, and combined in various ways.[8] Some needs, such as the need for food, are unquestionably natural, but as Hegel says, starvation is not the real issue. On the contrary, we must focus on wants and desires within a social framework where both their emergence and the style and extent of their satisfaction is far from being a natural affair:

> Poverty leaves them *more or less* deprived of all the *advantages* of society, of the opportunity of acquiring skill or education of any kind, as well as of the administration of justice, the public health services, and often even the consolations of religion, and so forth.[9]

Actually, civil society is almost by definition the realm of subjectivized needs or personal desires, and it does not appear to be the case that Hegel is speaking about any objective measure of the distribution of goods among people. Rather, he is interested in the satisfaction of desires (which is based on those goods); that is, in our subjective *advantages*. When one deals with this issue, one must keep in mind the general plan of civil society in the *Philosophy of Right*.

To see better how Hegel actually construes "poverty," let us review the three main factors that allegedly throw men into poverty. (1) Personal extravagance and foolishness, which imply unrealistic needs and desires, are important causes of poverty. This is a fitting thesis, since Hegel also tells us that civil society strengthens desires and multiplies them almost without a limit.[10] (He refers to the importance of advertising here.) Thus there is an ever-present danger of succumbing to artificial temptations to own and consume more and more until one's economic situation is ruined and the bitterness of mind grows intolerable.

What we actually have here is an indication of the existence of fake subjective poverty: Our dissatisfied agents want too much; they cannot really present any reasons why they should have all the comfort and luxury they expect to be available to them; therefore, they are not *really* subjectively poor. Of course, they will be poor if their pursuit of the luxuries of life prevents them from having the necessities they really need. (2) As Hegel says, random accidents, such as floods, storms, earthquakes, and other natural catastrophes, as well as wars and revolutions and other social disasters, sometime destroy investments and breed permanent economic difficulty. Though this second type of cause is possibly the least interesting of the causes of poverty, certainly no account of poverty would be complete without it.

I wish to clarify one point that I have mentioned twice: Those causes of poverty that we are discussing—accidental factors—illustrate nicely the important point that a person who is without some statistically interpreted "luxuries" but otherwise well off may really be *poor*. This idea hinges on the fact that the person may have a good reason to desire the valuable assets, so that what is a statistical luxury is not a luxury but a necessity to him. Let us take an example of a case where subjective relative poverty is not objective statistical poverty because the person in question is above the crucial statistical poverty line. A seriously handicapped farmer needs an expensive, specially equipped car so that he can drive to the city to get treatment and meet friends; otherwise his life is intolerable. But such cars are prohibitively expensive. The farmer is not objectively poor, but because he cannot afford the car and he subjectively suffers because of that economic problem, we may, and we should, call him poor. My point here is that this man's life-context is such a special one that the statistical poverty-criterion does not apply to him. Only the subjective criterion shows that he is genuinely relatively poor.

(3) Hegel's last poverty-inducing factor is clearly the most interesting of them all. There are structural and systematic social causes of poverty, such as the fact that overproduction of goods makes the market collapse and, consequently, a large number of workers will become unemployed. But their reemployment would again increase the production level and deepen the economic crisis. This dead end, suggests Hegel, shows where to look for an explanation of poverty: The economic system is protected by pushing some people out of its bounds. In this connection we can also understand what Hegel means by his enigmatic and, in its context, isolated comment: "The creation of a rabble of paupers . . . brings with it . . . conditions which greatly facilitate the concentration of disproportionate wealth in a few hands."[11] He never explains why and how this is supposed to happen. Hegel is not interested in economic theory. Nevertheless, for moral philosophy the import of this idea is clear enough; and three extra steps bring the point out more clearly: (1) "despite an excess of wealth civil society is not rich enough" to fight poverty successfully, (2) poverty takes "the form of a wrong done to one class by another," and (3) the poor have "vices which arise out of their plight and their sense of wrong."[12] Poverty cannot be prevented because some successful agents profit from it; yet this is morally wrong. Consequently, the rebellion of the poor has a definite moral point, however hidden this positive aspect ordinarily may be.

Hegel's final picture of relative poverty shows poverty as a dialectically reversed image of the original one: Subjective deprivation assumes now a systematic role in economic life so that there is good reason to suspect that *both* its causes and its effects are morally dubious and socially unjust. "Civil society affords a spectacle of extravagance and want as well as of the physical and ethical degeneration common to them both."[13]

At this point, one can remark that I have given a patently one-sided account of Hegel's idea of poverty. Civil society may be a wild and basically morally imperfect system of need satisfaction, but it can also be said that it is an institution that professes to take good care of its members. Social-policy measures are an essential feature of it. Therefore, as long so persons stay in the role of a participant in the game of competitive economic life, they are certain to get support and protection against its financial hazards. It is only after persons have dropped out of the economic system's bounds that their situation in civil society becomes alarming.

Well, all this is indeed true. Nevertheless, we must mark a difference between the real poor, or the rabble of paupers, and the temporarily not-so-successful members of the civil society. To put it in a more perspicuous way, economic life revolves around the so-called Corporations that resemble, among other things, modern labor unions and employers' organizations, whose main purpose is to take care of their members' long-range interests and goals, so far as these need collective support. (Also the police and other public authorities offer their help.) Hegel himself puts it in the following way:

> Within the Corporation the help which poverty receives loses its accidental character and the humiliation wrongfully associated with it. The wealthy perform their duties to their fellow associates.[14]

It is important to notice that Hegel describes the situation only among the corporation members; if he did not, his thought would be inconsistent. (In fact, some poverty does not receive help, as we have seen.) Yet, it remains true that within organized labor and capital poverty is no deep problem at all. But all this is irrelevant; for we are interested exactly in those cases in which the organic and smoothly delivered help to the poor is impossible. The key situations are those in which corporations have lost their grip on people. For then poverty will assume its humiliating character: The ugliness of material and cultural deprivation and the rudeness of the help it gets are just two sides of the one and the same coin.[15] (Hegel's illustration refers to people begging in the streets.) Furthermore, large-scale deep poverty cannot be prevented. The result is said to be the emergence of rebellious violence and the loss of the sense of right and wrong in human life. Civil society breeds an undercurrent of bitterness and hatred between "classes." And an ironic twist is revealed when we notice that we are dealing with subjective feelings more than with the life and death issues of absolute poverty.

Types and Nature of Violence

Our next step will be to introduce the notion of *violence* into our discussion. Hegel does not pay much attention to it in the present context, but certainly it lies buried beneath his ideas of poverty. Why does he not deal with the issue raised by social violence? I can see one very basic reason. Hegel is actually interested only in the *rational* part of social life. He does not develop the theme of the irrational or the immoral and unjust element of poverty because civil society is a mere preliminary stage of a dialectical development leading toward the state proper, in which individual and public interests are finally unified under the cover of one leading idea of what social life is and how it should be conducted. The universal state-interest is a consistent and comprehensive theory. In a rather mysterious way, all those egotistical agents of the free-enterprise system, now called "civil society," can adopt, or at least understand, the unified common-to-all state-interest. Hegel never even starts to explain how they could achieve that goal; on the contrary, he merely supposes that *if* the members of civil society are ideally rational they will accept their additional and, in a sense, primary status as state citizens. (Certainly they will do just that if they really are *rational* in Hegel's own special sense of the term, which, alas, can mean hardly anything but that they understand and accept Hegel's social theory: They join the state if they are rational, because to be rational is to do just that.)

Members of the civil society are also state citizens. Now, the social system governed by the state is necessarily perfectly just. The state is an ideal. All images of moral corruption and social injustice at the state level of the system are illusory, and their contradictions are resolved through the theory of the state. However, a rare exception to the rule that only the idealized harmony of particular interests is the proper subject matter of the dialectical social theory is poverty.

To avoid misunderstanding, let me emphasize the key point. No social institution, the state included, can be used to show either that poverty is avoidable or that its causes are ultimately understandable and normatively acceptable as meaningful and harmonious social facts. All this is vain hope. In relation to poverty both the affluent and the poor behave irrationally. The privileged class exploits the poor and thus indirectly denies their natural right to welfare for their families. The poor, having given up all hope of economic recovery and of their return to normal life within civil society, will rebel against the society, the state, and its laws and norms. This is the whole and final truth of modern poverty; no dialectical justification for poverty can be found at the later stages of Hegel's theorizing. Poverty is ultimately and finally a bad thing. No "invisible hand" works in the present context, like it does, according to Hegel, in a free market economy.

Poverty leads to violent behavior, and poverty is at least in cases a result of violence. If this is true, violence is many things. The poor fight the police in the streets, but no similar behavior can be witnessed in the case of the rich. We need to distinguish between several different types of violence. We can, *prima facie*, find four of them: *physical*, *psychological*, *social*, and *structural* violence. Moreover, two important points of view exist: "Violence" may be either a (negatively loaded) *normative* concept or a *descriptive* one; and violence is both a *process* and a *product*. As to this last twofold distinction, we distinguish between violent actions (or behavior) and violent states of affairs. Next, we can try to characterize "violence" in the following general way: "Violence" means *the use of force so that the subjective probability of the occurrence of intended or nonintended considerable personal harm increases.* I must add, however, that this definition is problematic, but we need one anyway. In general, I suspect that no satisfactory analytic definition can be given since "violence" is one of those complex social notions that is as to its meaning, tailormade for a wide variety of rhetorical uses. It is many different things, and what one calls "violent action" may tell as much about the speaker himself as about his object of interest. For example, war is violent, streets are violent, some horror movies are violent, and some divorces sever the links between the parents and the children violently. Often we just proscribe an action by calling it violent. Unquestionably, all this is true, but we are not interested in rhetoric.

Let us therefore go deeper into the real problems of violence. Our definition deals with the use or the *process* aspect of violence. Now, if one asks what "force" means, it is natural to suggest that it means physical force, although it may refer to psychological force, such as strong verbal abuse. Nevertheless, it seems plausible to say that the use of actual physical force, such as in beating, shooting, or torturing, constitutes the paradigmatic cases. Actual, not merely imagined or expected, application of excessive physical force constitutes the central case of all possible violence. If a certain other type of human action is violent, it is because it is *analogous* to the basic case described above. Thus we have a "process-oriented and reality centered analogy theory of violence." According to this idea, we say that real violence always has a point so that it is a harmful effect or a socially undesirable function. It is only because of real violence that its symbolic forms can emerge and appear frightening or stimulating.

Now, as to the *product* aspect of violence, in its most basic cases we can say that a violent state of affairs results from violent action. For example, a person living in a violent street will experience something like muggings, shootings, and rapes. In this way the violent end-state, the violent street, results from violent actions. It seems essential in these simple cases that actual use of violence occurs, for we cannot call a street violent before the trouble has started (but perhaps our intuitions are not too firm here).

Let me say next something about *psychological* violence. It is a type of violence, but it hardly deserves any basic or independent status of its own, as can be seen by recognizing the fact that we normally do not speak about psychological violence as mere violence. We typically add the qualifying explanatory adjective "psychological" in cases like that of a father accusing his children of being lazy and stupid in such a harsh manner that neurotic problems follow. If we make the psychological aspect explicit by adding "psychological" to qualify "violence," we express a reservation concerning the actual violence of the situation. The father is not *really* violent; he is *merely* psychologically violent. It is then relevant to notice that psychologically violent tactics often produce actual physical harm. For instance, brainwashing and "third-degree" interrogations cause physical damage. Moreover, physical maltreatment may well cause severe psychological problems. All this makes the analogy between direct physical violence and its psychological counterpart quite evident and strong. Psychological force works like real force. We are nevertheless dealing with an analogy. An army sergeant who virtually terrorizes the privates by his foul language is not a violent character just because of this aspect of his behavior. But if an army infantry training camp applies these methods so that psychological maltreatment brings about physical harm in *normal* men, we are justified in calling the institution psychologically violent. We have a well-grounded analogy to the basic idea behind all violence: that is, physical force and its undesirable effects.

If the psychological notion of violence is a rather uninteresting analogous extension of the basic notion, what about *social violence*? One might say, with good reason, that "social violence" is a special *product* notion whose meaningful use presupposes the processes of physical (and psychological) force. It applies to the context where the basic processes of violence function so as to shape the context in which they operate. The result can be called "violent" in some new social sense. Nevertheless, it seems senseless to maintain that there could be some special "social forces" independent of physical force, and that social violence occurs if and only if a situation exemplifies an excessive application of this social force so that some kind of injury ensues.

If we accept these preliminary points, we can say that "social violence" means *a state of a social institution (in the broad sense of the term) such that it embodies a systematic distribution of subjective harm to some of the members or participants as a result of the actual use of physical or psychological force, or violence.* For example, a landowner's private army legally drives his reluctant tenant farmers away from their village; such measures are a part of the normal functioning of the feudal social system. Actual force is used, and all action takes place within the limits of a social institution and between its members. Certainly, not all violence is institution-bound in this way. Much of it is more or less random and socially meaningless. Yet, social violence is violence within a social institution and, in this rather vague sense, meaningful. Notice that the rebellion of the poor as discussed by Hegel may qualify as genuine social violence, provided that poverty is so long-lasting and systematic that it forms an institution with its characteristic patterns of (mis)behavior. Hegel's account of poverty gives it this *systematic status* and qualifies the actions of the poor as social violence.

With this classification of the three forms of violence in hand, we may ask whether we could avoid the theoretical complications typical of "social violence" by simply reducing this problematic concept to that of *social power*. If this is possible, we can simplify our discussion of violence considerably. However, social violence is not social power or its subtype. Some social scientists support the opposite view; for example, Dennis

Wrong defines "power" as the "capacity of some persons to produce intended and foreseen effects on others."[16] He classifies the various forms of power in such a way that violence becomes *the use of physical force to produce intended and foreseen effects on others*.[17] His treatment of social violence is in line with mine, and let us therefore pretend that we accept Wrong's definition of social power and check what follows with respect to the notion of violence.

The main point is that, according to Wrong's definition of "power," violence as social power produces intended and foreseen effects on others. However, as it is easy to see, the occurrence of such effects is not a *necessary condition* of the existence of (the use of) violence: Cases exist such that violence is used without it being true either that (1) its effects are intentional and foreseen, or that (2) the relevant harm is experienced by others. If this is indeed the case, "violence" implies some conditions that do not hold for "social power," and therefore violence is not a subtype of power. Certainly it cannot be denied that violence is closely related to power, and I shall say something more about this later.

To separate violence from social power, we may argue as follows. First, as Wrong's definition of "power" clearly specifies, no agent has power over himself. In some sense, one certainly can influence one's own conduct, but this is not power in the presently intended social sense. "Power" means one's ability and capacity to act in the social realm; that is, to realize one's own preferences among and in opposition to other people's competing preferences. In this way, violence is not even in its social sense a form of social power, simply because one may act in a socially violent manner over and against oneself. If we look back to my suggested characterization of social violence, we see that self-directed social violence is perfectly possible (and the same is true of the more elementary types of violence). One glaring example suffices: fully institutionalized, ritual forms of suicide, such as the Japanese hara-kiri, which was committed by disgraced members of the soldier class. It was their explicit duty to perform this shocking act. It was a feature of their social role.

Second, the effects of violence need not be intended and foreseen. One may start to act intentionally and purposefully; say, one throws a chair through a closed window and the falling object kills an innocent passerby. This is violent action because it is highly probable that such action will cause harm, and its performance is based on physical force. And especially *if* the injury occurs, the end-state can be called violent. But whatever will happen in the street, it is neither intentional nor foreseen; therefore it cannot embody social power in Wrong's original sense. In sum, violence is not a subtype of social power because (i) one can act violently *against oneself* and (ii) one can be violent unintentionally; that is, the violent effects of one's action may be both unintended and unforeseen.

My second point can be extended to social violence quite naturally. For example, hockey is a violent game in the sense that fisticuffs are acceptable and expected even if they are against the rules of the game and they result in penalties to participants. Now, when a player starts a fight, it may be either for some tactical reason, which involves power-related considerations, or because of simple and pure anger. In this latter case, he need not consider the effects of his behavior as in some way desirable with respect to his or his team's plans and goals, and still we can say that his action is violent. Social violence need not be related to social power.

What is the real relation between power and violence? My suggestion is, to put it briefly, that violence is an *operational component* of certain forms of social power. For example, when A *coerces* B to do something against B's will, A may use a threat consisting of predicted violence against B. Agent A says that he will shoot B if B does not tell where his valuables are hidden. In this way, violence in its physical and psychological senses can have a role in the constitution of power relations in social settings. (This topic requires and deserves a fuller treatment, which I have tried to provide elsewhere.) [18]

Now, let us apply these considerations to our problems of poverty. My thesis is that *poverty* may be either (a) a dynamic factor in the exercise of social power or (b) a violent (social) state of affairs. If we take "power" and "violence" in their social sense, we can say that some people deliberately exploit others and actually *use* the poor, say, as slaves, for their own egotistical economic purposes. Hegel discusses this very possibility in his *Philosophy of Right.* But there is another type of situation: Suppose that colonists use considerable force to drive some primitive native tribes of a remote area away from their original hunting grounds and thereby reduce them to utter poverty. In this case, poverty is a mere *unintended* side effect of a violent process whose main goal is just to get rid of the people living in areas officially and legally reserved for more advanced productive purposes. In the first case, in contrast, poverty is a functional element in the intended exercise of social power, which may be generated in its turn by means of violence. Two points emerge at this stage. First, poverty may be something that helps more fortunate agents to realize their own will; that is, satisfy their needs and preferences in the competitive social world. Poverty may thus reflect the exercise of power. Second, poverty may be a result of the use of excessive force in such a way that a typically uneven distribution of economic losses indirectly ensues. Poverty may thus be a side effect of violence.

Structural Violence

The twofold account of the causes of poverty is too simple. Something important can be seen to be missing when we argue that poverty is either a purposefully used means or unintended result of violence. I do not mean merely that there exists a large number of other types of socially unjust factors that reduce men to the deprivation of welfare. Rather, we can find a poverty factor that is in line with the two discussed above but is not covered by my initial account of them. I have in mind a case in which *no overt force* (or violence) is used to generate intended or unintended poverty that still qualifies as a genuinely *violent* state of affairs. To put it in another way, the process and product aspects of violence seem to break apart in such a case. If this is possible, we certainly must focus on it and try to make sense of the situation. We have a major social phenomenon here: Let us call it *structural violence* and consider in what sense this new type of violence might be an extension of our earlier, more basic ones.

First, let us see how Johan Galtung defines a "broad notion of violence;" that is, violence that does not imply the use of force:

> violence is present when human beings are being influenced so that their actual somatic and mental realizations are below their potential realizations . . . . Thus, if a person died from tuberculosis in the eighteenth century it would be hard to conceive of this as violence since it might have been quite unavoidable, but if he dies from it today, despite all the medical resources in the world, then violence is present according to our definition. [Italics omitted] [19]

Second, it seems clear that "violence" has a normative use. "Violence" may mean "*unjust* use of force, as in deprivation of rights," or "acting or characterized by force *unlawfully* used" (*Webster*, italics added). Thus "violence" has a normative use such that any application of force that violates one's legitimate rights implies violence against the person. In spite of this undeniable fact, Galtung's definition is too broad. Not *all* personal harm, or violation of one's rights to self-development, qualifies as genuine violence. What Galtung seems to have in mind is simply *structural injustice*. Violence is only a subtype of injustice. [20]

How can we distinguish structural violence from injustice if we are not allowed to refer to physical force? I suggest that if the violation of person's rights is not serious, the situation is not violent. But if drastic injustice occurs, we may in some cases say that it exemplifies violence, even though no excessive, brute force is used in this social context.

On the basis of this preliminary discussion, let us forget the notion of the use of force in the present context of structural violence. This move guarantees an independent status to our most elusive violence notions, since now they cannot be collapsed into social violence, which does require the use of force. But there is a price to pay if we want to add this item to our list of the types of violence. As I indicated, no simple reference to an unjust social configuration is enough to identify it as *violent* in any proper sense of the term. This means that we must try to draw a line between those normative conditions that are essential and those that are inessential to the ascription of "violence" to social situations. We may now use our *analogy theory* of violence.

Let us start by recalling Steven Lukes's theory of three-dimensional power and applying its basic ideas in the slightly different realm of violence. [21] Its key idea is that power may have its effect on the social world even if no exercise of power is visible and even if the objects of power are not consciously disposed to struggle against the realization of the preferences of the (invisible) power wielders. The main point here is that no excessive force need be evident even when we have a full-fledged case of violence before us; viz., an instance of structural violence. We are ready to present a definition. There exists a special type of product violence, called "structural violence," such that (i) the end-state is not a result of any open use of excessive social force but which (ii) still violates the basic *prima facie* rights of people; and, moreover, (iii) the end-state resembles sufficiently those situations that follow from the actual use of physical force.

The third condition is bound to be difficult to explicate but is nevertheless absolutely essential. If we forget it, I see no hope of capturing the main point of the talk about structural violence. It is violence, and "violence" refers to an actually harmful use or result of (physical) force. We are interested in *results* now, and therefore we are entitled to forget the use aspect, which simplifies our task because we can say that a certain kind of injustice displayed by some typical social situations deserve to be called "violent" regardless of its genesis. Hence, condition (iii). Suppose a forest is turned into a corn field so that the natives living there see no other possibility but to leave their villages and move into a city slum. They will become desperately poor and deprived of all their earlier cultural and economic benefits. No violence was applied to them—suppose that no one really noticed their existence—yet their final end-state *resembles* the one that would follow from a direct use of physical violence against them. To destroy the forest and to take the natives as prisoners to the city would have exactly the type of consequences we call violent. Certainly if their material and cultural welfare is adequately taken care of in the city, and if they get compensation for what they lost, the natives cannot complain of violence (supposing that no force was used earlier). What they *can* complain of is that they suffer from unjust treatment simply because they do not like to live in a strange urban life to which they were never offered an alternative. But they cannot complain that they are victims of violence. This follows once we notice that violence has a strictly negative effect, which we characterized in terms of "personal harm" and its probability. Actual physical violence destroys welfare; and a partially corrected welfare situation, even if it remains clearly unjust, does not resemble the one following from the use of "real" violence. My notion of violence is, accordingly, a *serious* one. A violent agent (logically) cannot respect his object's welfare-oriented compensatory claims, except after the termination of the violent interaction. Violence can be more or less strong, but it appears to be a serious mistake to think that violent action could be compatible with the perpetrator's acceding to any of the victim's welfare claims within the situation in which violence occurs.

When we return to my example, we notice that, had it been the case that those people's urban poverty was brought about by means of actual violence (or force), then and only then could they argue that their partially corrected life situation qualifies as a violent one. This is what condition (iii) says: Only "simple" and uncorrected (sufficiently) serious injustice warrants one's ascription of "violence" to a social state of affairs. Another plausible-looking suggestion is that only *avoidable* and/or *deliberate* serious injustice indicates structural violence. A key factor now would be whether anybody cares.

My present definition of structural violence seems to make sense when applied to *absolute poverty*. We have the right to avoid it and it can be avoided, except in situations where a severe long-term shortage of goods occurs. In most cases, however, absolute poverty implies violence. This becomes clear when we realize that, if even moderate resources exist, the most dreadful aspects of the shortage are all-or-nothing affairs. Rather, small amounts of (say) food will resolve the problem totally, but if no food is provided death, will be unavoidable. This sharp line between the dissolution of the problem and total catastrophe makes absolute poverty an especially sensitive issue in relation to structural violence. (Moreover, "absolute poverty" is a comparative notion.) If affluent people care even a little about their poor fellows, no absolute poverty will exist; if they do not care, they make themselves guilty of structural violence. Incidentally, this conclusion supports the view that simple actions of omission may be interesting. The relevance of our present conclusion to the attitude we take in relation to third-world poverty is quite clear but cannot be dealt with now.[22]

What about *relative poverty*? Is there any connection between relative poverty and structural violence? I think that our answer will depend on the crucial questions of whether we think that relative poverty is *real* poverty in the sense that it harms us and that we have a strong *prima facie* right to avoid it, and whether it is avoidable in normal social circumstances. If all these clauses hold, we may say that relative poverty may be product violence in its structural sense. It is, however, not at all clear that relative poverty is never (*ceteris paribus*) excusable or acceptable from a moral perspective. Hegel's familiar idea that it is sometimes caused by our own extravagance provides a good illustration of what I mean. And if there is no real and unjust injury in evidence, the language of violence does not apply.

Thus it seems that the whole topic is ideologically loaded. The main issue is whether one allows the analogy to physical force to extend all the way to the structural product violence. It may seem sensible to maintain that some states of affairs manifesting relative poverty are such that they are sufficiently similar to the results of physical force to warrant the moral condemnation usually reserved for the users of such force; but is it really? One must be careful when answering this question. The reason is that if one extends the analogy to force too far, the result is a political radicalism that may justify the actual use of violence against such states of affairs that only *resemble* the effects of violence. It is easy to find examples of such cases in which relative poverty would justify the use of actual physical violence by the poor against more affluent agents who have as yet used no force against them. Moreover, it seems difficult indeed to imagine what kind of decision procedure is needed to settle the disputes between the relatively poor and relatively rich when one party claims to be a victim of violence and demands a right to reach accordingly, and the other party does not want to admit any responsibility. We may expect, however, that those who feel they are victims of structural violence and take the idea of violence seriously in this context will resort to force anyway. The victims of violence cannot be expected to negotiate, since it is an essential element of all violence that its user turns aside the considerations of his victim's welfare. And if the poor feel that this has happened to them, they need see no reason why they themselves should follow different moral principles in the course of their allegedly justified counteraction. The victims may demand revenge.

For these general reasons, I am convinced that all talk about structural violence must be taken seriously and a too quick and easy identification of (simple) injustice with (limitless) violence must be avoided. Galtung's ideas have paradoxical consequences to normative peace research. Nevertheless, I am not saying that relative poverty is never structural violence. I am saying only that in general it is not, but in some special cases of exploitation it may well qualify as violence. The problem is to pick out those cases on the grounds of a good social theory. Only then can we tell whether the scattered violence of Hegel's rabble of paupers is justifiable, along with the more sophisticated tactics of revolutionaries and the leaders of the economically oppressed countries and nations.

Notes

My thanks are due to Geoff Sayre McCord (University of Pittsburgh). The completion of the final draft of this paper was made possible by a generous research scholarship from the Center for Philosophy of Science, University of Pittsburgh, in 1982-83.

1. Hegel, *Philosophy of Right*, translated by T. M. Knox (New York: Oxford University Press, 1952).
2. N. Rescher, *Welfare* (Pittsburgh: Pittsburgh University Press, 1972), p. 94.
3. Ibid., p. 95.
4. R. Pinker, *Social Theory and Social Policy* (London: Heinemann Educational Books, 1971), p. 109.
5. Hegel, *Philosophy of Right*, #244.
6. Ibid., #244 Addition.
7. Ibid., #240 Addition.
8. Ibid., #190 and Addition.
9. Ibid., #241 (my italics).
10. Ibid., #191 Addition.
11. Ibid., #244.
12. Ibid., ##245, 244 Addition, and 241.
13. Ibid., #185.
14. Ibid., #253.
15. Ibid., ##245 and 253.
16. D. Wrong, *Power* (Oxford: Basil Blackwell, 1979), p. 24.
17. Ibid., p. 24.
18. A classic treatment of coercion is R. Nozick, "Coercion," in *Philosophy, Politics and Society*, Fourth Series. P. Laslett, W. G. Runciman, and Q. Skinner, eds. (Oxford: Basil Blackwell, 1972).

19. J. Galtung, *Peace: Research, Education, Action: Essays in Peace Research*, vol. 1 (Copenhagen: Christian Ejlers, 1975), pp. 110-1.

20. See B. Harrison's excellent paper "Violence and the Rule of Law," in *Violence*, J Shaffer, ed. (New York: David McKay Company, 1971), pp. 164 ff.

21. S. Lukes, *Power: A Radical View* (London and Basingstoke: Macmillan & Co., 1974).

22. See, for example, T. Honderich, *Violence for Equality* (Harmondsworth: Penguin, 1980), and J. Harris, *Violence and Responsibility* (London: Routledge and Kegan Paul, 1980).

Bibliography

Arendt, H. *On Violence.* San Diego, New York, and London: Harcourt Brace Jovanovich, 1970.

Canetti, E. *Crowds and Power.* New York: Continuum, 1981.

Fishkin, J. S. *The Limits of Obligation.* New Haven and London: Yale University Press, 1982.

Gaventa, J. *Power and Powerlessness.* Oxford University Press, 1980.

Hallie, P. P. *Cruelty.* Middletown: Wesleyan University Press, 1982.

Shue, H. *Basic Rights: Subsistence, Affluence, and U.S. Foreign Policy.* Princeton: Princeton University Press, 1980.

Taylor, M. *Community, Anarchy and Liberty.* Cambridge: Cambridge University Press, 1982.

4
Explorations of
The Definition of Poverty:
Comment

June Axinn
School of Social Work
University of Pennsylvania

An analysis of the concept of equality and consequently of the just allocation of resources in any society requires as a social-policy correlative a definition of what is to be taken as a minimally acceptable human standard of
living. In the United States today, the Reagan Administration's program-
matic use of the phrase "truly needy" has made the question of the definition of poverty a particularly urgent one. One can hardly discuss the existence or extent of any of our social welfare programs without some clarity
about the nature of the groups in society that are to be considered
deprived. The first policy analysis step would appear to be an exploration
of the meaning of poverty. What is poverty? More specifically, for pro-
grammatic purposes, who is to be counted as poor?

Timo Airaksinen develops poverty concepts to relate Hegel's views on
poverty and on violence. This commentary will move in another direction
and use those categories to analyze the official poverty standard, along
with the major suggested modifications, in use by the U.S. Government
since the era of the War on Poverty.[1]

In traditional fashion, Airaksinen distinguishes relative and absolute
poverty, explaining relative poverty as the inability to reach an
"acceptable" and "average" standard of living, whereas for absolute
poverty, the words used are "minimal" and "bare survival." To expand:
In economic terms what we are discussing when we talk of relative poverty
is economic distance. Individuals or groups are considered to be relatively
poor if their standard of living does not keep pace with the average. Absolute poverty, on the other hand, refers to a fixed, unchanging, minimal
market basket of goods. By relative poverty standards, if my neighbor acquired a new car and nothing else changed, I would be poorer; by an absolute definition, I would not.

Airaksinen goes on to some discussion of "objective" and "subjective"
criteria of poverty definitions and appears by "objective" to mean simply

group applicability of empirical measurements. He continues with the last set—the contrast between "real need" and "personal desire"—and here he opens up more complex questions. For while his paper presents the issue as one of individual cultural choice, from a policy perspective it might well be generalized as an issue dealing also with the role of expectations in both the short and the long run.

The federal government's poverty measure was developed in 1964 by the Social Security Administration. The government defined poverty first of all in terms of cash income (before taxes) for a family over the period of a year. The methodology involved basically pricing the cost of the economy food plan of the Department of Agriculture (based on both Recommended Dietary Allowances and low income food consumption patterns of 1955). It was then assumed, based on a Household Consumption Survey of the general population, also in 1955, that food expenditures were one-third of the total family budget. The minimum required income—the poverty line—was calculated at three times the economy food plan, with some adjustments for family size and a few other variables. This measure, priced in 1964, was adjusted backwards to 1959 for changes in the Consumer Price Index and has been similarly adjusted forward with only minor changes.

It is of historical interest perhaps that this index was devised in part in response to a tremendous increase in relative poverty. World War II and the period right after that, the early 1950s, were times of a great deal of economic growth. The war itself was a period of major income redistribution. By the late 1950s, however, it was clear that the assumption that resource redistribution would continue, or even that everyone would benefit from economic growth, was not true. Poverty, the "invisible poor" who were not "keeping up," was "rediscovered" and measures were being designed to "bring the poor into the mainstream." Relative poverty was the concern, but a market basket index was to be used for measurement. One result of using a fixed measure of poverty was that the poverty gap widened dramatically during the period. In 1959, the first year for which we have an official U.S. standard, a family of four was considered poor if it had less than $2,973 a year; median family income that same year was $5,417. Thus the poverty line was 55 percent of median income. By last year, median family income had risen to $22,020 and the poverty line for a family was $9,287, or only 42 percent of median family income. Economic distance between the poor and the average family has widened steadily.

The market basket of the poor's goods has remained the same over the years, with only the dollar value changing, despite the increased standard of living of everyone else. But in at least one sense this *cannot* be said to be an absolute standard. Consider how the market basket was selected in the first place. An absolute standard would be based on minimal nutrition and a maximum percentage of total income spent on food. But this index was based on the national average percentage of family food expenditure to total family income (after taxes)—the standard for the whole society, not the standard of the lowest income group. Thus the general standard—the most accessible, not the minimum—became the base, and indeed it is difficult to imagine a society constructing a minimum standard of living that would be completely context-free. Airaksinen argues that the very notion of absolute poverty is a vaguely comparative one. In this case it is more than that: it is in part truly relative.[2]

There are a host of other policy-choice questions underlying statistical decisions in the construction of the official poverty cutoff figures. Originally, a matrix of 124 separate poverty threshold figures was calculated. The size of the family unit (up to 7); the sex of the family head, the age of the family head (under or over 65), and the question of farm or nonfarm residence were the selected categories for special indexes. Since 1964, the size of the family unit for which extra income is considered necessary has increased (to 9), and the needs distinction between male- and female-headed families has been eliminated, as has the differential between farm and nonfarm families.

These changes were made for political, social, and economic reasons. As an example: Initially, in 1964 the poverty line for those residing on farms was set at 70 percent of that of families not on farms. The assumption was that farmers could (should?) grow their own food and had therefore less need for cash income. A readjustment of the indexes narrowed the difference to 85 percent in 1969, and it was eliminated completely in 1981. The current poverty threshold assumes that the need for cash income is the same in the city and in the country. The reasons were heavily political and involved the urgent wish of some officials to increase the eligibility for welfare programs of some farm-state constituents. One might, however, argue the matter on Airaksinen's grounds—that is, those who live in cities have a personal desire for that type of life—theirs is a choice which includes a choice of income possibilities and limitations. One might argue in a similar vein against special considerations for family size.

Interestingly, emphasis on the role of personal choice and personal needs did play a part in the early discussions of social insurance when it was decided that residency was a matter of personal taste and that therefore, despite dramatically different living costs in the different states, the United States would have one geographic standard of payment for old-age benefits. It has not, however, generally played an explicit part in the debates in the poverty literature of the last twenty-five years. These issues are more apt to arise now that the role of noncash income in the definition of poverty thresholds is being seriously considered.

The current Census Bureau definition is based only on cash income. And yet in the years since the introduction of the poverty measure, the dollar value of the major "in kind" transfer programs available to the poor—for food, housing, and medical care—has grown rapidly and currently far exceeds public assistance.[3] The bureau is now discussing the impact on our poverty count of including in the definition the value of some of these noncash benefits given to individuals, specifically, the value of food stamps, school lunches, housing subsidies, Medicaid, and Medicare. Clearly, which of these benefits are counted and how they are counted matters in both the poverty total and structure. Census estimates of poverty in 1979, for example, drop by amounts varying from 12.3 percent to 42.3 percent, depending on which noncash benefits are included and how they are valued.

Three ways of valuing noncash benefits have been suggested.

1. Market Value: The private-sector purchasing power of benefits is assumed to be the value of the in-kind transfer received by the individual. In the case of food stamps, for example, the dollar value of food coupons would be taken to be the value of the recipient of the food stamps. In the case of the free distribution of cheese, the market value would be determined by the market price of cheese. This technique puts the highest price tag on noncash transfers. The measure is objective, easily measurable. The difficulty is that the market price is determined by all consumers. This total group evaluation would in effect be counted as the individual value. Thus the values of the lowest economic class would be taken as identical with those of the entire consumer class.

2. Recipient or Cash Equivalent Value: This valuation is defined as the amount of money that would make the recipient just as well off as the noncash transfer. In the case of the free distribution of cheese the cash equivalent value is the amount of cash the recipient would take instead of the cheese. Implied ordinarily is the notion that in-kind transfers need to be discounted because they are not as valuable to their recipients as cash income would be (although one might hypothesize the reverse). When this variation is calculated, a hybrid process is used that involves components of average budgets and poverty budgets. While it allows for more differences in expenditure preferences between low income groups and the population at large than does straight market valuation, it is still a large group technique and assigns class values and choices to individuals. In any case, it yields a lower value on noncash benefits than a straight market valuation.

3. Poverty-Budget-Share Value: This valuation technique would limit the value assigned to a benefit to the proportional share it would normally assume in a poverty budget. In the case of the free distribution of cheese, the poverty-budget-share value would be a function of the amount of money the recipient usually spends on cheese (or a cheeselike commodity). The argument is that in setting the cash poverty line, at a fixed multiple of the economy food plan, a minimum level of other necessary commodities such as housing and medical care was implied. Therefore, this view holds, no value should be assigned to any one of these components that usurps the role of the other elements. Food, clothing, housing, and medical care are not considered substitutes for each other. The views and values of a panel of experts are assumed. This approach would put the lowest dollar value of the three on in-kind benefits and would thus have the smallest impact on the actual poverty count.

Calculating these values for 1979,[4] poverty on a cash-income basis (traditional Bureau of the Census definition) gave a poverty rate for the U.S. of 11.1 percent; When food stamps, school lunches, housing subsidies, Medicare, and Medicaid were added in, the rate dropped to 8.9 percent at a poverty-budget-share value, to 8.2 percent at a Cash Equivalent Value, and to 6.4 percent at Market Value. For the aged, who use Medicare and Medicaid extensively, the impact is even more dramatic, and their poverty rates for 1979 shift from 14.7 percent to as low as 4.5 percent depending on definitional variations. Note that under any valuation of in-kind benefits other than the third—poverty-share value—one could define the poor out of existence just by ensuring that they got sick enough.

But there is a still more basic question. If free school lunches are part of the income of the poor, is free tuition for their children part of the income of the professoriate? If Medicaid and Medicare, why not employer-paid health and dental insurance benefits; if housing rent subsidies, why not tax expenditures for mortgage payments? To the extent that poverty lines are relative—to the extent that they measure economic distance—then shouldn't noncash income be measured for all involved?

Most of the current discussion of poverty lines deals with issues of income distribution and income measurement. But other analyses have raised the question of whether or not wealth as well as income should be counted in some fashion in the evaluation of poverty. If so, the number and structure of the poor might shift. The percentage of aged who are counted poor might be different from the number under current income definitions, because their accumulation of assets is quite different from that of other income-poor groups. In any case, as Airaksinen has pointed out, these are subjective issues. And the loss of income can have dramatically different meaning under different poverty conditions.

It can mean different things for different time spans as well. There are some female heads of families who are transitionally poor, students who are poor but who may have an expectation of income in the near future, and some for whom poverty may be a lifetime phenomenon. Even on an objective basis, an annual measure of poverty may be inadequate, and we may require some measure of permanent income to incorporate the view that any standard of living is determined by accumulation over time of economic resources. This is particularly true if we make efforts to include less easily quantifiable factors.

In sum: Moving from a poverty index that is a cash measure to one that includes noncash benefits, adjusting the measure to include wealth as well as income, and shifting the index from an annual to a life-cycle scope is attractive. Conceptually, it increases the potential for measuring "well-being." It offers the opportunity to include important factors in material satisfaction. Such diverse things as home ownership, the expectation of an eventual career, or an individual's choice of solitary living might all be discounted in the formula. Politically, with the current emphasis on locating the "truly needy," the appeal of such a measure is apparent. For there is a temptation certainly to see all modifications in the definition as ways of solving the poverty problem. Instead of redistributing resources, distribution will be redefined. The difficulty is that all poverty indexes are relative in part, and in the end the distribution problem will not disappear semantically.

Notes

1. The official poverty standard is called the weighted average poverty threshold. It was developed at the Social Security Administration in 1964 and was revised by Federal Interagency Committees in 1969 and 1980; it is published annually. The most recent citation is: U.S. Bureau of the Census, Current Population Reports, Series P-60, No. 138, *Characteristics of the Population Below the Poverty Level: 1981* (Washington, D.C.: U.S. Government Printing Office, 1983).

2. There are many ideological inconsistencies in the design of the poverty index. It had one great virtue: It gave a result that was the "appropriate" economic distance from the median income at that time, and it fit the preconceived notion of the Council of Economic Advisers.

3. U.S. Bureau of the Census, Current Population Reports, Series P-60, No. 1361, *Characteristics of Households Receiving Selected Noncash Benefits: 1981* (Washington, D.C.: U.S. Government Printing Office, 1982).

4. U.S. Bureau of the Census, *Alternative Methods for Valuing Selected In-Kind Transfer Benefits and Measuring Their Effect on Poverty*, Technical Paper, No. 50, (Washington, D.C.: U.S. Government Printing Office, 1982).

Bibliography

Orshansky, Mollie. "Children of the Poor." *Social Security Bulletin*, vol. 26, no. 7 (July 1963).
— — —. "Counting the Poor: Another Look at the Poverty Profile." *Social Security Bulletin*, vol. 28, no. 1 (January 1965).
— — —. "Measuring Poverty: A Debate." *Public Welfare*, vol. 35, no. 2 (Spring 1977).
U.S. Bureau of the Census. *Alternative Methods for Valuing Selected In-Kind Transfer Benefits and Measuring Their Effect on Poverty.* Technical Paper No. 50. Washington, D.C.: U.S. Government Printing Office, 1982.
U.S. Congressional Budget Office. *Poverty Status of Families Under Alternative Definitions of Income.* Washinqton, D.C.: U.S. Government Printing Office, 1977.
U.S. Department of Health, Education and Welfare. *The Measure of Poverty: A Report to Congress as Mandated by the Education Amendments of 1974.* Washington, D.C.: U.S. Government Printing Office, 1976.
— — —. *The Measure of Poverty,* Technical Paper VII. "In-Kind Income and the Measurement of Poverty." Washington, D.C.: U.S. Government Printing Office, 1976.
— — —. *The Measurement of Poverty,* Technical Paper XIV. "Relative Measure of Poverty." Washington, D.C.: U.S. Government Printing Office, 1977.

Part II

Property and Responsibility

Economic justice can be broadly characterized as justice with respect to property. To discover what economic justice requires, it is necessary to ask a series of questions centering on property rights:
1. What rules ought to govern the acquisition of property? What kinds of thing is it permissible to own, and how can an individual legitimately come to own something?
2. What prerogatives ought the owner to enjoy? What are the owner's rightful permissions and immunities, and what are the limits on the owner's use of possessions?
3. What principles, if any, ought to direct redistribution? What are the grounds on which non-owners are justified in pressing claims against owners?

Together, answers to these questions tell us much about the just delineation of property rights and the just distribution of property.

The idea of property has a strong hold on our moral imagination. Following Locke's development of the labor theory of property, we are accustomed to consider ownership as requiring honest toil and often as a suitable reward for meritorious social contribution. Moreover, to the extent that we suppose present owners to have gained their wealth through steady labor and frugality, or in recognition of distinguished public careers, we are apt to conclude that the predicament of the destitute—those who own almost nothing and who fail to earn what they need—is their own fault. Because of character flaws that they are apparently content to indulge, these individuals lack the gumption to provide for their own welfare. Thus a popular idea of property, linking appropriation to industriousness and probity, colors our attitudes toward the wealthy and the poor, leading us to respect the former and to despise the latter.

And yet, despite this easy identification of poverty with indolence, ours is hardly a blind and carefree romance with bourgeois values. Much as we may admire it, we are also suspicious of wealth, for it can bring inordinate power, and it can tempt the rich into vulgar ostentation and depravity. Worse still, property is a locus of social divisiveness. Condemned to hopelessness and humiliation but treated to the ever-present spectacle of privilege, the impoverished may finally revolt against those they perceive as their oppressors. While it is easy to appreciate the importance of property rights, at least to the extent that they are necessary to protect the independence of citizens, many have qualms about unlimited accumulation and unrestricted use of private property. For economic dynasties together with social and environmental blight often result. The trouble with class stratification, in sum, is that it invites elitism, social decadence, and civil unrest.

How has this complex view of property arisen? Roughly, it has dovetailed with the familiar history of liberal Western democracy. From the fall of Imperial Rome until late in the seventeenth century, Europeans regarded sovereignty as an unassailable, because God-given, right. Not until Hobbes and then Locke and Rousseau mounted their powerful and systematic challenges to divine right, and not until commoners seized control of the English and French governments, did the hereditary political and economic dominion of the nobility finally succumb. The vacuum left by the defeat of the *ancien regime* was of course filled by an ambitious and energetic middle-class. Proclaiming the equality of mankind and demanding an opportunity to realize their potential in the marketplace, this new social stratum spurred the Industrial Revolution and profited mightily from it.

By the end of the nineteenth century, it became clear that liberal emancipation had not been wholly salutary. Former subsistence farmers had become the urban poor. Obliged to work cruel hours in unsafe factories for wages that left them in penury, they lived in squalor and died young. Their children, forced by economic necessity to join their parents in the sweatshops and unable to obtain education, were from a practical standpoint as trapped by the conditions into which they were born as the serfs were by feudalism. Meanwhile, the bourgeoisie lived in luxury and consolidated their position through the democratic political system they had erected. The formal equalization of opportunity and the opening of new avenues of advancement had created a novel but, for many, a no less rigid and stultifying social order. Because the few who replaced the aristocracy at the pinnacle of the social hierarchy drew their legitimacy largely from Locke's work-ethic conception of property, and yet at the same time because so many proved unable to better themselves in this redefined economic sphere, it is not surprising that property rights have come to be widely associated both with liberation and with oppression.

Marxists and libertarians alike reject this ambivalence about property, although they take diametrically opposed stands on property acquisition and use. Marxists condemn the accumulation of capital in private hands and deplore wage labor, whereas their libertarian opponents endorse the moral inviolability of property rights and are loath to restrict individual enrichment. The essays in Part II adopt a more moderate position. While the authors accept that large estates may be justifiable, they ask how formidable is the moral obstacle that property rights pose for those who favor the amelioration of poverty and the pursuit of other social goals. They grant neither that private ownership of the means of production should be ended nor that all expropriation is confiscation. Instead, they seek an account of property that is compatible with principled redistribution and social progress but that does not issue a carte blanche to governments to dismiss the claims of owners.

In "Property Rights and Social Welfare," Lawrence C. Becker's primary objective is to analyze property rights in a way that incorporates consequences into their justification. In the background of his discussion is a paradox about property rights and social welfare: Because property rights can withstand competing social welfare considerations, society may be barred from pursuing compelling projects because the costs of compensating intransigent property owners exceed what it can afford. When compelling social objectives are considered to outweigh a right, the right-holder is owed compensation. But if society cannot afford to compensate the right-holder, is it then just too bad for society? It would seem so. But—and this is Becker's central point—social-welfare considerations enter into every plausible justification for property rights. To the extent that they do, property rights are vulnerable to suspension for the sake of social welfare. This vulnerability is built into the right. Thus property rights need not obstruct society's aspirations and some urgent social projects can go forward unencumbered even though society cannot afford to compensate every affected property owner.

Building on Becker's essay, Diana T. Meyers's "A Sketch of a Rights Taxonomy" elaborates a method of classifying rights based on the distinction between a contoured right (a right constrained only by other rights) and a suspendable right (a right that social-welfare goals can nullify). Fundamental rights, the most stringent of rights that persons have simply in virtue of being human, are contoured only. Fundamental rights may be implemented in part by directly derivative rights which share the former's importance. They are also contoured but not suspendable. But indirectly derivative rights are justified by social-welfare considerations as well as by other rights, and conventional rights are instituted primarily to serve social goals. These latter two kinds of right are both contoured and suspendable. Meyers points out that the location of property rights on this spectrum depends in part on whether subsistence concerns are formulated as rights or as social goals. What strength property rights have thus depends on where they lie on this spectrum. She argues that champions of strong property rights must either accept an individual right to subsistence or accept weakened property rights that do not necessarily entitle owners to compensation when their property is condemned to promote social goals.

In "Rights, Responsibilities, and Redistribution," William Nelson focuses on three problems that arise in connection with property rights: what function rights serve in moral systems, how rights can be defended, and which purposes justify redistribution. He characterizes rights as grants of authority over specified sets of decisions, but he insists that the actions of right-holders are subject to criticism in the light of moral considerations that are independent of their rights. Carrying through his pluralistic approach to rights, Nelson contends further that we must evaluate proposed assignments of rights by anticipating what will happen as a result of granting them to certain persons. Will these individuals, by and large, exercise their rights for good or ill? Only insofar as we are confident that a proposed distribution of authority will work out for the best are we justified in implementing it. Ultimately, this emphasis on the uses to which people put their rights leads Nelson to favor redistribution of authority where (1) persons are likely to misuse their prerogatives and where (2) abuse has occurred and rectification of the harm is needed. Once moral responsibility is conceived as a system that may or may not be in equilibrium, rights and redistribution become the key means of maintaining a proper balance.

In "The Demands of Justice," Theodore Benditt relies heavily on the distinction between those things that are, in the interests of justice, good things for us to do, and those things that are demanded by justice. While there might be actions that would bring about a more just society and that ought therefore to be undertaken, it does not follow that society is unjust if it does not undertake them. Benditt holds that justice requires beneficence in "easy rescue cases," but that it does not require beneficence where the victim is a "chronic case" requiring "regular, ongoing care and attention." Apart from easy rescue cases and special obligations generated by voluntary undertakings, better-off individuals have no obligation to help poor ones. Thus the well-off members of society have no general obligation to help the chronically poor. However, if the poor are the victims "of a form of economic life that inevitably leads to some people losing out," then, because social life is itself responsible for the problem, those who have been so disadvantaged do have welfare rights against the rest of society. Technological unemployment and job-related injuries can thus create a basis for entitlement. But while society would be more just if it provided for the special needs created by old age and ordinary illness (disadvantages that are not socially caused), justice does not demand that it do so.

Bruce M. Landesman takes issue with Benditt's position, arguing that justice demands maximization of the equal well-being of all persons. It follows that the well-off can have obligations to promote the well-being of the poor even though social life has not caused their deprivation (as Benditt requires). Landesman suggests that Benditt's distinction between natural and socially induced deprivations may be difficult to draw in practice. And, from the standpoint of justice, the urgency of a deprivation and the cost of its rectification may be just as important as its cause. Rather than follow Benditt in characterizing measures as merely desirable for us to do in the interests of justice (but not demanded by it), Landesman maintains that whatever is good to do "on grounds of justice is at least prima facie obligatory." Landesman's "cosmic justice" holds that "rectifiable inequality between equally valuable human beings is unacceptable."

Marilyn Gwaltney's "The Actual and Potential Demands of Justice" takes aim at Benditt's use of an individualistic model of society. "Obligation is not a natural phenomenon like a stone or even anger, but is a social phenomenon that can exist only when people recognize the legitimacy and necessity of each other's existence." The Robinson Crusoe-like individuals who populate "state of nature" theories "do not have to recognize the necessity of each other's existence because they spring full-grown as adults from the heads of philosophers." Real human beings have had, as children within their families, the experience of interdependency. This social experience provides a more appropriate model for society. For whether or not the family can provide for the needs of its members depends on its resources. As the family's (and as society's) capacity to meet the needs of its members changes, so does the justifiability of claims against it. Thus a demand for recreational opportunity must be set aside until health deficiencies are attended to adequately. While the poor may not have a claim that you, as an individual, act to alleviate their poverty, at some level of community affluence they may have a claim that you so act as a citizen.

Exploring just such a dependency relationship, Kenneth Kipnis argues that some kinds of good—in particular, the expert help required for access to the judiciary—must be made available to all as a matter of justice. In "Distributive Justice and Civil Justice: Professional Responsibility and the Allocation of Legal Services," he argues that sophisticated legal systems will work serious injustices unless legal assistance is made available in civil cases. Kipnis discusses various ways in which such services might be made available to those who cannot afford them. In professionalized legal systems, such as that in the United States, a special duty to provide such services falls upon the legal profession in virtue of its exclusive monopoly on their distribution. Charity in free-market systems and state distribution of legal services in government agencies are other mechanisms. Kipnis points out that each approach sets its distinctive agenda of problems.

Diana T. Meyers

5

Property Rights and Social Welfare

Lawrence C. Becker
Department of Philosophy
Hollins College

The burden of this argument is that the conflict between social welfare and private property is not nearly as sharp as it seems. The illusion of a sharp conflict comes from a failure to understand one complex point: There are social welfare provisos attached to all justly acquired titles, and those provisos run with the titles indefinitely. Titles are self-adjusting with respect to social welfare.[1]

The Social Character of Property

Opponents of the welfare state argue that rights to private property severely restrict the state's power to tax and are part of the reason for rejecting altogether the legitimacy of so-called welfare rights.[2] Defenders of welfare rights, on the other hand, argue that rights to life and a minimal level of well-being are more important than property rights, and that social-welfare considerations (the "rights" of society) often override private rights in cases involving nonrenewable resources, clean air, clear water, "green space," and wilderness areas.[3]

The division of the house is not that simple of course. Libertarians worry about social welfare as well as property rights when the issue is economic blackmail.[4] Welfarists recognize the important connections between private rights, personal freedom and self-esteem, and the way in which many of their concerns can be cast into the language of property rights.[5] And legal theorists of all persuasions express concern about the takings clause of the Fifth Amendment—the clause that prohibits the taking of private property without due process of law, and requires the state to pay just compensation when it takes property for public purposes.[6] This constitutional provision, together with the recent expansion of the legal concept of property, can in principle be a serious obstacle to public welfare. The "new property" includes all sorts of things that were once considered mere privileges or governmental largesse, such as licenses of various sorts, Social Security, welfare benefits, and the value of an education.[7] If these things are property, how can the state legally "take" them through law reform? If an appeal procedure or compensation is required in all such cases, routine changes in the law would be impossibly burdensome.

In any case, most theorists imagine that there is in principle a sharp conflict between private rights to property and considerations of social welfare. The perception of that conflict leads the left wing to reject or restrict private property and the right wing to reject or restrict the welfare state.

Opposition to that "confict view" has been hampered by a vague, even empty, invocation of the so-called social character of property. The suggestion is that if private property is essentially "social," there may not be a serious conflict between property and welfare after all. This is obviously an important line of inquiry, but everything depends on having a clear concept of the social character of property.

That clarity has been hard to find. Some say, for example, that property rights are empty unless they are enforced through some social order. Since any "real" property right is therefore a socially enforced one, and since no social order is likely to enforce a right that runs counter to social welfare, enforcement will carry with it many social-welfare considerations. "Real" property rights, then, are social in this clear sense.

The problem with this account is that it is too weak. It is accepted by virtually everyone and therefore cannot help to resolve the current controversy. To say that "real" rights are enforced is not to say anything significant about which ones ought to be enforced. And disputes about that are precisely what the concept of the social character of property is supposed to help decide.

It will not do, moreover, to patch up the account by pointing out that, as a matter of fact, certain specific sorts of restrictions (tax liability, eminent domain, and so forth) have always been imposed on property by political orders and that we can therefore clearly characterize the role welfare considerations will play in the administration of property rights. That patch-up continues to beg the question of whether welfare should play such a prominent role. We have recently been invited, after all, to think of rights as trumps—as cards that take any trick constructed from considerations of prudence, or efficiency, or expedience, or social welfare.[8] The fact that no one actually does think of them quite that way—in the sense of actually acting as if the Two of Rights should trump the Ace of Negative Social Consequences—is not the point. Perhaps we should think so. Perhaps we should treat rights as trumps. If so, property has precious little "social" character.

Heroic metaphysical measures fare no better. The social character of property is not made clear by doctrines about rights emanating from the collective social body, or about property being held in trust for God. The former line in unacceptably vague. The latter rests on a religious faith that is inaccessible to many of us.

Property Rights and Social Welfare

A better way to understand the social character of property is to pay close attention to the social welfare provisos attached to all of the plausible justifications for property rights. Such attention will reveal that the conflict between private property and social welfare is not as severe (in theory) as is usually supposed.

The core of my argument for that contention is in this section, and it has three parts. The first defends the thesis that rights dominate, but do not trump, other sorts of moral considerations—including social welfare considerations. The second summarizes arguments (made elsewhere) that hold that all plausible accounts of justice in property acquisition are sensitive to social-welfare. The third argues that such sensitivity, in the form of social welfare provisos, is a permanent feature of individual rights to property. It is a feature that makes titles self-adjusting with respect to welfare. Concluding sections of the paper sharpen the general line of argument by replying to some objections and by discussing some connections to property law.

Rights Are Dominant, But Not Trumps

If individual rights never trump desires, or expedience, or considerations of social welfare, then there are no rights at all in the usual sense. Rights theorists are correct about that as a purely descriptive matter. Some sort of preemptive or dominant status is built into the ordinary conception of a right. It may not be possible to justify the inclusion of moral claims of that sort (i.e., rights) in a coherent moral theory, but that is a separate question.[9] My point here is merely that if there are rights, they are something like trumps, at least some of the time.

On the other hand, if rights were always trumps, it is hard to imagine that anyone would want to stay in the game. Surely it is irrational to hold that a trivial right should block the satisfaction of compelling social interests. (An argument for that assertion follows.)

The proper analogy (if we must stick to cards) is not that of a trump suit, but rather what might be called a dominant suit. Imagine a game in which spades outranks other suits in the following way: Any spade of a given number (say, a 10) outranks any other card of that number, but not any higher card. Rights are similar. They are by definition dominant over considerations of social welfare, efficiency, and prudence, but their dominance is limited by the strength of those other considerations. Compelling social interests outrank trivial individual rights.

This much is just common sense. It reflects the way we actually use the concept of a right, and that use (rather than the rights-as-trumps idea) seems straightforwardly justifiable. (a) After all, once it is granted that some rights are of relatively minor moral importance, it follows directly that they are outranked by things of major moral importance. (b) It is undeniable that some human needs (falling short of rights) are of major moral importance. (c) So it also follows that rights can in principle be outranked by other sorts of moral considerations. No doubt I have a right to the exclusive use of my private telephone. But the need of my neighbor for life-saving emergency medical care outranks that right. An operator, for example, may justifiably interrupt my conversation to put through an emergency call. That much is clear. What is not so clear is what this does to the concept of a right. There are, after all, at least two importantly different ways of thinking about this outranking business.

Overridingness.

One way is to insist that rights can sometimes justifiably be overridden (as in the emergency medical-care case), but that whenever we do that, no matter how good our reasons, we owe the right-holder some sort of compensation. If it is a trivial right we've overridden (such as my right to an uninterrupted phone call), no doubt a pro forma apology will suffice. If it is a significant right we've overridden, proportionately more is required by way of compensation.

This view is uncomfortable because it places a great constraint on the promotion of social welfare. If compensation is always required, even when individual rights are justifiably overridden, we will often be in the position of not being able to afford to do what is justifiable. That is, we will be in a position where social-welfare considerations (exclusive of the cost of paying compensation) mandate overriding the right, but the cost of compensation is prohibitive. And that seems unacceptably paradoxical.

Prima Facie Rights.

Another way of looking at the outranking business is to hold that rights are presumptively dominant, but that the presumption is a rebuttable one. The strength of the rebuttal required depends on the strength of the right, but once an adequate rebuttal has been made, there is no question of overriding a right and having to make compensation. There is no question of that because there is no right; the "prima facie" right has evaporated.

This view is also difficult to accept. The whole notion of a right seems to have been abandoned here in favor of a case-by-case assessment of what ought to be done. The notion of a prima facie right comes to little more than a procedural device for deciding who has the burden of proof. That is something, especially in the contexts of adjudication and ultimate justification,[10] but it is not much like what we ordinarily want to claim for the status of rights.

Limited Rights.

I shall take a somewhat different approach here. The theory of rights behind it is the first of the two above: that rights are dominant, but not trumps. They can therefore be overridden, but when they are overridden, no matter how justifiably, compensation is due. The scope of the compensation problem is reduced to manageable proportions by the fact that a concern for social welfare limits property rights from the very outset.

Property Acquisitions and Social-Welfare Provisos

For the purposes of this argument, let us assume that there are at least four sound and independent justifications for the acquisition of private property: two versions of the labor theory, an argument from utility, and an argument from political liberty.[11] This is enough to give the views presented here a strenuous test—more strenuous, certainly, than assuming the validity of only one form of justification. And nothing is lost by ignoring the miscellany of other putative justifications (e.g., first occupancy, personality, property-worthiness). Some of these others are unsound anyway, and the rest can be reduced to one or another of the four here assumed to be sound. But I shall not go over the arguments for that conclusion, because it seems clear that anything that might have to be added to this list of four justifications would only strengthen the argument to follow. Likewise, I shall not repeat the arguments designed to show the soundness of the justifications. I shall merely develop one important result of those arguments: Each of the four justifications contains a social-welfare proviso that constrains acquisitions.

(1) Utilitarian arguments are very open about it. In utility theory, what justifies my title to Greenridge is that it is somehow best for us all—best for aggregate welfare—if I have it. Clearly, if that is the justification for property, then social welfare is not a mere proviso—not a mere constraint on acquisitions. It is the whole issue.

(2) Locke's version of the labor theory justifies acquisitions only on the condition that enough and as good be left for others.[12] It is beyond dispute that the scarcity of resources and the level of competition for them (i.e., some social conditions) will in large measure determine whether a given acquisition can leave as much and as good for others. Changed social conditions can change the range of permissible acquisitions. That is exactly what is meant by a social-welfare proviso.

(3) Another version of the labor theory holds that laborers are entitled to property as a deserved reward for their work—but only if the property rights awarded them are a fitting and proportional reward.[13] What is fitting and proportional will depend in part on social conditions (e.g., scarcity). A little labor that has only minor and inessential benefit for others does not deserve the whole world as a reward. But what will count as a disproportionate reward will depend in part on how scarce the resources are and how essential the prize is to the welfare of others. So this too is a social welfare proviso.

(4) The argument from political liberty holds that any defensible system of liberty must allow people enough freedom to acquire some property. But this argument acknowledges immediately that some acquisitions by me may unjustifiably compromise your liberty. Think of my acquiring all the property surrounding yours, refusing you permission to cross my property, and thereby making you a de facto prisoner. Requiring me to grant you an easement to cross my property (by balloon?) is a simple recognition of the fact that no coherent theory of liberty can adopt a policy of unconditional acquisition. Which conditions will be necessary will depend in part on human needs, scarcity of essential resources, and the level of competition for them. In short, the liberty argument for property also contains a social-welfare proviso.

Each of the arguments that support acquisition, then, includes such a proviso. Property acquisitions are "social" in at least that clear and strong sense.

The Provisos Run with the Titles

What is often ignored, however, is the fact that what is true of acquisitions (with regard to social welfare) is also true of holdings and transfers. The social conditions that make it just for me to acquire the property are the same ones that make it just for me to retain it—or for others to acquire it from me.[14] If ever those conditions are not satisfied, my title is compromised. Social-welfare provisos run with titles.

To see this, think again of the arguments for justice in acquisition—for example, utility. If what justifies my getting title to Greenridge is in part the fact that it is best for us all if I have the title, then by definition, when it is no longer for the best that I have it, I have lost the justification for my title. Similarly for the labor theory: If what justifies my getting title is in part the fact that my having it causes no loss to others (or that my having title would be a fitting and proportional reward for my labor), then when my having it no longer meets those conditions, the justification for my title is gone. And the same is true for the political liberty argument. Social conditions in part justify my getting the property. When those conditions change, so does the justice of my having the property.

In general, then, the security of one's title to property is permanently limited from the outset by the social-welfare provisos on acquisitions. Property rights are permanently "social." (Nozick's theory recognizes this in principle. Recall his discussion of why the owner of the last water hole in the desert is not entitled to charge whatever he chooses for the water.)[15]

This point about the continuing force of provisos on acquisitions has often been missed. As a practical matter, no doubt this is partly because such provisos are often latent for long periods and thus forgotten by title-holders. (Think of homeowners' rage when they unexpectedly discover the social-welfare provisos administered by the local zoning board.) But it may also be the case that we are plagued by a deep confusion about the ontological status of rights: the notion that once justified, they can be cut free from their justifications to run their courses. It is as if we had in mind something like the deist's conception of the universe, in which a watchmaker God merely winds up the world and leaves it to run by itself. Rights are sometimes treated in an analogous way, as if, once acquired, they achieved an existence independent of the conditions that justified them and were therefore impervious to changes in those conditions.

But that is a false picture. The proper cosmic-scale analogy is rather to the Thomistic conception of the universe, in which the creative activity of God is necessary at every moment to sustain the world. Without it, the world would cease to exist. Rights are something like that. The justificatory work of the social-welfare provisos is necessary, at every moment, to sustain the legitimacy of the rights. Without it, the rights cease to exist.

Rights and Social Welfare

It is clear, then, that many apparent conflicts between property rights and social welfare may not be that at all. They may instead be cases in which limitations inherent in titles have unexpectedly become operative. A simple-minded illustration will make the point clearer. Suppose three people are alone on a desert island. There are three tracts of land, of equal size, fertility, access to fresh water, and convenience. Each person claims one as private property. Suppose further that those claims are justified in all the usual ways. The private property arrangement is best for all in the sense that it promotes peace and productivity. Each person equally deserves a tract as a reward for hard work. And the refusal of any two of the three to grant the other person ownership rights would be an unjustifiable infringement of liberty.

Now notice the provisos. Everything (in this case) is contingent on the rough equality of distribution. (We could change the case, of course, to make it depend instead on the special expertise and goodwill of one person—yielding, perhaps, a justification for monopoly.) But in the stated case, if there had been only two tracts, or if one or two had been infertile, the case for private ownership would not have been possible to make in the same way. (And let us assume for simplicity that it could not be made at all in any other way.)

Now suppose that after some years two of the tracts are rendered useless. The water sources dry up and the land cannot be farmed. The provisos on acquisition then come back into force. The conditions that once made the private ownership arrangement a justifiable one no longer obtain. The arrangement no longer promotes peace and productivity, no longer causes no loss to others, no longer is a fitting and proportional reward for labor. When the conditions that justify a right no longer obtain, there is no (justifiable) right.

Theoretical confusion about this is understandable. Social welfare limitations on titles are imposed at the level of general and specific justification: They are plain when we consider the question of how any system of property rights at all can be justified, or under what conditions it is justifiable for someone to have property rights in land, or nonrenewable resources, or ideas. We do not ordinarily think about these questions—and consequently about the social-welfare provisos—when we deal with particular titles. Instead, we think about the history of the title and about the consequences of enforcing or violating it. The issue before us therefore appears to be one of striking the proper balance between individual rights on the one side and public or state interests on the other. The compensation question arises with full force, then, and we are confronted with a paradoxical conflict between what we ought to do and what we can afford to do.

What I am suggesting is that an attempt to recover the "social character" of a title—in the form of the social-welfare provisos that run with it—is always in order when there is an apparent conflict between property rights and social welfare. If the conflict is real, as it sometimes surely is, then we play the dominance game. We compare the strength of the right to the strength of the conflicting considerations. If the right must be overridden, we pay compensation. But if the conflict is only an apparent one—if, that is, the limitations inherent in the title are precisely the social-welfare considerations at issue—then there is no right to be overridden and no compensation to be paid.

Objections and Replies

The consideration of a few objections may help to sharpen the point.

Rights Are Permanent

Objection.

The point of having rights as part of the moral landscape is lost if they are constantly threatened with extinction by changing conditions. Rights are meant to be fixed features of the landscape—bulwarks against the tides of public opinion, the expediency of the moment, the tyranny of the majority. No doubt social welfare is a crucial consideration in the initial distribution of rights. We must be careful about original acquisitions. But a right whose very legitimacy depends on the chance that a set of social conditions will remain unchanged—a set of conditions whose continuance depends in part upon the actions of others—is no right at all. Even if we must occasionally override rights in order to satisfy needs, we must recognize that we have overridden an important sort of moral injunction. And no matter how good our reasons were, we owe the injured right-holders some form of compensation. Once we lose that kind of security, we have lost the whole point of protecting people with rights.

Reply.

Rights are impervious to whole hosts of social changes—namely, the ones that did not figure in the justification of the right. And their sensitivity to changes in the conditions that did figure in the justification produces no fatal loss of security—any more than does the recognition that rights may occasionally have to be overridden. The reason that the loss of security is not fatal is partly, of course, that we are likely to profit from it as well as lose. (Your loss in private welfare is often my gain in social welfare.) But the conditions under which a right will "vanish" are also explicit in the justification of the right. We can in principle be aware of them, if we think clearly. That goes some way toward giving us the security we desire. And in any case, the situation here is no more threatening, or unusual, than our standard practice with respect to promises and contracts. They too are always conditional, and most of the conditions are implicit—simply "understood" rather than spoken. ("I'll come over to help you move the books tomorrow. Count on me at about noon." And what is understood, of course, is something like, "I'll do this unless I'm in bed with the flu, or . . .") Is the whole point of promising lost when these latent conditions emerge to excuse the promisor from the duty? I think not. We merely have to be careful about the kind of excusing conditions we permit.

Objection.

But what about changes in social conditions that are the fault of other people? Take the desert-island case again. Three people start with equal shares. One is prudent and thrives. The others are imprudent—perhaps even spiteful—and allow their water holes to dry up. Does the social-welfare proviso come into play to force the prudent one to share with the others?

Reply.

This objection is just a special case of two closely related general problems in moral philosophy: (1) To what extent is one obligated to save wrongdoers (or the foolish) from the consequences of their wrongs (or follies)? (2) To what extent is one obligated to help innocent third parties? Suppose (implausibly) that a hard line on these questions can be justified, giving the answer that one is under no obligation to save either the wrongdoers or innocent victims. (It would be "good" of one to help perhaps when an infant is abandoned on the doorstep. But it is not obligatory.) Would that damage the general point about provisos running with titles? Not at all. It would merely show that the provisos do not include the duty to rescue. So the objection is irrelevant. And in fact the general point about provisos running with titles is reinforced by a consideration of these fault cases. For example, when criminals violate my right to freedom, may they not be sanctioned in ways that, under other conditions, would constitute a violation of their rights? To recognize that a criminal act can change one's protections is to concede the point that provisos attached to the rights run with them thereafter.

Objection.

But the point of this objection may be that there are no social-welfare provisos at all on property acquisition, and therefore no provisos to run with titles. Suppose it is held, for example, that people are entitled to whatever they can get and keep, no strings attached. Then the thesis about provisos running with titles is irrelevant.

Reply.

Many amazing things can be "held." If that were all it took to defeat my arguments, there would be no point in making them. But the question is not what can be held; the question is what can be held with good reason.

And "provisoless acquisition" cannot be held with good reason. Consider: No coherent moral theory permits unconditional liberty.[16] One's liberty must always be limited by the liberty of others, even in highly inegalitarian societies. "Getting and keeping" things will therefore always be controlled, at a minimum, by the principles that coordinate people's liberties. What is that but a social-welfare proviso? Of course we may argue about the extent of the proviso—about whether it includes affirmative as well as negative duties of care, for example. (Am I obligated to care for the infant left on my doorstep?) But the existence of some provisos cannot reasonably be disputed.

Objection.

Perhaps. But conceding that is not enough to make your thesis interesting. Suppose that there are provisos on acquisition and they do run with titles, but they are so minimal that they never effect changes in acquired titles? Then there is no practical point in talking about self-adjusting titles.

Reply.

An adequate reply to that objection would be book-length: an argument designed to show that all the sound lines of justification for property acquisition do in fact contain robust social-welfare provisos. Readers who want such an argument may look at my *Property Rights*.[17] Here I can only be dismissive. I know of no sound line of reasoned justification for property that imposes merely minimal provisos. So once it is conceded that provisos run with titles, my thesis here has many interesting consequences.

"It'll Never Work"

Objection.

On the contrary, the supposed "interesting consequences" may well evaporate in practice. How can we possibly apply this thesis about provisos when we do not as a society or a nation under law have a coherent theory of justice in property acquisition? Some people are fond of the labor theory. Some take a utilitarian approach. Some are libertarians. In what sense, then, can one recover *the* social-welfare proviso for a given title? If we cannot recover it, we cannot know which conflicts are bogus (because they involve only the resurrection of a latent social-welfare proviso) and which conflicts are genuine.

Reply.

Two things may be said in answer. First, the fact that multiple lines of argument are used for property, in both legal and moral contexts, does not entail that property theory is incoherent. At most, it entails that the theory is complex. It is incoherent only if its multiple lines of argument are (a) equally plausible and (b) inconsistent. Second, we have some reason to believe that the arguments are consistent. The social-welfare provisos inherent in the various types of justification for property are strikingly similar. The "no-loss" requirement imposed by the traditional version of the labor theory has obvious similarities to the substance, if not the form, of the limitations imposed by the utility argument, the political liberty argument, and the proportionality requirement on the reward-for-labor argument. So even if the various lines of argument are equally sound, we should be able to coordinate them so as to avoid major conflicts. No doubt there are striking differences in the various lines of argument. But while we wait for a resolution to the coordination problem, perhaps we shall not go too far wrong if we simply adopt, for whole classes of cases, second-level principles about which of the provisos applies when.

For example, there are surely cases in which some of the standard justifications for property do not apply. With respect to inheritance, for instance, the labor theory has only limited application. The heirs have not earned the property or produced it. And the question of whether laborers morally acquire the right to control their property in perpetuity is certainly an open one. So all that may be left here is utility (and perhaps the political liberty argument, although that is doubtful). In such a case, recovering *the* social-welfare proviso would not be so difficult. And of course if one of these lines of argument emerges as the dominant one, the problem of finding the proviso is further simplified.

Objection.

Yes, but then this whole business begins to look vulnerable to special pleading. Won't people simply tend to reach for whichever provisos best suit their purposes? Threatened owners will pick the least restrictive ones; the state (or other challengers) will pick the most restrictive ones. How will those disputes be handled?

Reply.

If the process of adjudication is genuinely dialectical—if, that is, in genuinely problematic cases it is not rigged in advance in favor of one sort of outcome—then I see nothing wrong with this. And there is surely nothing unusual about it in our legal system. In fact, an adversarial system like ours is designed to handle such disputes.

Fairness
Objection.

But surely there is a question of fairness here that has been overlooked. No matter how true it may be that these provisos are inherent in rational justifications for property, people do not normally think of them—or at least not all of them—when they acquire property. Surely one's actual expectations, one's reasonable expectations given current social and legal practices, should count for something. Surely those expectations should control the process of reaching back to pluck the provisos out of some abstract theory or set of theories.

Reply.

When judges decide in negligence cases what counts as an appropriate standard of care, they apply the so-called reasonability standard. The question is not, "What did the defendant believe was the proper standard?" but rather, "What would reasonable people believe?" Reasonability is related to the actual beliefs of the populace as a whole, but it is not completely determined by those beliefs, and it is certainly not determined by the actual beliefs of the parties to ·the case. The situation here is analogous. Fairness requires that actual expectations be considered, but it does not require that these be determinative. After all, the expectations of the parties to a particular case may be bizarre, both with regard to what is generally believed and what sound theory can support. We cannot be hostage to unfounded opinions in property law any more than we can be hostage to them in criminal law.

The difficult question of fairness arises when theory conflicts with widely held long-standing beliefs. There we may have to move carefully. (Though I am uncomfortable with delay. Think of all the specious arguments for gradualism on civil-rights issues.) Property just is "social" in the sense that I have described. To the extent that we have, through the legal system or in other ways, collectively encouraged ourselves to think otherwise, we may (arguably) have to pay the price in genuine conflicts between rights and social welfare. But otherwise, we need not pay that price.

Provisos and Property Law

It is worth noting that property law for centuries has dealt with provisos that run with titles. The legal materials show a tendency to frame the issue in terms of a conflict between rights and social welfare—the same tendency that infects social and political philosophy. But the prevalence of the problem and the way courts have typically handled it should be enough to assure skeptical readers that my arguments are not at some lunatic fringe of empty theorizing. Changes in social conditions do sometimes change the law's estimate of one's property rights—in ways that exemplify exactly what I have called the emergence of latent social-welfare provisos. Two examples from land-use law should suffice to make the point.

Private Law

The first example concerns restrictive covenants, adopted by individual landowners and intended by them to run with title to the land even when they no longer own it.[18] Some such covenants (e.g., racially discriminatory ones) are unconstitutional.[19] But many types of restrictive covenants are quite legal and quite common—for example, those restricting land use to residential purposes[20] or defining obligations to a property-owner's association.[21] Such covenants, if properly drafted, can in principle be enforced by the law in perpetuity.[22]

The important point for present purposes is that courts may terminate such covenants, against the wishes of one or more of the interested parties, if another interested party petitions for the termination and "conditions" have changed sufficiently. The *Downs* v. *Kroeger* case[23] shows this as clearly as anyone could want to see it. In that case a private covenant restricting a piece of land to residential use was defeated by a showing (by owners not party to the original covenant) that the surrounding area had become a business area, greatly increasing the value of the restricted land as a business property and greatly decreasing its value as a residential property. The petitioners argued that changed conditions made the purpose of the original covenant impossible to achieve (with respect to their property), and that while enforcing the covenant would not benefit anyone significantly, it would impose a serious hardship on them. The court agreed, and even the vigorous dissent conceded the general principle.[24] Unless that decision and others like it are to be construed as cynical abuses of the rule against *ex post facto* legislation, they must be construed as attempts to determine whether social-welfare provisos implicit in the original covenant, and running with the title, have come into force through changed conditions.

Public Law

The other example concerns takings law. In this country, all titles to land are acquired under the condition that the land may be taken, with due process, for public purposes as long as just compensation is paid.[25] That condition expresses my position with regard to rights generally: that they dominate but do not trump other considerations, and that compensation is due when rights are overridden, no matter how good the reasons were for overriding them.

But there is another equally important constitutional restriction on titles. The government may regulate land use in ways that fall short of actual takings without paying compensation. (Translation: without, by its own reckoning, violating ownership rights.) And these regulations may change over time in ways unanticipated by, and unfortunate for, the owners.[26] The idea here is clearly comparable to my thesis about latent provisos. It is true that courts have often spoken as though the issue were simply one of degree; that is, that most regulations (e.g., taxes, zoning) do not rise to the level of a taking and therefore do not demand compensation.[27] But why not? Are we to say that the law may violate a citizen's property rights without compensation as long as the rights are "minor?" Or are we to say instead that a citizen's rights are always sensitive to changes in social conditions—sensitive in the sense that changed conditions can redefine the scope and character of those rights? The former alternative is an uncomfortable one for a legal system that takes rights seriously.[28] The latter alternative fits our system much better, and it is certainly the better choice.

A recent case clearly illustrates the importance of this theoretical issue. The case is *Loretto* v. *Teleprompter Manhattan Cable CATV Corp. et al.*[29] It concerns a New York statute that prohibits landlords from interfering with the installation of cable television facilities on their property, and it gives the State Commission on Cable Television the power to set a standard, nominal compensatory fee for such installations. The Supreme Court ruled that such mandatory installations constituted takings. The lines of argument in the majority opinion and in the dissent are instructive.

Briefly: Courts have repeatedly held that "[t]here is no set formula to determine where regulation ends and taking begins."[30] But in the *Loretto* case the Court, citing recent precedents as well as legal history,[31] denied that the issue is to be determined solely by balancing public benefits against private harms. Instead, it affirmed what it took to be the traditional rule that any permanent physical occupation of property, authorized by the government, is a taking for which compensation must be made, no matter how minor the damage to the owner or how great the public benefit. (See p. 6 of the Slip Opinion.) The Court thus asserts in effect that rights dominate other considerations, but it fails to consider any social-welfare provisos that might be relevant to this case. Without a recognition of such provisos (whether or not they change the result in this case), the Court's strong stand on the dominance of rights could lead to some rather dangerous results, as noted by Justice Blackmun in his dissent. Blackmun's opposition, however, relies on a "balancing of interests" doctrine in which it is all too clear that rights turn out to be little more than procedural devices for assigning the burden of proof. The resultant conflict of jurisprudential theories is unnecessarily difficult to resolve. Those who want a robust theory of rights will reject the balancing test and assume that any dangerous consequences that might follow are just necessary evils. Those who accept the balancing test (in order to get the consequences they think are correct case by case) will assume that it is a watered-down theory of rights that is the necessary evil. My thesis is that we can have a robust theory of rights and also weigh the consequences case by case—by recognizing the provisos inherent in titles.

In fact, I suspect that the practice that I recommend here is already in place, even if the proper theoretical foundation for it is not. But like all practice based on bad theory, current property-rights practice is vulnerable to unnecessary confusion, conflict, and error. Recognizing that the theoretical conflict between rights and welfare is not nearly as severe as it often seems will not make the practical problems disappear. But it should make them more tractable.

Notes

1. An earlier version of this paper was presented to the Jurisprudence Section of the Association of American Law Schools, at their annual meetings in January, 1982.

2. See Roger Pilon, "Ordering Rights Consistently," *Georgia Law Review* 13 (1979): 1171.

3. See Joseph L. Sax, "Takings, Private Property and Public Rights," *Yale Law Journal* 81 (1971): 149. See also William Blackstone, ed., *Philosophy and Environmental Crisis* (Athens: University of Georgia Press, 1974).

4. Consider the implications of Nozick's discussion of the Lockean proviso. *Anarchy, State and Utopia* (New York: Basic Books, 1975), pp. 178-82.

5. C. B. Macpherson, "Human Rights as Property Rights," *Dissent* 24 (1977): 72-77.

6. See Bruce Ackerman, *Private Property and the Constitution* (New Haven: Yale University Press, 1977).

7. See the articles on takings law in Bruce Ackerman, ed., *Economic Foundations of Property Law* (Boston: Little, Brown, 1975).

8. The metaphor is Ronald Dworkin's, in his *Taking Rights Seriously* (Cambridge: Harvard University Press, 1977), p. xi.

9. For a sustained argument against the significance of rights as a moral category, see Raymond Frey, *Rights and Interests* (Oxford: Oxford University Press, 1980).

10. In adjudication, with its demands on resources and time, burden-of-proof questions are often crucial. A system of criminal law in which individuals, pitted against the state in an adversarial system, had the primary burden of proof would be grossly unfair. Likewise, when the question at issue is an "ultimate" one (e.g., whether we can know anything at all), deciding who has the burden of proof is often tantamount to deciding which "side" will win.

11. See my *Property Rights: Philosophic Foundations* (London: Routledge and Kegan Paul, 1977).

12. John Locke, *Two Treatises of Government, Second Treatise*, chap. V.

13. For a developed presentation of the desert argument, see *Property Rights*, pp. 48-56.

14. With the exception of the condition, attached only to original acquisition, that the object acquired be unowned.

15. *Anarchy, State and Utopia*, pp. 178-82.

16. I assume that nihilism is not a moral theory but rather the rejection of moral theory, and of reason as applied to moral problems.

17. Specifically, chaps. 3-7.

18. A. James Casner and W. Barton Leach, eds., *Cases and Text on Property*, 2d ed. (Boston: Little, Brown, 1969), chap. 32.

19. Ibid., pp. 986-1023.

20. See *Downs* v. *Kroeger*, 200 Cal. 743, 254 P. 1101 (1927), and cases cited therein. Compare *Redfern Lawns Civic Assn.* v. *Currie Pontiac Co.*, 328 Mich. 463, 44 N.W. 2d 8 (1950).

21. See *Neponsit Property Owners' Assn., Inc.* v. *Emigrant Industrial Savings Bank*, 278 N.Y. 248, 115 N.E. 2d 793 (1938).

22. Casner and Leach, p. 993, n. 3.

23. 200 Cal. 743, 254 P. 1101 (1927).

24. Ibid. Three of the seven justices dissented vigorously—not on the ground that changed conditions could not terminate covenants, but on the ground that in this case the changes were not of the sort that could justify termination.

25. The Constitution of the United States, Amendment V: "No person shall be . . . deprived of . . . property, without due process of law; nor shall private property be taken for public use without just compensation." This is applicable to the states through Amendment XIV. See *Missouri Pacific Ry. Co.* v. *Nebraska*, 164 U.S. 403 (1896).

26. *Village of Euclid* v. *Ambler Realty Co.*, 272 U.S. 365 (1926), zoning for industrial purposes; *Berman* v. *Parker*, 348 U.S. 26 (1954), zoning to develop a better balanced, more attractive neighborhood.

27. *Pennsylvania Coal Co.* v. *Mahon*, 260 U.S. 393, 413-416 (1922). For analysis of takings law generally, see Joseph L. Sax, "Takings and the Police Power," *Yale Law Journal* 74 (1964): 36; Frank I. Michelman, "Property, Utility and Fairness: Comments on the Ethical

Foundations of 'Just Compensation' Law," *Harvard Law Review* 80 (1968): 1165; and Joseph L. Sax, "Takings, Private Property and Public Rights," *Yale Law Journal* 81 (1971): 149. In his 1971 article, Sax analyzes takings problems in terms of a conflict between private rights to property and certain "public" rights. While this is arguably an improvement on a straight private-right vs. social-welfare analysis, it leads to unnecessarily frequent conflict of rights situations. My analysis does not.

28. See the discussion of fairness in Michelman, "Property, Utility and Fairness," n. 22, and the general line of argument in Ronald Dworkin, *Taking Rights Seriously*, chap. 7.

29. U.S. (30, June 1982) No. 81-244.

30. *Goldblatt* v. *Town of Hempstead*, 369 U.S. 590, at 594 (1962).

31. E.g., *Penn Central Transportation Co.* v. *New York City*, 438 U.S. 104 (1978).

Bibliography

Ackerman, Bruce. *Private Property and the Constitution*. New Haven, Yale University Press, 1977.

———, ed. *Economic Foundations of Property Law*. Boston; Little, Brown, 1975.

Becker, Lawrence C. *Property Rights: Philosophic Foundations*. London: Routledge and Kegan Paul, 1977.

———, and Kipnis, Kenneth, eds. *Property: Cases, Concepts, Critiques*. Englewood Cliffs, N.J.: Prentice-Hall, 1984.

Held, Virginia, ed. *Property, Profits, and Justice*. Belmont, Calif.: Wadsworth, 1980.

Pennock, J. Roland, and Chapman, John W., eds. *Property*, Nomos XXII (New York: New York University Press, 1980).

6

A Sketch of a Rights Taxonomy

Diana T. Meyers
Department of Government
Cornell University

Among the most formidable problems in rights theory is that of adjudicating conflicts between rights and conflicts between rights and social goals. Rawls favors modeling this problem on a jigsaw puzzle composed of interlocking pieces representing such primary social goods as personal and political liberty, opportunity, and wealth. Once these parts have been cut to fit together, no further problems of adjudication remain. Dworkin recommends a card game model in which rights trump social goals up to a point. Only when the urgency of social goals approximates but does not decisively exceed that of rights is there a problem of adjudication. Becker combines and modifies these two models.

Becker holds that no right can be justified unless its formulation includes social-welfare provisos that suspend the right when they are germane.[1] However, since Becker also holds that not all pertinent social-welfare considerations are built into rights, rights can compete with social welfare. When these conflicts arise, either of two dispositions is possible: (1) the right takes precedence over the collective good, and the right-holder should be accorded the good his right confers; or (2) the collective good outweighs the right, and the right-holder should be compensated for being deprived of the good his right confers. According to Becker, social welfare figures both in the jigsaw puzzle of codified principles and in the card game of ad hoc conflict resolution.

An objection to this understanding of rights—one Becker addresses at some length—is that rights, especially human rights, are widely regarded as moral constants impervious to circumstantial vicissitudes. Yet, since everyone concedes that no substantive rights are absolute, philosophers have turned to procedural guarantees or to rights possession to account for this much-vaunted constancy. Becker rightly dismisses procedures, for they too are defeasible. Also, he attacks rights possession on the grounds that any right's protections are liable to suspension in the name of social welfare. To replace these forms of security, Becker proposes the dominance of rights over social welfare and the predictability of rights suspensions dictated by social welfare. Since the reasons for suspending a right rarely obtain and, when they do, invoke the original justification of the right with which any right-holder can familiarize himself if he troubles to inquire into the matter, right-holders are not likely to lose their rights and need not be taken by surprise if their rights vanish. The tenability of this unified view of rights ultimately depends on how various rights are justified.

Before turning to the problem of the justifications underpinning rights, it is necessary to examine Becker's claim that persons can anticipate social welfare incursions on their rights. Since predicting how future events might bear on rights is haphazard guesswork, and since assessing the impact of aggregate well-being on individual rights is a subtle and controversy-ridden enterprise, Becker's position is puzzling. I suspect, however, that this opacity daunts him less than it does me mainly because he adopts an exceedingly broad view of social welfare. Illustrating the constraints social welfare imposes on a person's right to swing a baseball bat in the park, he notes that this right does not authorize clobbering innocent passersby. But no social-welfare proviso intervenes here. Rather, other persons' rights to life prevail over free bat-swinging prerogatives. Insofar as each of us knows what rights persons have and how these rights rank relative to one another, we can anticipate ways in which our exercising our rights might violate someone else's rights and rule out these impermissible actions in advance.

Still, some relations between rights do not admit of neat codification. Which individuals have this or that right may be open to dispute (does the fetus have a right to life?), and the stringency rating of others' rights may vary with circumstances (the force of an assailant's rights plummets for the duration of the attack, but how far his rights are weakened depends on the viciousness of the attack). To the extent that such uncertainty clouds rights, it is impossible to include comprehensive rules of rights interaction in the formulation of each right. Likewise, the impact teleological social-welfare considerations have on rights resists systematization, for unfolding circumstances frequently and unexpectedly create novel aids to social well-being and precipitate social distress where harmony had flourished. Becker's confidence in the transparency of social-welfare considerations would not be warranted, it seems, if he had confined the class of social welfare considerations to social-welfare goals.

To capture the distinctions adumbrated above, it is useful to settle on some terminology. When the protections and prerogatives a right confers are constrained by a set of more stringent rights, I shall say that the latter contours the former. Contoured rights do not comprise unrestricted guarantees that are sometimes chiseled away and later restored; the sculpting of a contoured right is completed before the right is released to right-holders. At most, such rights may require a bit of polishing in light of right-holders' experience with them. Becker's right to swing a bat is a case in point.

Similar but importantly different is suspendability. A claim right or a liberty that affords protections and prerogatives that may evaporate when they obstruct attainment of the greater good of all is suspendable. Though a person who has a suspendable right knows in advance that his right is liable to suspension, he may not know precisely which social conditions would extinguish it. For example, a popular decision to construct a museum where a park had been would suspend a person's right to swing a bat in that park. Whereas anyone can predict that sometime or other he will be obliged to schedule his bat-play in deference to others' rights, no one could predict that a museum project would eventually supplant a park's contribution to social welfare and altogether suspend his athletic liberty at that locale. In the case of suspendable rights, not only is it possible that the guarantees they have afforded will be temporarily or permanently eliminated, but also the occasions generating these changes may arise unforeseeably. Because the class of actions and policies that may enhance social welfare is vast and indefinite, suspendable rights provide little security unless they are subservient to prespecified types of social-welfare goals.

Apart from these internal rights qualifications, there are reasons external to rights that can justify infringements. Infringeable rights may be superseded by competition from other rights or by considerations of aggregate welfare. But since the justifiability of an infringement does not extinguish the right, infringeable rights entitle aggrieved right-holders to acknowledgment in the aftermath of abridgments.

In denying that any rights are absolute, Becker affirms (and I agree) that even the most important rights are infringeable. However, Becker's ambiguous use of the expression 'social welfare' leaves it in doubt whether he means to hold that all rights are both contoured and suspendable and therefore that other rights and social goals enter into the justifications of all rights. While the categories of rights I have delineated—contoured, suspendable, and infringeable—are not mutually exclusive, I shall urge that Becker is mistaken if he supposes that all rights fall into all of them.

Notably, Becker's remarks about punishment verge on classifying basic human rights as suspendable as well as contoured.[2] As evidence that some sort of proviso is integral to fundamental personal liberties, Becker cites our assent to the practice of jailing convicted rights-violaters. However, it is unclear what he thinks preempts the offender's liberty of movement: social welfare, which requires that crime be deterred and that public outrage be vindicated, or contouring rights, which generate an obligation to avenge the criminal's misuse of his victim's rights? Yet, it makes all the difference. For the exigencies of crime deterrence and popular catharsis are not dispositive and cannot suspend basic personal liberties.

To see that excessive frequency and unpredictability are not the only limits on suspendability, it suffices to reflect on what might aptly be called sadistic punishments. What if deterring potential kidnappers required torturing convicted kidnappers slowly to death? Such a practice would seem clearly to breach limits on the amount and kind of degradation that can be routinely inflicted on persons to promote the greater good of all. If so, social-welfare provisos are themselves constrained by rights.

Our response to the plight of the innocent convict casts further doubt on the claim that any teleological considerations are built into basic personal liberties. Suppose that the publicity surrounding the conviction and incarceration of an alleged rights-violator dissuades some other individuals from committing the same crime. But suppose it turns out that this individual did not commit the crime for which he was imprisoned. Disclosure of the convict's innocence would halt the deterrent effect of his punishment but would not diminish the deterrent effect it had already had. Furthermore, the revelation of this miscarriage of justice would not sabotage the deterrent power of subsequent punishments unless it were perceived to be part of a pattern of capricious judicial administration. That a convict is innocent is not a morally barren discovery precisely because accumulated social benefits cannot suspend basic personal liberties. If suspension of these rights were contingent upon whether or not this state of affairs was conducive to law-abidingness and an innocent individual's imprisonment had deterred crime without indirectly promoting it, enforcement officials could dismiss the harm the prisoner had endured as a socially beneficial error, all things considered. Though punishing the innocent could not be instituted as a general practice since it would lack deterrent efficacy, on those occasions when punishing an innocent person yielded counterbalancing social benefits this prisoner's rights would be suspended, and he would not be wronged. But no one thinks that gains in social welfare wipe the moral slate clean when basic personal liberties have been impinged upon in this way.

Becker is right to urge that if acquisition of a right depends on meeting social-welfare qualifications, keeping the right does too. Nevertheless, there is reason to believe that some rights are not encumbered with social-welfare provisos. If the adage attributing human rights to persons simply in virtue of their humanity can be given a cogent interpretation, these rights are independent of social welfare, and, to use Becker's language, all conflicts between these rights and the collective good are real. On the other hand, the justifications of some derivative rights and all conventional rights include appeals to social welfare that must be incorporated in the content of these rights. Rights can be located on a spectrum ranging from fundamental rights, which are justified without appeal to social welfare, to conventional rights, which are recognized chiefly to promote social welfare. At the latter end of the array are rights like the right to drive through an intersection when the light is green—instituted merely for the sake of public order and convenience—while at the opposite pole are rights like the right to life—recognized because they are vital to the integrity of the individual.

Derivative rights, lying between fundamental and conventional ones, are of two kinds. They may be directly implied by fundamental rights, in which case their justifications contain no welfare component, or they may require the added support of social-welfare considerations, in which case their justifications combine an appeal to social goals with rights-based reasoning. A prime example of a directly derivative right is the right to a fair trial. Because capital punishment, corporal punishment, and imprisonment abridge fundamental rights, and because these abridgments would be wrongful violations if there were not reason to believe the convict guilty, enforcement agents must accord defendants a fair trial in order to respect the fundamental rights of the accused individual. In contrast, the right to vote in contested elections for government offices appears to be an indirectly derivative right. It helps to defend citizens against tyrannical abrogations of more fundamental rights, but it also enables right-holders to advance other interests through the democratic process. Accordingly, while the franchise is constrained by other rights, it can properly be suspended, at least temporarily, to stave off disaster.

Fundamental rights and directly derivative rights are qualified, if at all, only by other equally or more fundamental rights (they are contoured but not suspendable), whereas indirectly derivative rights and conventional rights are qualified by social-welfare considerations as well as by other rights (they are both contoured and suspendable). Inasmuch as all rights would be inadmissible without their respective qualifications, the ways in which these qualifications trim rights do not constitute abridgments. Still, these mutually adjusted and, in some instances, welfare-sensitive rights are not absolute. In the cases of some rights, only the most far-fetched circumstances would permit them to be infringed. Nevertheless, since some rights priorities cannot be fixed in advance, and since welfare considerations can balloon sufficiently to override rights that usually exclude consequentialist balancing, abridgments which, though justified, do not extinguish the affected right remain possible. All rights being infringeable, the right-holder's position in the aftermath of infringement needs explication.

Once again, rights spread out along a graduated scale. Infringing a fundamental right necessarily degrades the right-holder: to infringe a fundamental right is to compromise a right-holder's humanity. As such, this act invariably calls for recognition of the right-holder as a victim. Because directly derivative rights are instrumental in respecting fundamental rights, abridgments of the former often translate into abridgments of the latter. Unfair trials are more likely than fair ones to issue in erroneous convictions and illicit punishments. Still, the wrong an innocent convict suffers is not identical to the harm infringement of a directly derivative right inflicts. By itself, the peril in which abridgments of these derivative rights place fundamental rights victimizes the right-holder. Anyone who is forced to submit to irregular procedures when his fundamental rights are at stake is subjected to severe mental anguish that ought to be assuaged once the need for the infringement has passed. Infringements of directly derivative rights are not as devastating as infringements of fundamental rights, and persons who undergo only the former are plainly owed less consideration than persons who also suffer the latter type of abridgment. Still, both of these measures disrupt the lives of right-holders in a manner that requires that these individuals be acknowledged as victims.

Indirectly derivative rights stand at a further remove from fundamental rights and from the critical interests of right-holders, and the obligation to acknowledge the victims of these rights abridgments weakens commensurately. Surely, the cancellation of an election would not necessarily victimize every voter. Only if this step is an extravagant response to a minor crisis, or presages the indefinite usurpation of democratic political authority, or frees officials to violate other rights does it seem appropriate to regard voters as victims. Finally, since extensive social-welfare provisions are built into conventional rights, it is virtually impossible to abridge these rights, and suspensions do not support any acknowledgment of the right-holder unless, coincidentally, these reversals injure this individual's interests.[3] Because the tribulation of being denied passage through an intersection when the light is green is no worse than other trivial frustrations independent of any right, only exceptional circumstances could generate a duty to recognize a stalled driver as a victim.

Various factors must be taken into account in deciding how to acknowledge a victim of a rights infringement. Sometimes an explanation or apology seems appropriate; sometimes anything less than reparations seems inadequate. The form this recognition ought to take depends on factors like the harm inflicted by the abridgment, the reason for the abridgment, and the resources available to the abridgers. However, as the tie between the abridged right and fundamental rights becomes progressively attenuated, the victimization right-holders experience becomes less palpable, less threatening to the integrity of the right-holder. Accordingly, the consideration owed the right-holder wanes until eventually none at all may be owed him. In some quarters, the proposition that a rights infringement entails an obligation to compensate the discomfited right-holder is taken to be axiomatic. Becker apparently subscribes to this view. Unfortunately, in failing to appreciate the variety of rights, this position also fails to provide a basis for appraising what consideration aggrieved right-holders are entitled to demand.

Many controversies about property rights are illuminated when they are interpreted as problems about where to locate property rights on the the rights spectrum I have sketched. Locke and his followers write as if property rights belong among the fundamental rights or, at any rate, among the directly derivative rights; however, neither of these classifications can be reconciled with these theorists' rejection of a right to satisfaction of basic needs. Other rights contour fundamental and directly derivative rights, but no welfare considerations can suspend them. Yet, as Becker observes, everyone agrees that the right to life constrains but does not abridge ownership prerogatives (I may use my knife to chop vegetables, but not to stab you), and also that extreme and urgent need curtails property rights in the same way (I cannot charge exorbitant prices for water if I own the sole well on the desert). Since fundamental and directly derivative rights are contoured but not suspendable, the second of these qualifications poses an insuperable obstacle to classifying property rights as fundamental or directly derivative rights unless this qualification stems from a right to satisfaction of basic needs which is itself fundamental or directly derivative. Partisans of strong property rights thus confront a dilemma. Either they must admit individual welfare rights into the empyrean alongside property rights, or they must concede that property rights are indirectly derivative in order to deny all fundamental rights to positive aid.

To consign property rights to the indirectly derivative category is to incorporate social welfare considerations into the conceptions of these rights. How powerful these provisos will be—whether they will include environmental protection, historical preservation, and the like—hinges on the degree to which the collective good must be accommodated in order to justify property ownership. Wherever the line between internal qualifications (that is, suspendability) and external rivalry (that is, infringeability) is drawn, it is important to reiterate that abridgments of indirectly derivative rights do not necessarily entitle right-holders to substantial compensation. These abridgments may skirt the right-holder's crucial and inextricable concerns and may inflict only negligible harm on this individual. If so, he could claim only *pro forma* recognition as a victim.

Of course, it remains possible that property rights are just conventional rights. In that case, the longevity of these rights mirrors their social usefulness, and any restitution deemed appropriate in the wake of suspensions is dictated by further calculations of social welfare, not by the erstwhile rights. This cavalier treatment of property rights is appealing because it efficiently disposes of all worries about social intervention in resource management. However, our intuitions about some forms of dispossession controvert it. The consternation we feel about demolishing homes to make way for economically desirable roads suggests that property rights have deeper moral roots. Not only do people need shelter to survive, but also their homes are emotional centers from which social networks radiate. It is understandable, then, that many people find the loss of a home severely disorienting and that having a home taken for others' economic gain only exacerbates the trauma. To capture this type of victimization in the moral lexicon, property rights must be elevated to the status of indirectly derivative rights.

My own view is that there are rights to satisfaction of basic needs that help to justify property rights, but that social-welfare considerations must be superadded to complete the reasoning for these rights. Assuming that persons are entitled to sufficient goods and services to satisfy their basic needs, rudimentary property rights entitling persons to use their allotments for this purpose and enjoining others not to interfere in this activity must be acknowledged. Furthermore, property rights may prove instrumental in enabling a society to attain a level of prosperity at which it can implement rights to basic necessities. Still, these two arguments sharply restrict property acquisition and use. To loosen these constraints, broad social benefits, such as personal independence and diverse consumer goods, must be adduced. Together, these arguments install property rights among the indirectly derivative rights. If I understand Becker correctly, he would concur with this conclusion. My objective in this essay has been to refine and situate this result in the broader context of rights theory.

Notes

1. My thesis addresses 'Property Rights and Social Welfare' by Lawrence Becker in this volume.

2. It is worth noting that, if this is Becker's view, he is not alone in holding it. Rawls, too, contends that all rights are suspendable. Assuming that there are circumstances in which Rawls's general conception of justice—basic liberties and equal opportunity may be traded off in the interest of economic gains—should be implemented rather than his special conception of justice—equal liberties, fair equality of opportunity, and the difference principle in lexical order—Rawls must grant that no right bars suspension for the sake of social welfare. Though he could reply that his general conception of justice does not run afoul of the right to equal concern and respect which therefore is not suspendable, this right is merely an exhortation to impartiality until it is fleshed out with rights and other principles. As such, its nonsuspendability is normatively empty.

3. Though it has sometimes been supposed that in virtue of their importance fundamental rights must be absolute, it is more plausible to hold that in virtue of their unimportance some conventional rights are absolute. An absolute right can be contoured and suspendable, but it cannot be infringeable; that is, subject to justifiable overriding. Accordingly, a conventional right contoured to give way to any other right and suspendable in the name of any social goal would be absolute, since no moral consideration external to the right would remain to justify infringing it. That persons would gain little from such an absolute right shows how utterly misguided this characterization of a natural right is. *

7

Rights, Responsibilities And Redistribution

William Nelson
Department of Philosophy
University of Houston

We have sometimes been encouraged to believe that natural rights theories of justice differ fundamentally in kind from liberal, egalitarian theories. The latter, we are told, are *patterned* theories, while the former are *process* theories, and patterned theories are said to involve extensive limitations on liberty, while process theories do not.[1] However, at least in the case of the best-known examples of each kind of theory, this way of contrasting them is inaccurate. The role of "pure procedural justice" in Rawls's theory makes it a kind of entitlement theory, and the "Lockean proviso" in Nozick's entitlement theory functions as a kind of "end-state" constraint on the exercise of entitlements.[2] Moreover, though it is easy to see that rights like property rights increase the liberty of their possessors in some respects, it is equally easy to see that they decrease the liberty of others. Considerations of liberty do not speak unambiguously in favor of the property rights or other alleged natural rights in the so-called libertarian tradition.

That property rights limit liberty is not, of course, a sufficient reason to reject them. Indeed, one respect in which natural rights theorists and liberal proponents of redistribution do *not* differ is in their commitment to property rights. After all, proponents of redistribution clearly intend that the recipients of income transfers will have rights over what they receive. In general, theorists in both traditions face the same basic question: How can the various rights, limitations on rights, and restrictions on liberty to which they are respectively committed be justified? The particular question for the liberal is how it is possible to justify both property rights and redistribution within the same theory.

Perhaps it should not be so difficult to answer this question. For surely, it will be said, property rights are *not unlimited*, and they are *not absolute*. These are distinct points, and each requires further elaboration: What is the ground for limitations on property rights, and, if they are not absolute, what considerations justify their infringement? The first of these questions I will turn to later. I shall begin by considering Judith Thomson's discussion of the second.[3] Suppose you own a locked box, and suppose it contains a supply of some drug—a supply more than ample for your future purposes. Suppose, further, that a small child desperately needs a dose of the drug, or she will die. Surely, says Thomson, I may break into the box and take a small dose of the drug for the child. I may do so without your permission and even against your express wishes. I do not act wrongly in doing so, though perhaps I (and others) should compensate you to some extent for the value of the drug used. Hence, Thomson concludes, it is not in every case morally wrong to infringe a property right, and so, such rights are not absolute. By analogy, it is at least imaginable that we might be morally justified in taxing people against their will to save lives or avert some other catastrophe.

It is hard not to agree with Thomson in the matter of the drug and the child. Not only is it not wrong to take the drug, it might even be wrong not to take it. However, as Thomson notes, we need to be careful in generalizing from this case. Given that you have an ample supply of the drug, that the child will die without it and will be saved by it, the case for taking the drug is compelling. In the absence of one or more of these conditions, it might not be. In short, while there are some cases in which it is not wrong to infringe a right, there may not be many.

There is something further to note here. In describing her example, Thomson never denies that you have a right to the drug and the box. Though it may not be wrong to take the drug, it nevertheless is yours. In taking the drug, I do infringe one of your rights. Why does Thomson say this? Is it not unnecessarily paradoxical to say that we act rightly in taking the drug while also insisting that you have a right to it? A person's rights, it is sometimes said, operate as constraints or as barriers that define the absolute limits of the permissible for others. Yet, Thomson says, you have a right to the drug, *and* we may take it. How can it be permissible for us to take it if there is a moral barrier that prohibits taking it? And what good reason do we have to believe that there is such a barrier anyway? Since there is ample reason for me to take the drug, why is there not equally good reason to deny that you have a right to the drug at all—that anyone can have a right to goods like this?

Questions like these, of course, could be raised about many kinds of rights other than just property rights. The questions include questions of at least two kinds. First, there are conceptual questions about how we are to understand the relation between assertions about your rights and assertions about what I (or you) may or must do. The answers to these questions are relevant to whether there is something paradoxical about Thomson's view—the view that I may take the drug *and* that you have a right to it. The second kind of question is whether there is reason to believe in any rights at all. The problem is that rights—at least rights construed as barriers or constraints—drastically limit the freedom of others to act. This is true of rights in general, and it is certainly true of property rights in particular. Property rights interfere with individual liberty to use resources to good purpose. How can there be an objection to someone's making good use of a resource? True, the owner of the resource—the person with a right to it—may have in mind a different use for it, and it may even be a good use. But that in itself does not distinguish him from many others.

Consider the first of the two questions just raised: What is being asserted when it is said that you have a right to the drug in the box? Suppose someone asks whether the girl in the example ought to be given the drug. The reply "it is your drug" or "you have a right to the drug in the box" is not a direct reply to this question.[4] It is not even a direct reply if it is asked whether *I* should give the drug to the child. It is certainly not an appropriate reply if *you* ask whether the child ought to be given the drug. Your knowing that you own the drug does not settle the question of what you should do with it. It does not even settle the question of what I should or may do with it; for (to take the simplest case) you may have given me permission to use it in some way, or in any of a number of ways, or even in whatever way I want. That you have a right to the drug, then, does not, *by itself*, imply much of anything about what I, or you, may or must do with it. What does it imply?

In general, I believe such rights can be analyzed in terms of Hohfeldian categories.[5] They consist, typically, of powers (like the power to transfer or waive), immunities (the absence of a power on the part of others to do such things), and duties of noninterference (the absence of liberties to use without permission) on the part of others. If it is your drug, others are not at liberty (unless granted permission) to do certain things with it, and others lack the power to alter certain rights and duties regarding the drug. (Different rights will involve different combinations of these elements.) In general, then, to have a right is to have an area of control, free from interference by others. It is to have, I shall say, a certain authority.[6] If it is your drug, it is your choice what is to be done with it. But this does *not* mean you cannot choose wrongly or stupidly. It does not mean you are at liberty to do any of the things you have a right to do. One can act with authority but not as one should, or one can act without authority but well. I may act without authority if I break open your box and give the drug to the child, but I may be doing with the drug what should be done with it—what *you* should have done with it.

The idea that statements about rights (many of them, anyhow) are statements about authority (in the sense I have tried to elucidate) dispels some of the air of paradox surrounding Thomson's conclusion. That you have a right to the drug and that I act rightly in taking it are not straightforward contraries. And even if I take it without your permission, I may at least be doing with the drug what should be done with it. Judgments about who properly has control over certain decisions and judgments about how the decisions should be made represent different, but complementary kinds of judgment.

None of this means, of course, that there is nothing wrong with my taking the drug without your permission, even if I do the right thing with it. If it is yours, and I am not joint owner, then I am not at liberty to take it.

But it can still be true that what I do with it is what should be done with it. Given that that judgment may be a correct judgment, the question we now need to confront is the second of the two questions mentioned above: Why are there any rights? Why assume there are *two* questions to be answered: What is to be done, and who is authorized to make the decision? To ask this question is not yet to question any particular assignment of authority—to suggest that we move to a different system from the one generally recognized now. Many alternatives are possible, including alternatives in which a large number of decisions now reserved to individuals must instead be made by some collective procedure like majority vote. But to justify shifting to some such alternative, we would need an argument to show that the alternative is superior. The question I am now asking is why we need any assignment.

It is sometimes thought that rights are important mainly as a protection for the interests of their possessor: They.secure their possessor against interference in matters of particular concern. Hence, the question whether we should recognize rights has been seen as the question whether certain individual interests are sufficiently important to deserve special protection in competition with the interests of others or of society at large. But it is not clear to me that this is the right way to view the matter. In granting a right, we are indeed leaving an individual (or, in the case of rights jointly held, two or more) in control of certain resources or decisions. We deprive others of the authority to make those decisions. But we may also believe that the person with the right should exercise it in certain ways, perhaps with the interests of others in mind. (Consider the case of a trustee, appointed to use his or her judgment in exercising certain rights or powers in the interests of some third party.) What I want to suggest, then, is that whether we should grant rights depends not solely on whether individuals have special interests that need to be protected at all costs against the interests of others. It depends, rather, on what might be gained (or lost) for people in general by the division of control and authority implicit in a given assignment of rights.

Whether people should have rights is one question; how and to what purpose they should exercise them is another. It may not be just one's own business how one exercises one's rights. And so, an assignment of rights is also potentially a determination of who can be required to do what and who is to be held responsible for what omissions. But, if only you have a right to do something, and only you can be held responsible (ordinarily) for failure to do it, it may still be highly desirable or even required that it be done. And if you fail to do it, it may then be highly desirable that I do it. Though these judgments need not be contradictory, it is clear that there is a serious practical tension within any moral view that allows for both. Thus it is natural to prefer a theory that eliminates this tension by eliminating rights altogether. The paradigm of a theory that does that is, of course, utilitarianism.

Viewed from the perspective of a conception of rights like mine, utilitarianism occupies an interesting position. To believe in rights is to believe that some people are barred from making certain decisions, even if these would otherwise be right. This does not preclude rights held jointly, as when two or more persons control the use of some resource, each entitled to use it as he or she wishes, but no one else is entitled to do so. What utilitarianism holds, in effect, is that we are all joint owners of all resources—that we are all entitled to make any decision. (Though it does not hold that anyone who makes a decision makes the right one.) Does that mean that utilitarianism recognizes rights after all? I think not, for rights consist in, and get their significance from, the fact that some people are excluded from making some decisions, while others are not.

Utilitarianism is, at best, a limiting case of a theory recognizing rights. What it lacks, but what full-fledged rights theories have, is any moral limit on the options one may (or must) consider in applying principles of right conduct. For the same reasons, it lacks limits on the omissions for which one can be held responsible. Perhaps more important, whatever one's purposes—whether they are self-interested or include the interests of others—the absence of rights means that one's ability to plan and carry out long-term projects may be seriously hampered. For such projects often require that one take some action now (like an investment decision) that makes sense only on the assumption that certain other actions will be possible later. But that is exactly what is precluded by the absence of rights. Not only are all options potentially mine, but none is certainly mine. While rights, as understood here, do not determine the purposes for which one acts, they do determine what one has, and can expect to have, to work with. Without some such determination, it is hard to see how coherent, long-term planning and coordinated action are possible.

It might be objected still that it is wrong to rule out interference with someone's protected sphere of authority when he is exercising his rights badly. I grant that there may be occasions, like the one Thomson describes, in which it would be best to interfere. But such cases may not be common. It is important to note that many of our responsibilities and obligations do not require that we do or refrain from doing some relatively specific act. And so, others will not often be in a position to appreciate, on a specific occasion, whether we are exercising our rights as we should and whether they can interfere for the better. Much of what we must do is to carry out relatively long-term projects (provide for our old age, raise our children decently, or get a paper revised and completed in time for a publication deadline). What we do at a particular time will be well (or ill) advised only relative to other things we have done or plan to do. If we are acting badly and an improvement is possible, it would be only by someone else's taking over our affairs in general and imposing on them a new direction or more coherent organization. But that would require *that* person's having exclusive control over the relevant matters; that is, having rights.

If I am right, then, we are left with some kind of mixed theory—a theory that recognizes both individual or collective rights and also principles of conduct that cut across these rights. The idea that one of these aspects of morality might be eliminated entirely or reduced to the other seems mistaken. But that does not mean there are no important overlaps between the two, that they derive from completely distinct, irreconcilable concerns, and that there is no hope of mitigating the conflict between the two.

Justifying Rights

What rights and principles of conduct are there? How much potential conflict is there between rights and principles of conduct? To what extent are they congruent so that there is little chance that people exercising their rights will act wrongly? To answer these questions, we need to consider what kinds of rights and principles can be justified.

I have suggested an analogy between individual rights, like property rights, and what I have called collective rights, like the right of the members of a group that decisions be made by a procedure such as majority vote. In each case, the existence of the right amounts to a grant of authority over a certain range of decisions. In each case, at least typically, there is room for discretion so that people have a number of distinct, mutually exclusive ways of exercising their authority while still acting within its limits. For this reason, there is room for objections to what one does even when one acts within one's rights.

When people in a democracy believe that voters or their representatives have exercised their authority badly, they sometimes seek to curtail those powers, as by constitutional amendment. Something similar happens when people object to the way others exercise individual rights, of speech, say, or of property. Such objections, of course, tend to call forth passionate defenses of the systems (democracy, property rights) in question. Among the defenders in each case, it is possible to find both those who treat the rights as something like natural rights and those who defend them with what might be regarded as utilitarian arguments: Some think it just obvious that certain modes of acquisition automatically give full title to what is thus acquired, and others similarly think it just obvious that people have a right to a voice in any decision that affects them.[7] Some, on the other hand, defend property rights on the ground that, for example, they promote productive effort or encourage individual responsibility, while others defend democracy on the ground that it tends to produce just legislation and civic virtue. Not surprisingly, those who take property rights to be natural rights, defensible regardless of their effects or of how they are exercised, are skeptical of arguments for democracy and are likely to accept it only when its powers are narrowly circumscribed. Those who think it obvious that most decisions should be made by democratic procedures are equally skeptical of private-property rights.[8]

From a detached perspective, neither party to this dispute occupies a strong position. What is at stake is the proper distribution of authority and control in society. The defender of property rights believes that individuals should have exclusive, dictatorial control over distinct goods and decisions. The defender of a thorough-going democracy believes no group smaller than the whole of those affected should be able to control anything—that every decision should be turned over to a political process. It is noteworthy, though, that many parties to the dispute believe that *some* assignment of authority is to be evaluated, and perhaps rejected, on broadly consequentialist grounds. They may think their favorite rights (perhaps property rights) are justified independently of their likely consequences; but they will reject other rights (like democratic rights to participate in making certain decisions) on the ground that the resulting decisions may undermine property rights. Why the asymmetry? Why isn't it always at least relevant to the evaluation of a given assignment of authority whether the authority will be exercised to good purpose, consistent with other moral requirements?

Relatively few people are willing to make it a matter of absolute principle that social decisions are to be made by a democratic procedure. They are not willing to insist on it merely because it gives people an equal voice in decisions, or merely because they accept some further principle about some supposed right to participate in collective decisions; nor, finally, do they think that we must acquiesce in decisions democratically arrived at merely because of the procedures followed. Most people will grant on reflection that people as they are, or not very different, might vote to do terrible things; and most will grant that this possibility is at least relevant to whether we should accept democracy. Almost no one favors a pure democracy not hedged around with a written bill of rights or strong traditions of liberty and limited government. Even in the best of circumstances, we think the authority to make decisions democratically must be limited, and it must be limited to prevent its being exercised in impermissible ways.

If the foregoing ideas about the evaluation of democracy are reasonable—and I think they are—it is hard to see why similar considerations should not apply to the justification or evaluation of property rights and other exclusive rights. These rights are also in large part grants of authority to make decisions. Consider the right to life. We think life is almost always valuable to the person whose life is in question, and we think people are sufficiently good judges of what is good for them that they want to preserve their lives when (and perhaps only when) their lives are valuable for them. If this were not the case, would we be as willing as we are to grant people a right to life—a right not to be killed against one's will? Would it be reasonable to grant such a right? Or, again, suppose people are rational in their judgments as to the desirability of preserving their own lives, but suppose that life for one person is often incompatible with life for another—or even that lives are in short supply but are transferable so that, for its duration, a given life might "belong" to more than one person. In *that* case would it be reasonable to grant each person unlimited authority to decide questions about "his" or "her" life or death? As things stand, there is relatively little room for abuse or misuse of one's right to life, and so there is relatively little likelihood that it will be misused. But if this were not true, uncritical acceptance of this right would be less reasonable.

There are many arguments available, for those who do not disdain argument, in support of rights of private property. They provide an incentive to make productive use of resources; they generate a more or less rational system of prices for goods and resources; and they make for autonomous control of one's life and thus promote coherent and meaningful lives. These are good arguments, but they rest on empirical assumptions that might be false and that probably need qualification. Moreover, if these effects of property rights are good, there may be other effects that are not good. If one set of effects is to be considered, so is the other.

Let me recapitulate. I take the position that rights are to be understood mainly in terms of the authority to make and act on certain decisions. So understood, it is hard to imagine accepting a theory that does not recognize rights, either implicitly or explicitly. There is clearly room for controversy, however, as to the proper distribution of authority and as to whether people should have exclusive or nonexclusive, private or collective, forms of authority. (It is our decisions on these substantive matters that will determine in the end whether we agree with Thomson's characterization of the moral issues in the case of the little girl and the drug.)

How should we decide on the proper distribution of authority? I have stressed the analogy between rights of private property and rights to govern, claiming that the former constitute a kind of sovereignty over a restricted territory. Hence, I have concluded that the evaluation of a system of property rights should proceed in the same way as the evaluation of a proposed system of government. In particular, if, as I think, the justification of a form of government like democracy depends heavily on contingent facts about how people are likely to use the authority to govern in such a system, so also the justification of property rights must depend heavily on such facts. Where do these ideas lead us?

First, if we are to choose among different possible allocations of authority on the basis of their likely effects, we must do so from the standpoint of some more general conception of what effects are desirable. I have committed myself to no such general conception and, in particular, not to either aggregative utilitarianism or Rawlsian contractarianism. Any adequate approach to justification must include a substantive (though maybe not determinate) conception of the good, but a theory of the good without a conception of how it is to be applied to the task of justification is of no use. Rawls's contract theory contains both.[9]

Second, not only have I not defended any particular account of what rights people have, but I have also not discussed specific duties, responsibilities, or desirable character traits. To defend a system of rights, we will have to show that it will result in good consequences. To show this, we will need to make assumptions about how people exercising the rights in question will act, and we will also need to consider the consequences of this kind of behavior, in the aggregate, given background assumptions about the society in which the system of rights is to be set. Accepting a system of rights on the basis of such calculations, then, seems to involve also accepting standards of behavior, at least insofar as these standards dictate how people are to exercise their rights. A theory of rights involves a theory of responsibilities, and since how one behaves depends on one's character, it involves a commitment to at least a partial conception of the virtues.

In general, then, the task of justifying rights will require that we look at whole systems of rights and at the way they work together; and our decisions about rights will not be independent of our decisions about other moral issues, like what responsibilities people have and what the virtues are. Now, this "holistic" approach to justification and, in particular, the idea that the primary subject of moral appraisal is the whole system of rights and responsibilities is one of the basic ideas that underlies Rawls's work. I have arrived at the idea, however, neither by assuming a patterned theory of justice nor by assuming a contractarian approach to justification. What I have argued is that it is unreasonable in justifying them not to take into account how and to what effect they will be exercised.

Rights and Redistribution

A system of government—a system or procedure for making and executing public policy—involves an assignment of rights. It authorizes certain people, either individually or collectively, to make and carry out certain decisions. It is doubtful that any assignment of authority will automatically result in good decisions, even if that assignment is based on a conception of what kind of decision ought to be made and on the assumption that those authorized to make decisions will tend to make them well. In particular, those of us who believe in democracy, and believe in it because we think it less likely than other systems to result in awful legislation, nevertheless believe that it sometimes does or can. When we switch from the example of political rights to that of individual rights, it again seems likely that any assignment of rights will be subject to abuse, whether intentional or unintentional. And, again, this seems likely even if the assignment of rights is based on reasonable expectations about how they will be exercised.

It seems likely, then, that if we grant any interesting rights at all, we will find ourselves in the position, sometimes, of saying that a person ought not to have done what he had a right to do, or even that someone else ought to violate his rights in order to do what needs to be done. Of course, we avoid this possibility if we accept only trivial, "limiting case" rights, as utilitarianism might seem to do, or if we accept a theory with nothing but rights, like some natural rights theories. But there is also another interesting possibility. Given an appropriately simple conception of what kind of outcome is desirable, we might be able to devise a system of authority that would automatically produce the desirable outcome. We would then have a case of what Rawls has called "perfect procedural justice."

It has been thought that something like this happens in the case of private property in a free market, where, given certain assumptions, the exercise of private-property rights will automatically result in a Pareto optimal allocation of goods and resources. By analogy, people have sometimes thought of defending political democracy with legalized buying and selling of votes on the ground that it will yield Pareto optimal outcomes.[10] And others, with a different conception of what goals are desirable, might think that the outcome of the political process cannot be unjust so long as the process is properly constrained by a bill of rights. The general idea running through all of these attempts at justification is that some system of rights, properly constrained or limited or embedded in appropriate background institutions or in a certain kind of culture, will always yield the desired outcomes. People, acting as they are bound to act under the circumstances, and remaining within the bounds of their legitimate authority, will always act as they should.

This is an extraordinarily attractive idea, but few people have been satisfied with specific attempts to apply it. For one thing, the claim that a given system will automatically yield the right outcome usually depends on empirical assumptions that turn out to be false. Thus, for example, the free exercise of property rights by rational maximizers automatically yields Pareto optimal outcomes only if there are no externalities. (Pollution is an example of an externality—in this case, an external *cost*. When there are external costs, someone is able to make use of resources, thereby imposing costs on other potential users without compensating them.) The problem is that there are externalities, and it is difficult to eliminate them in any systematic way. Moreover, attempts to devise a system of rights that can be exercised only in desirable ways usually involve some rather narrow and simple conception of what is morally required—conceptions that are bound to be challenged by someone else as inadequate. The Pareto criterion is a case in point. So also is the idea that any outcome of the political process consistent with the constraints in the Bill of Rights satisfies all moral requirements appropriate to legislation.

One way to extend this idea, applying it to social and political systems as a whole, is to add to the kinds of constraints on rights I have mentioned. Thus, for example, in addition to constitutional constraints on legislative authority of the sort found in the Bill of Rights, and in addition to seeing that markets remain open and competitive, we could impose positive requirements to the effect that minimum family income should not fall below some fixed (relative or absolute) level. Perhaps *then* there would be no room for an exercise of rights that was seriously immoral or unjust, and so there might be an argument for redistribution if it played an essential role in making our system a case of perfect procedural justice. This actually seems to be something like the position that Rawls takes in *A Theory of Justice*. As he sees it, given that the basic structure is just (that, for example, basic liberties are guaranteed and an appropriate minimum income is established), whatever results from either the political process or the market is not unjust. Granted, Rawls speaks of this as a case of "*pure* procedural justice," not "perfect," but explaining why it is a case of pure procedural justice, or even what that means, turns out to be problematic.[11] I think there is something to be said, therefore, for reading Rawls differently: The requirements of justice are satisfied when liberties are respected and when no one falls below a reasonable economic level. The reason that all outcomes of a just system are just is that unjust outcomes are ruled out by systematic constraints.

It might be objected to Rawls—or to Rawls as I have just interpreted him—that even if an appropriate distribution (etc.) is guaranteed, people are bound to misuse their rights. They will mismanage their own lives, they will be callous or greedy, they will do a bad job of raising their children, or they will destroy the natural beauty of the land. All sorts of things will go wrong in a just society. It could be replied, of course, that the problems I have imagined are not matters of *injustice* and so do not constitute objections to the Rawlsian position I have described. They are, however, relevant to the kind of justification of rights that I envisage, since they do concern the extent to which people will live well or even flourish under the constrained system of rights Rawls requires.

The points I want to make at this stage are these: First, if we agree that rights need justification, and we agree that their defense must depend in part on how and to what effect they are likely to be used, it is certainly appropriate and proper to limit or constrain them in such a way that the most serious bad outcomes are ruled out, and that the likelihood of good consequences is increased. Required redistribution is one kind of constraint that is likely to be justified. Second, however, if we do not arbitrarily limit the range of consequences that concern us, it is highly unlikely that we will find an assignment of rights, however limited and constrained, such that there is no possibility of their being exercised in objectionable ways. Hence, there are likely to be cases in which people act within their rights and still act immorally, or at least not as they should given the results. These cases provide us with a second kind of role for redistribution; namely, that of a remedy for the damage done when people, misusing their rights, produce or fail to prevent bad consequences. In some of these cases, redistribution will serve not as part of a system of constraints on justified rights but, rather, will involve an infringement of rights.

That these two grounds for redistribution are different should be clear. Thomson mentions only (something like) the second. But there is clearly a place for each. If we agree that rights are to be justified in terms of their consequences (in terms, I want to say, of the way they contribute to peoples' ability to live decent lives), it is surely possible that rights will have to be constrained and limited in various ways. And it is certainly plausible that some regular, required redistribution might be one of the most effective, least intrusive kinds of constraint. That is, the system of rights best designed to make human well-being possible may be a system that incorporates some significant level of redistribution. But it by no means follows that people will not, in fact, intentionally or unintentionally, misuse their rights. In some cases, of course, only those who act irresponsibly will be harmed; and in those cases there is perhaps no ground for further interference. In other cases, people will suffer through no fault of their own, but as a result of the irresponsibility of others, or even just because of unusual circumstances that distort the normal process by which responsible behavior and respect for rights contributes to human well-being. Here I think forced redistribution to compensate for these distortions can again be justified, given the underlying aims I presuppose. But this kind of redistribution should seldom be necessary if people exercise their rights as they should. And so, it is not unreasonable to characterize it, as does Thomson, as an infringement of rights on which people should normally be able to rely.

Notes

1. See Robert Nozick, *Anarchy, State and Utopia* (New York: Basic Books, 1974), pp. 150-64.

2. On the "Lockean Proviso," see ibid., pp. 178-82. On pure procedural justice, see John Rawls, *A Theory of Justice* (Cambridge: Harvard University Press, 1971), pp. 85-86.

    On patterns and entitlements in the work of Rawls and Nozick, see William Nelson, "The Very Idea of Pure Procedural Justice," *Ethics* 90 (1980): 502-11, esp. 510-11; and Arthur Kuflik, "Process and End State in the Theory of Economic Justice," *Social Theory and Practice* 8 (1982): 73-94.

3. "Some Ruminations on Rights," *Arizona Law Review* 19 (1977): 45-60.

4. See Jeremy Waldron, "A Right to Do Wrong," *Ethics* 92 (1981): 21-39. Much of what I say here about the relation between rights and right conduct is suggested by the ideas in this paper.

5. W. N. Hohfeld, *Fundamental Legal Conceptions* (New Haven: Yale University Press, 1919).

6. I am grateful to Carl Wellman for forcing me to think more carefully about how to analyze this notion of authority. I am afraid he would still regard the term as inappropriate, but I cannot think of a better one.

7. See William Nelson, *On Justifying Democracy* (Boston: Routledge and Kegan Paul, 1980), pp. 45-48, for a discussion of theories of democracy like this.

8. Cf. Carol Gould, "Contemporary Legal Conceptions of Property and Their Implications for Democracy," *Journal of Philosophy* 77 (1980): 716-28.

9. Authors as different as Thomas Scanlon and Alasdair MacIntyre have recently stressed the fundamental importance of human good and human interests in moral theory. For the former, see "Rights, Goals and Fairness" in Stuart Hampshire, ed., *Public and Private Morality* (New York: Cambridge University Press, 1978). For the latter, see *After Virtue* (Notre Dame: University of Notre Dame Press, 1981). While MacIntyre urges that we cannot begin rational discussion of moral issues without a shared conception of the good, he proposes no conception of how it is to function in moral argument. Do we maximize good in the aggregate? Seek to promote the good for each?

    Rawls, in *A Theory of Justice*, emphasizes the importance of the latter question, and his contract theory is supposed to provide an answer. The contract theory, however, does in various ways involve a commitment to a certain theory of the good. Rawls is aware, for example, that a just society will not be neutral among all possible systems of desire. See

"Fairness to Goodness," *Philosophical Review* 84 (1975): 536-554.
10. See Nelson, *On Justifying Democracy*, chap. V, for examples of such theories.
11. See Nelson, "The Very Idea of Pure Procedural Justice," (n. 2 above).

Bibliography

Brody, Baruch. "Work Requirements and Welfare Rights." In Peter G. Brown et al., *Income Support: Conceptual and Policy Issues*, pp. 247-58. Totowa, N.J.: Rowman and Littlefield, 1981.
Gibbard, Allan. "Natural Property Rights." *Nous* 10 (1976): 77-86.
Kuflik, Arthur. "Process and End State in the Theory of Economic Justice." *Social Theory and Practice* 8 (1982): 73-94.
Nelson, William. "The Very Idea of Pure Procedural Justice." *Ethics* 90 (1980): 502-11.
Nozick, Robert. *Anarchy, State and Utopia*. New York: Basic Books, 1974.
Rawls, John. "The Basic Structure as Subject." *American Philosophical Quarterly* 14 (1977): 159-66.
―――. "Fairness to Goodness." *Philosophical Review* 84 (1975): 536-554.
―――. *A Theory of Justice*. Cambridge, Mass.: Harvard University Press, 1971.
Scanlon, Thomas. "Preference and Urgency." *Journal of Philosophy* 72 (1975): 655-68.
―――. "Rights, Goals and Fairness." In Stuart Hampshire, ed., pp. 93-112. *Public and Private Morality*. New York: Cambridge University Press, 1978.

8

The Demands of Justice:
The Difference that Social Life Makes

Theodore M. Benditt
Department of Philosophy
University of Alabama in Birmingham

The Right to Life as a Reason

Some people believe that everyone is entitled to welfare, or to the alleviation of poverty, or to the fulfillment of basic needs on the ground that everyone has a right to life. The right to life, it is held, is not merely a right not to be killed (that is, it is not merely a negative right), but it is also a positive right—a right to be provided the necessities of life, and even, some would say, a right to be provided with the necessities of a decent or tolerably good life.

But the claim that one is entitled to welfare *because* one has a right to life flirts with being a confusion. The fundamental question regarding welfare is whether anyone is justified in insisting that others provide it. If someone were to say that he is justified in insisting that others provide him welfare *on the ground that* he has a right to it, then he is indeed confused, for to say that he has a right *is* just to say that he is justified in insisting on it. Far from showing that he is justified in insisting on being provided welfare, he is simply repeating himself. Similarly with respect to the right to life, insofar as it is said to be a positive right. The fundamental question is whether one is justified in insisting on being provided with the necessities of life, and to say that one is so justified because he has a right to life is simply to repeat oneself.

The foregoing also reveals the error in trying to think in general terms of 'the right to life,' and, having satisfied oneself in some way that such a right exists, *then* going on to find out what such a right entails. For the proper question is always "What is one justified either in doing or insisting that others do," and this cannot be answered in any significant way by pointing to the right to life, unless defenses have already been given of each element of that right. Of course, if this defense has been given, there is hardly any point in appealing to the right to life.

It goes without saying, I hope, that there is no logical or conceptual confusion in the idea that I may, for example, be justified in insisting that you not stab me (a negative right) but not in insisting that you feed me. These don't *have* to go together. It may be that one is justified in insisting in both cases—but the point is that if one is, it is not because both are comprehended by a general right to life. I don't mind repeating myself by saying that to maintain otherwise is merely to repeat oneself.

So the central question is: Are you justified (and if so, why) in insisting that I do something to promote your welfare? And the very important related question is: Must the society do certain things to promote your welfare? A fundamental strand of libertarian thought on these questions, to be taken up later, is that there is no right to any individual's acting so as to alleviate another's poverty, *and so* there is no right to the society or the state doing so. These matters will be taken up in a while, after some points about the notion of justice and some further matters concerning rights are brought out.

The Obligatory and the (Merely) Desirable

It is a familiar idea that there is a distinction between what is obligatory and what it would be good to do even though it is not obligatory. This is evident in cases of heroic acts. And it is also evident in cases that are quite trivial from the moral point of view—for example, giving someone the time of day. But it is also a phenomenon in a wide variety of other, not so trivial cases. Daily, there are many things it would be good of me to do, but which I do not *have* to do. Situations arise in which I could help someone, but I don't want to—I don't feel up to it, or I'd rather relax. I'm not imagining cases in which someone is in dire circumstances; in such cases I may be obligated. What I'm imagining are the probably numerous cases in which the gains (or prevention of losses) to others would more than offset any short- or long-term reduction of my utility, and yet I need not put myself out. It might be better if I were to do so, there are good reasons for me to do so, I ought to do so, but I don't have to, morally speaking. The conception of morality that I am outlining is one in which not everything (even beyond the heroic and the trivial) is obligatory. Many things are morally required, to be sure; but there is also, morally speaking, a lot of space in which we are free from obligation even when the good of others presses on us. Here a better person would act, but we are not morally required to do so.

This distinction—between what is obligatory and what is (merely) good—is intimately connected with the notion of rights. People have rights, which they can *exercise* (in the case of liberty rights) or *insist on* (in the case of so-called claim rights). Now it is important to be clear that having a right is one thing and exercising it (or insisting on it) is another thing. What this means is that a person can have a right even though it would be better if he didn't exercise it; that is, a person can have a right that he ought not to exercise (or insist on). Notice that the ought/obligation distinction comes in here: Though a person perhaps ought not to exercise a right that he has, he is under no obligation not to do so. For if he were obligated not to exercise it, that would mean that he did not have the right in the first place.

There are two additional matters concerning the distinction between having a right and exercising a right. First, even if there are good reasons not to exercise a right, the existence of these reasons need not defeat the claim that there is a right; the right may still exist. Second, what this means is that *it is up to the right-holder* whether or not to exercise his right. Exercising it may mean acting badly, acting as he oughtn't, but it is still up to him. That he would be acting as he oughtn't does not mean that he lacks the right so to act. Having a right, then, means being in a position, morally speaking, to act badly.

It is my contention that the distinction just noted with respect to rights is also to be observed with respect to justice: that within the area of justice there are matters that are obligatory and others that are good, or desirable, but not obligatory.

Justice Is Not Always Obligatory

To begin with, note that there is a curious disparity in some of the ways in which we talk about justice. On the one hand, we sometimes say that something is unjust because it violates someone's rights. This is what is involved in a number of the instances of justice and injustice identified by Mill in the last chapter of *Utilitarianism.* "It is just to respect, unjust to violate, the *legal rights* of anyone;" "a second case of injustice consists in taking or withholding from any person that to which he has a *moral right,*" and "it is confessedly unjust to *break faith* with anyone: to violate an engagement . . . or disappoint expectations raised by our own conduct." The other two cases cited by Mill may also be instances of injustice due to violation of an antecedent right: "it is universally considered just that each person should obtain that (whether good or evil) which he *deserves,*" particularly from those to whom he has done good or evil, as the case may be. And finally, Mill says, "it is, by universal declaration, inconsistent with justice to be partial."[1]

These instances of justice show that, contrary to what some philosophers have said, we cannot regard a person's rights simply as what he is entitled to as a matter of justice. Could we, though, say that justice is simply respecting people's rights? It would seem not, since we sometimes say that something is wrong (or even that it violates someone's rights) because it is unjust. In these cases the injustice typically consists in equality being violated in some way. A failure of equal treatment is an injustice and for *that* reason a violation of someone's rights. In these cases there is nothing a person is in a position to lay claim to apart from principles of justice. The wrong is created by the violation of those principles and as such constitutes a violation of his rights—the right in question being the right to just treatment. Putting the point in an aphorism, the distinction is between that which is unjust because a violation of someone's rights, and that which is a violation of someone's rights because unjust.

Joel Feinberg has drawn a related (though perhaps not the same) distinction—a distinction between what he calls comparative and noncomparative justice. "In all cases," Feinberg says, "justice consists of giving a person his due, but in some cases one's due is determined independently of that of other people, while in other cases, a person's due is determinable *only* by reference to his relations to other persons."[2] Whereas comparative justice involves equality in the treatment of the members of a class, non-comparative justice does not. To determine what noncomparative justice requires, we measure an individual against objective standards and judge him "(as we say) 'on his merits'."[3] The clearest examples of noncomparative justice, Feinberg says, are "cases of unfair punishments and rewards, merit grading, and derogatory judgments,"[4] whereas comparative justice consists in some sort of arbitrary and invidious discrimination.

What we appear to have, then, is two notions of, or perhaps only branches of, justice, and it is a good question (which Feinberg tries to answer) why both of them are kinds of *justice*. I will focus on comparative justice, and in particular on the element of there being a wrong—and especially a violation of rights—because there is injustice. That is, I will focus on the idea that there is a *right* to justice.

It is widely held by philosophers that justice is something that is demanded of us, or of society, and that it can be claimed as a right. Accordingly, the only question, for these philosophers, is to determine exactly what justice is, and when we know this we will know what is demanded of us. This procedure seems to me, however, to be mistaken: we cannot assume in *advance* that *whatever* justice turns out to be, it will be something that is demanded of us. In other words, we cannot answer the question "What is demanded of us?" or the question "What does society *owe* its members?" merely by finding out what is encompassed within the idea of justice. If we find that *a*, *b*, and *c* are comprehended by the notion of justice, we must still go on to ask as a separate question which, if any, of these is demanded of us.

For it might well be the case, as I think it indeed is, that though there are some aspects of justice that are demanded of us, there are other aspects that are not. Justice in the latter case is to be regarded as an ideal, a way in which a society can be better. Justice at this end of the spectrum is thus desirable but not demanded, not owed, not something to which anyone has a right. The relevant notions of justice and injustice are contraries, not contradictories. A society that is less just than it could be is not necessarily unjust (at least in the sense of violating anyone's rights). It *might* be unjust (for example, if it were not to accord certain important elements of due process in criminal matters) but other sorts of deficiencies connected with justice might not violate anyone's rights. If there were two inhabited planets in the universe, far apart and having no contact with one another, and one were rich and the other poor, the universe would not be as just as it could be, but it would not be unjust either. Or if we prefer to say that there is injustice here in a sense, the important point is that no one is guilty of the injustice, for it imposes no demand on anyone, and no one's rights are violated.

The Continuity Thesis

The question we must answer, then, is: Which elements of justice make demands on us, and which do not? When *must* we do things—and especially, when must we make resources available—for others, and when would it be simply a good thing for us to do this, though not required of us?

Opinions on this vary considerably. There are some who hold that everyone has a right to the satisfaction of basic needs, to a decent standard of living, and/or to some sort of equality with respect to resources—either to equality of welfare or to equality of shares. At the other end of the spectrum there are those who think that there are no positive rights (rights of recipience) to resources, absent some sort of agreement or other voluntary undertaking. I hold with neither of these, at least in their boldest forms.

There are, I believe, situations in which, even absent an agreement or other voluntary undertaking, a person has a right that another come forward on his behalf. Such a right is a right of beneficence. But there are also cases in which, though there are pressing needs, there is no such right. The sort of case in which I think there is a right of beneficence is the so-called easy rescue case. If someone is in imminent danger, for which I am in no way responsible but from which I can easily extricate that person with no risk to myself, then I believe that I am morally required to do so, and even that the other person might be justified in insisting on my so doing (i.e., that he has a right to it). But think, on the other hand, of an individual who is, as the expression goes, down on his luck. Imagine such a person—in poor health, unable to hold a job, with few resources, and no prospects. Are you morally required to help him get on his feet: to feed him, clothe him, help him find a job, monitor his progress, provide emotional support, and do whatever it takes? I take it that no individual is morally required to do this.

The difference between the easy rescue case and the case of a person who is down on his luck is that the needs of the latter are ongoing. The person is in need of regular, ongoing care and attention. His is a chronic case. The distinction is between the adventitious case, the emergency, where there may be an obligation, and the chronic, ongoing case, in which there is not. For one is seldom required to organize his life for the benefit of another, and especially so where that other is a stranger. Of course, all credit is due to those who are willing to take on such burdens; the point is that we are seldom, if ever, required to do so.[5]

Now, though there are sometimes rights to beneficence, there are cases, as we see, in which no one—that is, no individual—is required to come forward. But if there is no *individual* who is required to come forward to relieve those whose lives have become difficult in certain ways, then can the society as a whole be required to come forward? And if so, why? How can the society be required to do what none of its members individually are required to do?

Some of the things that state-of-nature theorists such as Robert Nozick have said on this matter seem to me to be on the mark with respect to the foregoing question. In one of Nozick's well-known examples, he asks us to imagine ten Robinson Crusoes on separate islands, having no connec_ tion with one another save for some recently discovered communication equipment.[6] Nozick asks us to imagine that there are differences in the levels of well-being of these Robinson Crusoes, owing perhaps to differences in abilities or to the natural endowments of the islands. Would any of these Robinson Crusoes, Nozick asks, be justified in insisting that some of the others transfer resources to them? Nozick answers that they would not, and I agree. There is clearly a sense in which the little world consisting of the ten Robinson Crusoes would be more just (or fairer) if things were distributed more equally, or if they were in proportion to effort or to need. But this does not translate into a requirement that the better off make transfers to the less well off.

Many people want to say that Nozick is correct about the moral situation in the state of nature, but that does not say anything about the moral situation in a society, which is entirely different from a state of nature. Now it is easy to agree that the situations are rather different. But the question is what exactly has made the moral difference. How is it that individuals have no obligation to provide resources for the good of others when they are all in a state of nature, but they do have such an obligation when they constitute a society? What many people feel about this is that a society is significantly different from a state of nature in that it is complex and interdependent, such that one person's well being is tied up with another's and no one can get along very well without the cooperation (or something like that) of others. And yet it is not clear to some—certainly not to Nozick—why this creates obligations that otherwise would not exist. This is a good question. In a state of nature I have no obligation to promote your well-being (apart perhaps from cases of easy rescue and apart from some voluntary undertakings), and neither does anyone else. And in society I likewise (with the same exceptions) have no such obligation, and neither does anyone else. And yet, some say, the *society* (that is, all of us together, when we exist in a social state) *does* have such an obligation. But why? What has really changed, other than that the society is better able to provide the needed resources?

Rights Against Society

My aim is to give an argument for certain welfare rights against society that calls upon the idea of a state of nature (though the argument is not a social-contract argument). In preparation for the argument it will be useful to explain the notions of a society and of a state of nature, at least as those notions will be used here. Many social theorists have tried to give an analysis of what a society is and then to use the favored analysis as the underpinning for certain social and political principles. It is not my intention, though, to allow a particular conception of what a society is to play a determinative role in the argument for welfare rights. Instead, I will play down the role of the concept of society in the argument and embrace straightforwardly certain moral ideas as underlying welfare rights.

The central idea I want to advance is that if you are to have a right to the society's acting so as to promote your welfare, there must be some sort of *connection* between you and your problem, on the one hand, and the society on the other. In other words, if you are to have any legitimate claims against the society, then it must be on the ground that social life itself is in some relevant way responsible for the problem for which you seek relief. Once we have identified such a connection (if there is one) between the individual and the society, we can hope to determine from the character of the connection just what rights against the society a person might have.

There is a wide variety of possible ongoing interrelationships among people that might lead us to say that a society exists. Imagine a number of individuals (or perhaps families) living self-sufficiently in isolation (though I am not claiming that historically societies arise from such states of affairs). Now imagine that a variety of ties develop among various of these individuals and/or families, including projects such as common schooling, common prayer, protection, and a variety of economic relationships. We can imagine continual development along these lines, though not necessarily in a straight line. After all, some projects fail, some relationships deteriorate. But historically the trend has been toward greater interrelationship and complexity.

It is not profitable to conjecture exactly when, along this continuum of interrelationships from isolation to great complexity, a society comes into existence. I myself would be willing to say that a society exists at the stage of loose conglomerations pursuing certain common ends. But there is one point in the progression that is of special significance. At some point individuals who are largely self-sufficient must make a choice whether to continue being self-sufficient or to, as it were, specialize—by, for example, moving to a single cash crop, or moving from farming to laboring. This is a critical point because it is the point at which an individual ties his livelihood and welfare to the welfare of others and thereby becomes committed to the success of something beyond himself—namely, a set of relationships among people. When enough people have made the move from self-sufficiency to specialization (it is not important to specify how many is enough), there exists what I will call a *collective.*

The question of rights against society is, then, the question of whether a collective has any obligations to the individuals who constitute it. That is, the question is whether a person who becomes committed to the success of a collective in the way outlined above is justified in insisting that the collective do certain things on his behalf. I take it that if the case can be made for those who initially, and as a matter of choice, participate in the set of economic relationships that constitute the collective, then it is readily made for those who (like most of us) are born into a world in which they find themselves already dependent on the collective for their livelihoods.

The case for rights against the collective does not rest on any undertaking, explicit or implicit, on the part of the collective or of any of its members. One does not 'join' the collective in any formal sense; membership is not *de jure*. Rather, one enters simply by entering into economic relationships with other individuals; membership is *de facto*. Further, the reason for entering a collective is (almost) entirely self-interested: One enters a collective expecting to gain, believing that he will do better by specializing rather than by remaining self-sufficient.

The case for rights against the collective rests on the following three grounds. First, while some may not succeed in the economic life of a collective, the success of those who do succeed depends on the participation of others, for without the others there is no collective. Everyone who enters a collective expects to benefit thereby, and thus expects to benefit from the participation of others. Thus everyone who succeeds both expects to benefit, and does benefit, from the participation of others. Second, inevitably some people do not succeed in the economic life of a collective. Sometimes that is the fault of the individual, but sometimes it is not the fault, or not entirely the fault, of the individual, and in such cases we can say that the individual is not only a loser in the economic life of the collective but also its victim. As a simple example, consider the individual who has acquired a set of skills that at one time were useful in the economic life of the collective, but which are useful no longer. What is a person who is a victim of the economic institutions of a collective to do? I take it that it is a moral principle of some importance that a person must make reasonable efforts to help himself before he will be justified in insisting that others do things to promote his welfare. So if leaving the collective and returning to self-sufficiency is an option, then that is what he must do. But what if that is not an option? Then the collective does have obligations regarding his welfare. The third element of the ground of rights against the collective, then, is that there are no reasonable options to the economic life of the collective; that is, one is dependent on the collective. In sum, then, what I contend is that a person has welfare rights (of some sort) against the collective only when he is a victim of a form of economic life that inevitably leads to some people losing out.

Kinds of Rights Against the Collective

Given the foregoing principle, we are now in a position to determine some of the things to which people have rights against the society. What we have to look for are the deficiencies in a person's welfare that are attributable to his or her involvement in the collective. Take the example of the individual whose skills were once useful in the economic life of the collective and now have become useless. Such an individual is a victim of the economic life of the collective, and he has a right to some sort of effort by the collective on his behalf, perhaps retraining. Similarly, a person who suffers a job-related injury, or an industrial ailment such as black lung disease, is a victim of the economic life of the collective and has a right to medical attention.

Sometimes people become victims of the economic life of the collective because of general economic conditions. Business slowdowns can produce unemployment, and people have rights in connection with such occurrences. Different economic systems deal in different ways with these situations. Some, either by law or by tradition, insulate people against loss of their jobs. Direct payments to the unemployed is another way of dealing with the problem; this is the 'solution' favored in our own society. The principles outlined earlier imply that one or another of these ways of dealing with the problem are morally required. Thus, if unemployment is to be permitted, there must be compensation to the unemployed. Unemployment compensation does, though, raise some problems of its own, among which are what the level of compensation should be and how long it should last. The optimal situation, of course, is for everyone who loses his job to find another. Most people would, I assume, return to work as soon as they could. Some, however, would not, and for these individuals incentives are needed. Inevitably situations arise in which incentives designed to discourage malingering adversely affect those who do want to find jobs but have so far been unsuccessful. Here, as often happens, a choice must be made between seeing that those who are deserving get what they are legitimately entitled to, and seeing that those who are not deserving do not get what they are not legitimately entitled to. But however this is resolved does not affect the principles requiring unemployment compensation.

Having indicated some of the rights against society that an individual *does* have, I will now proceed to matters that are *not* rights against society. Maintenance during retirement (a pension) is *not* one of the rights supported by the principles I have advanced, despite the fact that many people are heard to voice the complaint, "I have worked hard all my life, so I am entitled to a decent retirement." The reason that there is no right to a retirement income is that outside a social collective one would be stuck with having to provide for his own retirement (inability to work because of age), and so no *special* problems are created with respect to this by virtue of one's association with the collective. On the other hand, retirees do have a right that their retirement incomes (wherever they come from) not be (seriously) diluted by inflation. The dislocations that result from inflation should be shared out; retirees have a right that the economic life of the community not be carried on in such a way that they are harmed disproportionately.

It is not the case that, in general, people have the right to have their basic needs satisfied, including their needs for food, shelter, clothing, and medical care. No individual can be called upon to provide these things just because someone else needs them, and neither can the society be called upon, unless, somehow, one's relation to the society has something to do with the existence of these needs. So if, for example, one is impoverished through misfortune, or one's health is poor, there is no right to welfare to relieve these conditions. Having said this, though, I hasten to add that a good society, a caring society, would certainly provide these things. A society that did provide these necessities would be more just. But this is one of those elements of justice, referred to earlier, that are not required of a society and cannot be demanded of it.

Similar remarks apply to equality. A more equal society is a more just society, and, at least to that extent, a better society. But the question that must be answered is not whether the just is the equal (which, at least in part, it is), but whether anyone is justified in insisting on it, whether it is owed to anyone. For my part, I cannot see that in general there is a right to equality of either resources or welfare. No one would have a right to equality in a state of nature—or, more realistically, no one living in isolation has a right to equality. Likewise, no one would be justified in insisting that another share anything with him simply on the ground that that would make them more equal. Accordingly, no one has a right that the collective seek to equalize resources or welfare.

There can, to be sure, be instances in which a person does have a right to equality. Take, for example, the case discussed by Professor Gregory Vlastos in his article "Justice and Equality."[7] An individual who has been threatened is in need of additional police protection in order to make him as safe as others are. Such an individual, according to Vlastos, has a right to be equal to others in this respect because, whatever his merit, his human worth is equal to that of any other person. Now I agree with Vlastos in this. But let me explain how I think we should look at the matter. What we have here is a social distributing agency, distributing, in this case, police protection. The resources are already in the hands of the agency, which has only to deploy them appropriately. And I agree that for *this* resource, *already* in the hands of the social distributing agency, there is what could be called a right to equality: each person has a right to a level of protection that is the equal of anyone else's.

This is not, however, the sort of right to equality that lies behind egalitarianism. For nothing Vlastos says supports the view that anyone has a right to the existence of that social distributing agency in the first place. No one, that is, has a right to the establishment of a police force. The only right regarding police protection that anyone has is that *if* the society is going to make that good available, it must be distributed equally. The right is, then, only a right to *conditional* equality. However equal you and I are in our human worth, that does not justify me in insisting that you, or you in conjunction with everyone else (including me), establish a security force. A fortiori, the equality of our human worth does not support any rights to the relief of poverty, health care, or many other aspects of our welfare.

There are many ways in which the acts and laws of a society *affect* distribution even where no social distribution agency, with control over resources, has been established. In these cases, too, the society is required to adhere to principles of justice, including the presumption that everyone is equal and that deviations from equality must therefore be justified. But, again, this is a right to *conditional* equality. *If* the society acts in such a way as to affect distribution, it must treat people equally (or at least presume equality). But this does not mean that the society *must* do anything to affect distribution.

Similar considerations support a right to equality of opportunity, which is another right that is conditional. Often when a society undertakes to do something, either because it must or because it is desirable to do so, no matter how fairly the undertaking is carried out, some people gain significant advantages vis-a-vis others. When public offices are established, power and a better than average share of resources are part of the package. And when a society establishes, for example, a medical school, those selected on the basis of their ability gain great prestige and a better than average share of resources. Furthermore, the families of the individuals gaining these positions realize great advantages, and their offspring are at a competitive advantage in the next generation. Because of this, everyone in the society is justified in insisting that, so far as possible, this competitive advantage be neutralized. The best way to do this, of course, though not a perfect solution, is to move toward equalizing educational opportunities. In short, whenever the society, for good and sufficient reason, undertakes something that makes a significant distributive difference, it incurs an obligation to equalize opportunities to gain the greater rewards.

I have argued thus far that there are rights to welfare when, and to the extent that, a person's difficulties are of a sort that are the inevitable product of the economic life of the collective. But there is no general right to welfare, though a society is just and better if it provides more in the way of welfare than it must. I have also argued that there are rights to conditional equality, including equality of opportunity, but no general right to equality; that is, no right in general to the society's establishing mechanisms designed to make holdings or welfare more equal. Again, of course, a society is more just and better if it is more equal. But there are also certain demands that fall on a society that are straightforwardly demands of *justice*. These demands derive from the idea of *justice as reciprocity*.

Both John Rawls, in his *A Theory of Justice*, and Robert Nozick, in *Anarchy, State and Utopia*, suggest the notion of justice as reciprocity. The notion that I am interested in is Nozick's idea that there should be a balance between the value of what a person gives and the value of what he gets (or takes). (Rawls has two notions of reciprocity that are quite different from one another. At one point Rawls says that the difference principle, being a principle of mutual benefit, expresses a conception of reciprocity.[8] Much later in his book he connects the idea of reciprocity with the idea of answering in kind.[9] The latter notion may embrace the same sort of conception we find in Nozick's notion of reciprocity.) That there should be a balance between the value of what a person gives and what he gets seems to be not merely desirable, but at least sometimes to be required. It is something that can be a person's right, both in a state of nature and in society.

Examples are easy to find in which there is no doubt that there is a right based on reciprocity. Suppose a group of people is using a common kitchen, and one of them eats some of the food of another thinking it is his own. This person owes the other the value of the food taken. Here we have a genuine obligation of justice.

In most transactions people enter into they determine their own rates of exchange. Usually in such cases no obligation to give value for value arises, the situation being controlled, at least so far as the rights and obligations are concerned, by the agreement. Thus even if there is some disparity in the values of the goods being exchanged, one is obligated to go through with it and the other has a right to the performance. Sometimes, however, the disparity in the values being exchanged is so great that the agreement is regarded as not binding, and if one party has already performed, the other party may not be obligated to the extent of the agreement, but only to something that is closer to reciprocity. The reason for this is that agreements are binding only when voluntary. A great disparity in value raises doubts about the voluntariness of the agreement. There is a tendency in such cases to treat the exchange as if it had occurred in the absence of an agreement, in which case the principle of reciprocity would govern. What this shows, I think, is that the principle of reciprocity underlies all transactions, serving as a focal point from which agreements must not (morally speaking) deviate too greatly. This is a *right* of justice that everyone has, in or out of society.

Summary

The implication intended by my title "The Demands of Justice: The Difference that Social Life Makes," is that though some elements of justice are required, others are desirable but not morally required. That is one of the views for which I have argued.

The elements of justice that are morally required, and to which an individual has a right, are three: (1) Reciprocity. A person, whether in or outside a society, is justified in insisting, unless a voluntary agreement supersedes, that there be a balance between the value of what he gives and the value of what he gets. (2) Conditional equality. If a society distributes a good or acts in such a way as to affect distribution, one is justified in insisting that he be presumed to be equal to everyone else. (3) Certain elements of welfare. A person is justified in insisting that a social collective on which he is dependent support deficiencies in his welfare that are attributable to his being a victim of the economic life of the collective.

Notes

1. John Stuart Mill, *Utilitarianism*, Oskar Piest, ed. (Indianapolis: Bobbs-Merrill, 1957), pp. 54-57.

2. Joel Feinberg, *Rights, Justice, and the Bounds of Liberty* (Princeton: Princeton University Press, 1980), p. 266.

3. Ibid., p. 268.

4. Ibid.

5. I have discussed the right to beneficence at greater length in Chapter 6 of my book *Rights* (Totowa, N.J.: Rowman and Littlefield, 1982). On the question of a legal duty to rescue, see my "Liability for Failing to Rescue," *Law and Philosophy* 1 (1982): 391-418.

6. Robert Nozick, *Anarchy, State and Utopia* (New York: Basic Books, 1974), p. 185.

7. Gregory Vlastos, "Justice and Equality," in *Social Justice*, Richard B. Brandt, ed. (Englewood Cliffs, N.J.: Prentice-Hall, 1962), pp. 41-53.

8. John Rawls, *A Theory of Justice* (Cambridge: Harvard University Press, 1971), p. 102.

9. Ibid., p. 494.

Bibliography

Benditt, Theodore M. "Liability for Failing to Rescue." *Law and Philosophy* 1 (1982): 391-418.

Benditt, Theodore M. *Rights*. Totowa, N.J.: Rowman and Littlefield, 1982.

Daniels, Norman. "Health-Care Needs and Distributive Justice." *Philosophy & Public Affairs* 10 (1981): 146-79.

Feinberg, Joel. *Rights, Justice, and the Bounds of Liberty*. Princeton: Princeton University Press, 1980.

Golding, Martin. "The Concept of Rights: A Historical Sketch." In *Bioethics and Human Rights*, Elsie and Bertram Bandman, eds. Boston: Little, Brown, 1978. pp. 44-50.

Lyons, David. ed. *Rights*. Belmont, Calif.: Wadsworth, 1979.

Vlastos, Gregory. "Justice and Equality." In *Social Justice*, Richard B. Brandt, ed., pp. 31-72. Englewood Cliffs, N.J.: Prentice-Hall, 1962.

9

Justice: Cosmic or Communal?

Bruce M. Landesman
Department of Philosophy
University of Utah

What are the ground rules to be used for determining the scope and breadth of justice? What human activities does it cover, how much does it demand, what duties does it require? How are conflicting "intuitions" on these matters to be adjudicated? These questions are raised by Theodore Benditt's "The Demands of Justice: The Difference that Social Life Makes" when he tells us that we have a claim against society on grounds of justice only if "social life itself is in some relevant way responsible for the problems for which (we) seek relief." And Richard DeGeorge has also argued in "Property and Global Justice" that there is no injustice in some nations being rich and others poor if there is no constitution uniting them and

> no background institutions in accordance with which redistribution among nations takes place and benefits and burdens distributed. In the absence of such institutions, and further in the absence of a true community among all nations, there is neither distributive justice nor injustice, since such justice is a function of some system. (p. 5)[1]

Both these claims suggest that inequalities—even basic and fundamental ones—are a matter of injustice, demanding rectification only if there is interdependence ("true community") and/or the well-off are responsible for the situation of the deprived. Benditt summarizes this by reference to Nozick's example of ten Robinson Crusoes on ten separate islands who have different levels of well-being resulting from differences in ability or in the natural resources of the islands. Benditt agrees with Nozick in holding that, because of the absence of relationships between them, none of the Crusoes would be "justified in insisting that some of the others transfer resources to them." (He does say, however, that such a transfer would make the outcome more just or fairer, a point I'll discuss below.)

My intuitions disagree. I'm inclined to think it is unjust that Crusoe A be well off and Crusoe B be impoverished and that justice demands that A help B. More generally, I'm inclined to think that the "basic truth" about justice is expressed by the following egalitarian ideal: the equal well-being of all persons at the highest possible level of well-being; that is, maximum equal well-being. And I'm inclined to think that justice demands the promotion and protection of such a state of affairs.[2] The project of explicating and defending such a view of justice is certainly a big one, and I won't be so foolish as to try to undertake it here. But let me just note that the project has three parts: First, the ideal needs to be clarified, specified, applied. A theory of the good needs to be developed and the concept of well-being given content. Second, a basic argument for at least prima facie equality needs to be given. Something must be said about what is so good "in itself" about equal well-being. The standard egalitarian intuition is that the similarities between human beings are morally a great deal more significant than the differences that develop between them; that their alikeness in being conscious, in being subject to pleasure and pain, fulfillment and frustration, and in having conscious aims and purposes—"life-plans"—makes a condition in which some are more able to fulfill their plans than others unjustifiable, or at least difficult to justify. Third, the theory needs to be defended against the standard criticisms: that it is impossible to attain such equality; or that such equality would be highly inefficient; or that it overlooks morally significant claims of desert or merit; or that it is incompatible with liberty and democracy. Whether the theory can overcome some of these typical criticisms and even incorporate some of the values they rely on into a basically egalitarian framework is, for the egalitarian-minded, the fundamental question.

Benditt seems to accept the egalitarian ideal, at least to some extent, for he says that "a more equal society is a more just society, and, at least to that extent, a better society." And he says that redistribution among the Crusoes could lead to greater justice. But, he says, it is not the sort of justice it is obligatory to bring about. And this is his major claim: Not all of what is 'right' or 'good' on grounds of justice is obligatory. Some just states of affairs are such that we are obligated, required to promote and maintain them, but others are only desirable: We act well if we promote them, we are better persons if we do than if we do not, but we have no duty to do this. How, then, do we distinguish the obligatory from the merely desirable states of justice? His criterion is that we have duties to promote justice only when a person's deficiency in welfare is "attributable to his involvement in the collective." Consistent with this he tells us that if "one is impoverished through misfortune, or one's health is poor, there is no right to welfare to relieve these conditions." A society that did provide such help would be more caring and more just than one that did not, he says, but this is not one of the elements of justice required of society.

I find this consequence of Benditt's view unsatisfactory at the level of moral intuitions. Now, one way to respond to his view would be to hold that the disadvantages that result from misfortune or ill health are not unconnected to social institutions. Poor health could be responded to in such a way that it is not a disadvantage, and what is a misfortune in one form of social organization may be a mark of distinction in another. So one might be able to bring these deficiencies under the category of obligatory justice even on Benditt's terms; that is, accepting his criterion of causation by the collective as the necessary condition for duties. And in general it is arguable that the distinction between natural and socially induced deprivations will be difficult to draw for creatures who are social beings as we are. Even if it can be drawn, very little would fall into the category of nonsocial deprivations.

I would like, however, to push a different and more fundamental criticism. Consider the fact that a certain proportion of people are born with various physical handicaps that make it difficult for them to achieve their life-plans. They start life at a disadvantage compared with nonhandicapped persons. But suppose that a moderate expenditure of funds to provide both training and special facilities (such as ramps for wheelchairs) would for many cancel the disadvantage. (We assume, furthermore, that the disadvantage is not the result of the collective.) Why shouldn't the provision of training and facilities be seen as a societal obligation on grounds of (egalitarian) justice? Benditt would presumably think that such provision is not obligatory, though he would hold that someone whose job skills are no longer adequate because of changed economic circumstances is owed help on grounds of justice. Why obligatory aid in one case, but not in the other? At least at the level of 'intuitions,' the distinction seems arbitrary.

Generalizing a bit, we should note that with regard to a particular inequality, we can distinguish at least three different dimensions for the deprivation: its cause (whether social or natural); its urgency; and the cost of rectifying it. Suppose in a given case the cause is not social, but the need is urgent and the cost of help is small. Then it may very well seem that the help ought to be provided, that it is a duty. On the other hand, a socially induced deprivation, which, however, is not urgent and would be expensive to rectify, may not seem to require action. What this shows is that there are other ways of distinguishing between the obligatory and desirable elements of justice, and Benditt has not given us enough ground for concluding that the cause of the inequality should play the dominant or only role in making the distinction.

Turning now to the view that there is a basic distinction between the obligatory and merely desirable elements of justice, we should note that this is at least verbally strange. We naturally speak of what justice calls for, requires, demands. If justice involves X, it is natural to think that we or someone are obligated to promote and maintain X. Justice 'speaks' in terms of duty, not desirability. In fact, if we thought of some inequality that there was no duty to remove it but that it would be a good thing for it to be removed, we might say that the inequality is not unjust, but merely undesirable. That is, we have the alternative locution of saying that things not *demanded* by justice are not demanded by *justice*, but are good on some other moral value.

This criticism may well be rejected as merely verbal (that is, it may be right that we speak of justice as demanding things, but we should change the concept to recognize the duty-desirability distinction), so I will not press it. Another alternative to Benditt's, and one which I do hold, is that whatever is good on grounds of justice is at least prima facie obligatory, but may not be obligatory, all things considered. It may not be obligatory, all things considered, because its provision is too expensive or is only possible at too great a sacrifice of other values. On an egalitarian view of justice, every inequality of well-being ought to be undone, other things being equal, but, unfortunately, things are not always equal. This way of understanding the matter accounts for Benditt's intuitions that not every element of justice is ultimately obligatory, but it is not subject to the criticism that what has been picked out as decisive—causation by the 'collective'—is arbitrary, or at least of no greater significance than other factors. There are a number of factors, a plurality of difficult-to-weigh considerations, which make it sometimes permissible not to promote what is, other things being equal, a duty to promote.

I suppose that what is ultimately behind Benditt's view is the idea that justice has basically to do with dividing up the fruits and burdens of social cooperation. Rawls clearly starts from this perspective and sees principles of social justice as ways of defining "the appropriate benefits and burdens of social cooperation." From this perspective a notion of justice that looks at how people fare independently of their interconnections might be dismissed as a concept of "cosmic justice" (even "poetic justice"), an ideal of how things ought to be, but involving no obligations or requirements. But for the dismissal of this view, some argument is needed. If some people are born into well-heeled, comfortable, affluent societies through no 'merit' of their own, and others—who possess every bit as much 'intrinsic worth' as the former—are born into poor and deprived societies through no fault of *their* own, it is not obvious that the former owe nothing, in justice, to the latter. A cosmic 'crime' might demand a quite secular rectification. If the ultimate principle that Benditt (and Rawls) relies on is that individuals owe nothing to other individuals unless they are in some way responsible for their ills, then this individualist dictum needs to be explicitly brought out and some of its counterintuitive consequences faced (consider, for example, good Samaritan rescue cases).

I do not wish to deny that the interconnectedness of people, or lack thereof, is relevant to determining our actual ("all things considered") duties to others with regard to justice. My inclination is to think that it is one of a plurality of considerations relevant to the matter, along with such things as cost, urgency, the likely effectiveness of aid, and the degree of responsibility people have for their own misfortune. This is a different way of understanding the scope of justice·and the duties involved than the way Benditt gives us, and my argument with him, in short, is that this way is just as intuitively plausible as his and that he has not (yet) given us enough further argument to persuade us to adopt his point of view.

Notes

1. Richard DeGeorge, "Property and Global Justice," unpublished manuscript.
2. For a formulation and partial defense of this ideal, see my "Egalitarianism," *Canadian Journal of Philosophy* 13 (1983): 27-56.

10
Actual and Potential Demands Of Justice: A Response to Theodore M. Benditt

Marilyn Gwaltney
Niagara Frontier Regional Center
Empire State College

In his essay "The Demands of Justice," Professor Benditt concludes that some demands of justice are morally required, while others are simply desirable. His understanding of the morally required demands of justice is limited to those that an individual can demand as a right either of other individuals or of society.

Benditt's argument for limiting the demands of justice rests upon the assumption that we are not morally obligated to rescue another person if the act of rescuing that person would be dangerous to us. The mere fact that another person is in need does not obligate us as individuals to help that person without considering the effect that giving aid would have on our welfare.

There are many reasons one can give for saying that justice cannot generally demand that an individual sacrifice his or her own *basic* well-being in order to provide for the well-being of another individual. For one thing, such sacrifice becomes an act that cancels itself out, simply replacing one person's well-being with that of another. For another, in individual charity, the relationship of freedom and equality between giver and recipient is disturbed, and justice generally cannot demand that.

So I agree with Benditt that "there clearly are cases in which a person does not, simply by virtue of his needs, have rights against some other individual." There is, however, no logical connection between that assertion and assertions about the individual's rights against society. To assert such a connection is to commit the fallacy of composition. Elsewhere, however, Benditt makes a different statement: "there is no right to any individual's acting so as to alleviate another's poverty." From this it *does* follow that "there is no right to the society or the state doing so."

There is a difference between the two sets of statements. The first set of statements involves making inferences from the properties of individual resources to the properties of social resources. The change in quantity results in a qualitative change. While the well-being of an individual may be diminished in supporting another person, the well-being of society will be enhanced, it will have more members who are better off.

The second set of statements involves inferences about the source of society's power to act. A society cannot act to gather or distribute resources unless some individuals act to do so. If society is to provide for the well-being of the unfortunate, then I must at least vote for the allocation of resources for welfare and pay my taxes. If the tax structure is fair, then my own well-being will not be unduly threatened. Thus if the poor have no right to demand that I at least vote for welfare programs of some sort, then indeed they have no right to demand that society alleviate their poverty.

However, I think that the poor *do* have the right to demand that I act, not as an individual, but as a citizen, to alleviate their poverty.

In considering the possibility of such obligation as I have asserted, Benditt looks to the state of nature. He illustrates the state of nature with Nozick's example of ten Robinson Crusoes on separate islands with no connection except communications equipment. The question is, is there an obligation for the better-off Crusoes to transfer resources to the worse-off Crusoes? The answer is obviously no since they do not have the means to do so. As Kant pointed out, ought implies can; conversely, cannot implies an obligation cannot exist since there is no means to carry it out. Clearly Benditt's understanding of the state of nature is that of a collection of separate individuals with no intrinsic connection with each other.

But where did this picture of the state of nature come from? It has a long and honorable history, at least back to Hobbes and Locke. No one argues that it is historically accurate. It is only a model for purposes of philosophical argument. But why choose this model? When thinking about this model of the state of nature as a collection of separate individuals, the image that comes to mind is that of frontiersmen or of adolescent males before joining a team, the army, or getting a job. It is really a most peculiar model, and it is not surprising that Benditt and Nozick cannot find any ground for obligation in a model of a nonsociety. Obligation is not a natural phenomenon like a stone or even anger; it is a social phenomenon that can exist only when people recognize the legitimacy and necessity of each other's existence.

The individuals that exist in the traditional state of nature certainly do not have to recognize the necessity of each other's existence because they spring full-grown as adults from the heads of philosophers. But real human beings come into the world helpless and dependent on at least one other person and usually more. The child certainly recognizes the legitimacy and necessity of its parents, and the parents confer legitimacy and necessity on the child by giving it life and raising it.

Thus, it seems to me, the family is a better model of the state of nature than the Robinson Crusoe model or the frontiersman. But the family is a society and cannot be a model for a nonsociety. The conclusion I draw from this is that state-of-nature theories are inherently false and are philosophically useless for thinking about rights and obligations. Human beings are *essentially* social and interdependent although after a period of necessary dependence we may, if we are appropriately endowed physically and mentally, be able to survive in isolation and even in a hostile environment. But this lonely and isolated existence is abstract even when it must be lived, and it is certainly no place to look for the sources of obligation or rights, since such an existence *means* that obligations and rights have either been repudiated or torn away.

In proposing the family as a substitute for the state of nature as a starting point in thinking about human rights, I am *not* proposing any particular form or duration of the family. I am only proposing that we must take into account the fact that *everyone* has *always* entered the world dependent on someone else and of necessity remains dependent for a number of years. Even Ik mothers nurse their children for three years before abandoning them to peer groups.[1]

It is unintelligible to appeal to life outside the social collective to justify denying a right to pensions or provisions for one's basic needs. But Benditt's view of life within the social collective is almost as atomistic, mechanistic, and ahistorical as his view of life in the state of nature. He seems rigidly to separate economic activity from the rest of life. He then ties any right to welfare to participation in economic life. Since he would deny the *right* to welfare to those who are poor through misfortune, to the retired and the disabled, I assume he means the participation of the individual and would not include proxy participation through parents, grandparents, or spouses. Thus he would deny the right to aid those who are inherently unable to participate in economic life. Benditt's welfare principle is simply an expansion of his principle of reciprocity and is essentially limited to unemployment insurance. The right to welfare is based solely on one's own economic contributions.

But why should participation in economic life carry with it such rights? Every individual comes into the world helpless and dependent. Everything necessary for economic independence comes from other people, either as genetic endowment, preexisting knowledge, or an economic and social environment. And all of this affects our motivation and choices to a large degree, if not totally. If most of what we are has its origins in other people, on what basis can anyone claim rights to more than anyone else?

If we think about economic rights within the family, we could say everyone has equal rights to the basic goods of life—food, clothing, and shelter. In a family, some people are producers as well as consumers (adults), and others are primarily consumers (children and the ill). The producers in the family often require additional resources as a condition for providing for the needs of the entire family; that is, they will need tools, and perhaps transportation, extra clothing, and extra food and bedding. The right the individual has to these additional resources is derived from their necessity for producing for the group. The producer thus has a right to additional resources only insofar as they result in an increase in basic goods for everyone; he or she has no right to any more basic goods for personal use and satisfaction than anyone else in the group. If there are surplus resources above what is needed to provide the means of production and the very basic goods of life, then it would seem that justice requires those extra resources be distributed in the following priorities: (1) rectification of deficiencies in health; (2) basic education to those who require it; (3) increased food and clothing for everyone; (4) improved shelter for the group; (5) recreation for everyone; (6) luxury items either by lottery or by saving until everyone could have equivalent luxuries.

In nonindustrial economies there are few members of society who are of necessity purely consumers. Children contribute to the work of the group and old people do not retire unless they are very disabled, and even then they can serve as educators. Thus one could argue that it is possible for human beings to organize themselves in such a way that virtually everyone has a right to welfare under Benditt's criteria except for infants, toddlers, and the very disabled. By changing the means and mode of production, we have defined some people as consumers only. To penalize those people by denying them welfare rights is unjust when they could have those rights if the economy were differently organized.

As for the rights of children, since they do not effect their own conception and birth, children are not responsible for their lives during their period of dependency. Since society in general needs children at least as future producers, it is society that is responsible for their lives. Thus children do have a right to demand welfare on the grounds that they are needed for the future life of the social collective. The retired are entitled to the same rights on the grounds that they were needed by the social collective in the past.

Benditt denies that there is a right to welfare if one is poor as a result of misfortune (which includes ill-health). This is a strange notion of justice indeed. Benditt's justice demands that the person who loses everything in a flood or tornado is not entitled to welfare, while the person who loses everything because of a change in technology or markets does have a right to welfare. (This is just the opposite of federal disaster-relief programs.)

Of course, Benditt believes a society that does provide for the unfortunate is a better and more caring society, but the unfortunate cannot *demand* that care, they have no *right* to it. Now, I agree with Benditt that suffering a misfortune is not the same thing as suffering an injustice. Injustice is the result of the action or inaction of some person or group of persons. Someone has to be at fault in cases of injustice. Misfortune by definition is a situation in which no fault can be assigned. Benditt infers that therefore there is no right to demand that any person or group of persons rectify the consequences of the misfortune. However, most people would agree that we are as responsible for actions we fail to perform as for those we do perform. The misfortune of human beings causes them to suffer, and suffering is surely an evil, even if no one's fault. To fail to alleviate suffering in a fellow human being when we can without causing undue suffering to ourselves is surely immoral, if anything is. (Benditt recognizes the duty to rescue even in a state of nature.) This implies that we have a duty to alleviate suffering if we can, which implies a corresponding right by the sufferer of the misfortune. Like the duty to rescue, the duty to alleviate suffering is limited by the ability and resources of the alleviator. Thus the duty of society in this respect is much greater than the duty of the individual, since the ability and resources of society are much greater.

I think what Benditt is legitimately trying to point out is that there are some demands of justice that we as individuals or as a society have either insufficient resources or ability or both to satisfy at any given point in history, and that in such a situation there is no obligation to act and thus no corresponding rights. Now, I think Benditt is correct about this, but he confuses the issues by having a static, ahistorical view of society and the individual. He gets stuck in the one-dimensional world of the state of nature and thus does not make much progress in unraveling the problem. Rather than put absolute limits on the demands of justice as Benditt does and then talk about less just societies in which no rights are violated, it makes more sense to think in terms of the actual and potential demands of justice. Potential demands must be acknowledged and planned for in the light of changing capacity. The absolute limits placed on the demands of justice by Benditt relieve us of any obligation to reexamine our rights and duties in the face of changing resources and abilities. The limits become a justification for the *status quo*.

Notes

1. Colin M. Turnbull, *Mountain People* (New York: Simon & Schuster, 1972).

Bibliography

Gewirth, Alan. *Reason and Morality.* Chicago: The University of Chicago Press, 1978.

Heilbroner, Robert L. *The Making of Economic Society*, 6th ed. Englewood Cliffs, N.J.: Prentice-Hall, 1980.

Marx, Karl. *Economic and Philosophical Manuscripts of 1844*, translated by Martin Milligan, edited with Introduction by Dirk J. Struik. New York: International Publishers, 1964.

Meszaros, Istvan. *Marx's Theory of Alienation.* London: Merlin Press, 1970.

Reamer, Frederic G. *Ethical Dilemmas in Social Service.* New York: Columbia University Press, 1982.

Somerville, John, and Santoni, Ronald E., eds. *Social and Political Philosophy.* Garden City, N.Y.: Doubleday, 1963.

Turnbull, Colin M. *Mountain People.* New York: Simon and Schuster, 1972.

11

Distributive Justice and Civil Justice: Professional Responsibility and The Distribution of Legal Services

Kenneth Kipnis
Department of Philosophy
University of Hawaii at Manoa

When goods or services of any type are distributed in society (henceforth, the term "goods" will refer to both), a choice must be made whether these will enter the market to be bought and sold there, or whether they will be distributed or rationed wholly or in part in accordance with some principle other than the ability and willingness to pay the market price. Few would question that with respect to some goods—after shave lotion, for example—market mechanisms are a reasonable and appropriate means of distribution. In efforts to maximize their profits designers, manufacturers, and distributors compete with one another to produce the highest-quality goods at the lowest cost. Purchasers in turn make independent judgments about whether the goods offered for sale are worth their price. For some other goods, however—childhood vaccinations, secondary education, firefighting services—distributions are not nearly so dependent upon transactions made between the end-users of the goods and their suppliers. We can distinguish therefore between market systems of distribution and rationing systems, understanding by that latter term all systems in which ability and willingness to pay for the goods are not the sole preconditions for receipt.

In some cases, the justification for a rationing system involves an appeal to goals that are shared, more or less, by the community as a whole. We may all be more secure if fires in our community are contained as quickly as possible. The public interest in speed and efficiency here is not served if purchasers of fire protection services must negotiate with sellers while homes, businesses, and factories go up in flames. In a second category, the justification of rationing systems involves an appeal to some right. The arguments can be made that police protection services, legal services in serious criminal proceedings and elementary education must be provided where the need arises, not merely because it is in the public interest that this be done, but, rather, because the beneficiary of the good has some type of right, some entitlement to it. The victim who is being beaten up has a right to the assistance of a law enforcement officer. Those accused of criminal wrongs have a right to legal assistance in proceedings that would be unfairly imposed in the absence of such help. And children arguably have a right to be taught skills that are essential to a decent life in the society that we will leave for them.

In a third category of case—and it will be one of these that will interest us here—nonmarket mechanisms may be justified, not by an appeal to a right enjoyed by the beneficiary of the good, but, rather, by appeal to a duty or special responsibility assumed by those designated to provide the good. We may wish to say, for example, that where it is vital to their well-being, children should receive medical care, not because they have some kind of inherent right to health care (we may believe that no one does), but, rather, because in becoming parents, mothers and fathers have assumed a responsibility to provide that care. The child is what lawyers would call a "third-party beneficiary."

In the United States, legal services in civil proceedings are for the most part made available through market distribution systems. To be sure, many attorneys and firms provide services at reduced fees or for no fees at all to people who might otherwise have to go without needed legal advice or representation. Additionally, private organizations (the American Civil Liberties Union or the National Association for the Advancement of Colored People) and government-funded organizations like the Legal Services Corporation also make available legal services without reliance upon market pricing systems in distribution. In its state and national bar associations, the organized bar has played a role in the provision of legal services to those who cannot obtain them because of an inability to pay. While it is clear that legal services in civil matters have been made available outside of market distribution systems, it is less clear that these services have been adequate to meet the general needs for them. But it will not be our purpose here to explore the dimensions of such shortcomings. Rather, our central concern will be to identify who it is that has central responsibility for the provision of such services, the form that such responsibility takes, and the grounds for that obligation.

Let us accept that our community has committed itself to an adversary system of adjudication. For the sake of the discussion that follows, we assume that a public commitment to adjudication secures for each member of the community the following four rights: (1) the right to submit certain types of complaint to a judge or tribunal, (2) the right to have the other party to the dispute summoned to court to answer the complaint, (3) the right to have the judge make a decision in the case, and, if it is favorable, (4) the right to have the judge's decision enforced. Let us further assume that in an adversary system of adjudication responsibility for gathering evidence and marshaling arguments rests with the parties to the dispute. It is the judge's job however (1) to create a forum in which the parties can argue their cases, (2) to issue a decision in the case, (3) to declare a rule applicable in all relevantly similar cases, and

(4) to disclose the reasoning behind the decision. Finally, we assume that the overriding purpose of such a system is to make it as likely as possible that the judge's declaration of the rights of the parties will be a just decision and as likely as possible that it will be accepted by the parties to the dispute and by the community as a whole.

The Conditions of Information and Exercise

It would seem that for any legal system worthy of respect, the protection and support that the community provides for some should be made available to all whose claims are similar. To the extent that the community fails to make this protection so available, it fails to provide equal protection: It fails to be just. Two conditions must be met if the protection afforded by legal rights is to be available to all with sound claims to it. First, it should be possible for citizens to obtain, at least generally, *information* about what the law requires or permits. There may be some cases, as when the law is unsettled, when only educated guesses are possible: Adequate authoritative information is not available because it does not exist. To be sure, even when rights are problematic, a commitment to adjudication secures for members of the community a right to an authoritative clarifying judgment in the event of a dispute. But when information does exist, it should be possible for a member of the community to find out what the legal standards are. Legal rights have little value (and legal obligations can be unfairly perilous) to those who cannot find out which ones they have.

Second, when members of the community have a legal right to something that has been denied to them, it should be possible for them to obtain whatever protection and support the community guarantees to them as a matter of law. In other words, it should be possible for them to *exercise* what rights they have. Thus if Potter has the legal right that Watson not build the tall orange fence on the boundary separating their two lots, it should be possible for her to commence some community-constituted process that will have as its effect the rectification of Watson's wrong. Potter might be able to invoke some legal requirement that Watson remove, relocate, or repaint his fence or that he compensate her for a continuing encroachment upon her interests. If the community is serious in its commitment to adjudication as a means of clarifying and securing legal rights for its citizenry, it must begin by securing generally for all citizens a right to information about what the law permits and requires, and a right as well to appeal to the law to secure that which the law guarantees to them.

Adversarial systems seem to have the serious disadvantage that complaints may not be made and cases may be wrongly decided if the party in the right doesn't bring the case or loses it because of an inability to present intelligibly and persuasively what is, in fact, a solid case. Some citizens—let us call them nonparticipants—may be effectively excluded from the courts because of inadequate resources of one kind or another. Since the judge in an adversarial proceeding depends upon the parties to do the investigative work and to present the results to the court in a useful way, serious injustices may be tolerated when they shouldn't be or cases may be wrongly decided if one of the parties is unable to meet the requirements of adversarial adjudication. Where this happens, the judicial system may serve generally to protect some perpetrators of injustice; may serve, in other words, to further injustice. Certain sectors of the community may be forced to put up with wrongs that the rest of us would not tolerate for an instant. Being unable to participate in the mechanism that the community provides for the settling of disputes, these persons will be exposed to wrongs without the prospect of legal recourse.

If such wrongs are to be rectified, measures will have to be taken that are outside the law. However, if in taking "direct action," wrongs are committed against those who are not similarly excluded from participation in the system, then the system will protect the victims of the nonparticipants in a way that it won't protect the nonparticipants when they are victimized. One thinks of the looting and destruction in America's periodic ghetto riots. Inquisitorial systems of adjudication seem not to have these same problems, since one official has the responsibility for doing the work of both sides, investigating the facts and interpreting the law. Injustice stemming from inequality in the resources of the parties is thus less likely to occur in these nonadversarial systems. If the community opts for an adversarial model, it will have to address this distinctive problem.

At the broadest level, adversarial legal systems can meet the conditions of information and exercise in several ways. Because each of these approaches ameliorates some difficulties while exacerbating others, they may be thought of as representing different agendas: With what kinds of problem do we wish to be occupied? The first solution is that of the "convivial" legal system.[1] In such a system care is taken so that people can generally be expected to understand their legal positions with respect to most matters and to be able to function within the legal system without assistance. This is brought about by (1) employing programs of mass legal education to ensure that virtually everyone has the knowledge and skill that are needed, and (2) opting for a simple legal system so that only minimal instruction is required.

The system can be kept simple using a number of methods. Judges can be limited in the degree to which they are able to become specialists. They might receive only a small amount of specialized training, perhaps only after they are selected. And they could be rotated in and out of short single terms in office. Because in terms of training and experience judges would not be all that different from the litigants, courtroom discourse would not differ strikingly from the language of everyday life. Indeed, experience in the courtroom, as litigant and as judge, might be fairly commonplace among members of such a community. A convivial arrangement has the advantage that each person would know just about everything anyone would need to know about the legal system: both what the law was on most matters and how to function in the courts. It would have the disadvantage—perhaps this is a disadvantage—that legal relationships and their derivative social institutions could never be so complicated as to require a specialist to understand what is involved in them.[2] Difficult-to-discern injustices might persist because the expertise required to identify and deal with them might not be developed. In essence, a convivial system meets the conditions of information and exercise by means of mass legal education and simplicity.

On the other hand, the community could choose to make no effort whatever to educate the general public to the point at which it has an adequate understanding of the provisions of the law and the niceties of legal procedure. The legal system itself could be permitted to become as complicated as it may, with only highly educated and experienced specialists sitting on the bench. In such a "sophisticated" system, the ordinary person cannot be expected to understand his or her legal position with respect to many matters, and neither can the layman be expected to secure, all alone, what the law guarantees. In a legal system like this, justice requires that there exist some mechanism for making available both information about the requirements of the law and skilled legal assistance. Without such a mechanism, a sophisticated legal system cannot be justified. Justice can thus require that a sophisticated adversarial system of adjudication be a "professionalized" system.[3]

Sophisticated Adversarial Systems

Unlike the convivial arrangement, sophisticated legal systems do not provide for mass legal education, nor do they incorporate structural features that serve to limit the complexity of the system. Accordingly, in order to meet the conditions of information and exercise, they must provide for some sort of intermediary between laypersons and what will generally be a mysterious and intimidating legal system. There are three main approaches to the provision of such an intermediary: the free market, the liberal profession, and the public agency.

The Free Market. In the absence of mass legal education, judicial specialists create the need for lawyers. Just as—historically—shoemakers and repairers of appliances can materialize without invitation, so pettifoggers will appear about the courts to make specialized services available to those who have business there. In exchange for a fee, these self-designated attorneys will give legal advice, draft legal documents, and, with the court's permission, represent clients before the judge. It is important to note that these "proto-professionals" differ greatly from what we now know as attorneys. For example, they will not have standardized educational experiences, nor will they be certified in familiar ways. Though some may have been to "law school," completion of such a course of study will not be a prerequisite to the practice of law. Just as anyone can hold himself out as a gardener or as an automobile front-end specialist—and let the buyer beware!—so pettifoggers will fall all along the spectra of competence and integrity. There will be virtually no formal restrictions on entry into the field. Of course, some may not be able to earn a living in the legal services business and will turn to other callings. Consumer services may alleviate some of the problems created by variations in quality, selling information to potential clients about the relative merits of attorneys. Still, the purchaser of legal services will generally have no assurance (except for the word of the attorney) that the goods received are of their putative quality.

Should pettifoggers decide to organize, their distinctive form of society will be the "trade association," set up to further the economic interests of the membership. The trade as a whole may have problems that are best addressed by means of some kind of collective action. Perhaps there are too many people entering the business, causing excessive competition and driving down the average income of the membership. Perhaps a few "rotten apples" have given pettifoggery a bad name and there is therefore a public-relations problem that needs attention. Perhaps programs can be set up that will help lawyers keep current on legal developments. A legal-services trade has the advantage that it may require little attention by the larger community. If disparities in financial resources are not too large among the citizenry, if the costs of litigaton are not great, and if reliable information is readily available concerning the quality of practicing lawyers, the conditions of information and exercise can be met.

Sectors of the community that are without adequate legal services will almost naturally generate their own specialists as legal tradesmen seek out untapped markets. On the other hand, where poverty is significant in sectors of the community or where legal services are for other reasons not made available by market forces, the problems may be more difficult. Still, the proto-professional lawyer may nobly offer legal services "pro bono publico" (for the good of the public). A sufficient level of such charity may serve adequately to address the community's concern to meet the conditions of information and exercise. It is important to note that pettifoggers would seem not to be under an obligation to do work for anyone except for their paying customers. Appliance-repair services need not fix the electric mixers of those too poor to pay for the work. If the gratuitous charity of the legal trade will not suffice, the community can always decide to subsidize the purchase of legal services for those too poor to pay.

The Liberal Profession. The development of a trade into a profession is a lengthy process,[4] and occupations can be located at virtually any point along the continuum. In American legal history, the process of professionalization can perhaps be said to have begun in 1870 with the organization of the Association of the Bar of the City of New York.[5] Samuel J. Tilden, addressing the first meeting of the first modern legal professional association, warned:

> Sir, [I] should not be unwilling that the Bar should combine to restore any power or influence which it has lost, except such power and influence as it may have deservedly lost. As a class, as a portion of a community, I do not desire to see the Bar combined, except for two objects. The one is to elevate itself—to elevate its own standards; the other object is for the common and public good. For itself, nothing; for that noble and generous and elevated profession of which it is the representative, everything.
>
> Sir, it cannot be doubted—we can none of us shut our eyes to the fact—that there has been, in the last quarter of a century, a serious decline in the

character, in the training, in the education, and in the morality of our Bar; and the first work for this Association to do is to elevate the profession to a higher and a better standard. If the Bar is to become merely a method of making money, making it in the most convenient way possible; but making it at all hazards, then the Bar is degraded. If the Bar is to be merely an institution that seeks to win causes and to win them by backdoor access to the judiciary, then it is not only degraded, but it is corrupt.[6]

Tilden's language signals a new role for the bar, a new conception of the responsibility of lawyers, a striking departure from the idea of lawyering as a trade, and a commitment to the development of the liberal legal profession. The transition from something close to what we have described as a "free market" to the modern legal profession took many decades, but the three critical steps in the process are roughly as follows.

First, organized practitioners within the trade begin to make a *claim to maximal competence.* Through representatives, one begins to hear that a certain discrete class of lawyers, in virtue of superior training, education, and experience, exceeds in skill all others in legal knowledge and skill. Two conditions must be satisfied before such a claim can be made: (1) there must be some organization of practitioners within the favored class; not necessarily all, but enough to warrant a claim to speak for the whole class. And (2) there must be some criterion for deciding who belongs to the class of favored practitioners and who does not. (In the end, this evolves into an elaborate gatekeeping procedure involving education, accreditation of schools, and certification of new members.) The esoteric nature of the legal knowledge and skill possessed by this select class of practitioners implies that those outside the favored class simply lack the standing to make sound judgments about the competence of these specialists. As the claim to maximal competence becomes generally accepted, it becomes more and more reasonable to let the select class of practitioners certify and evaluate itself, excluding from practice those of dubious expertise. The organization of favored practitioners stands ready to assume this responsibility.

Second, since in a society that is committed to a sophisticated adversarial system special legal knowledge and skill are vital to the achievement of justice, the process of professionalization requires that the profession make a *public commitment* to use its distinctive abilities in the realization of that significant social value. The profession pledges to give due attention to the special responsibilities it will assume in ensuring that the system of adversarial adjudication succeeds in its task of justly addressing conflicts emerging within the community. Typically these commitments are expressed in the codes of ethics that have become virtually the hallmark of professionalism itself. Thus the American Bar Association's Code of Professional Responsibility begins with the language:

The continued existence of a free and democratic society depends upon recognition of the concept that justice is based upon the rule of law grounded in respect for the dignity of the individual and his capacity through reason for enlightened self-government. Law so grounded makes justice possible, for only through such law does the dignity of the individual attain respect and protection. Without it, individual rights become subject to unrestrained power, respect for law is destroyed, and rational self-government is impossible. . . .

Lawyers, as guardians of the law, play a vital role in the preservation of society. The fulfillment of this role requires an understanding by lawyers of their relationship with and functions in our legal system. A consequent obligation of lawyers is to maintain the highest standards of ethical conduct.

Thus in characterizing itself as a guardian of the law, a guardian of the foundation of justice, the legal profession represents itself as dedicated to an ideal of social service.

Third and most important, the process of professionalization requires that the community recognize the favored members of the profession as the sole means by which legal skill and knowledge are to be applied. This exclusive *social reliance* upon licensed attorneys is based upon the preceding two stages. For if there is confidence that the favored members of the class of practitioners possess maximal competence in matters legal, and if there is trust that these same lawyers are reliably committed to the responsible application of their distinctive skills, then there will seem to be neither the ability nor the need to designate nonprofessionals as overseers of professional practice. No one is competent to do the job, and we don't need to have it done in the first place. As the profession secures trust and confidence, it takes control over the selection and training of candidates, the accreditation of professional schools and programs, the certification of new members, and the promulgation and enforcement of standards of professional conduct. It becomes, in essence, an unregulated legal monopoly with respect to legal services, unauthorized practice being a criminal offense. In the end, of course, it is the citizenry who, through representatives, delegate responsibility to professions of relieve them of it. Though permission to practice in the courts—admission to the bar—is initially granted by the judiciary, the privileges that lawyers enjoy can be ratified, extended, and revoked by legislatures.[7]

It is helpful to compare the monopoly status of public utilities with the standing of the professionalized bar.[8] Corporations that operate as public utilities receive from the community an exclusive legal right to distribute some good or service within a defined geographical area. It is a great advantage to the corporation to have the assurance that it will not face competition and, because of this, it may be able to keep its costs low and achieve economies of scale. From the point of view of the citizenry however, the deal makes sense only if the corporation assumes the responsibility of providing reasonable service to all those within its area. As the United States Supreme Court put it in 1918:

Corporations which devote their property to a public use may not pick and choose, serving only the portions of the territory covered by their franchises which it is presently profitable for them to serve, and restricting the development of the remaining portions by leaving their inhabitants in discomfort without the service which they alone can render.[9]

Without the commitment to provide service, the granting of the exclusive right to the corporation—the barring of all others from entering the market—does not make sense.

Likewise, in the absence of a commitment from the legal profession to provide service to all who need it, the granting of an exclusive right to the bar becomes a decision to exclude some sectors of the community from participation in the system of adjudication. Where only attorneys are permitted to advise and represent members of the community, but where no attorneys will agree to serve some community members with need for legal assistance, the community does not meet the conditions of information and exercise and is to that extent unjust. One mechanism for meeting the two conditions is a responsible legal profession. Those in it would possess the knowledge and skill that the ordinary members of the community would lack. They would have an exclusive right to counsel and represent clients in legal matters. And finally, the profession as a whole would acknowledge its obligation to serve adequately as the necessary intermediary between the public and an otherwise inaccessible judiciary. Understood in this way, the liberal legal profession serves as an integral part of the legal system: Though they retain their autonomy, lawyers are *officers* of the court. Thus a serious failure of the legal profession is a serious failure of the legal system. The standards of practice that the profession as a whole imposes upon its members must ensure that the counseling and representational services that must be made available if the legal system is to make sense are made available to the public in an adequate way.

Speaking through professional associations in codes of ethics, lawyers have acknowledged the bar's duty to serve all members of the community. Thus the first Ethical Consideration of the American Bar Association's Code of Professional Responsibility begins:

> A basic tenet of the professional responsibility of lawyers is that *every person* in our society should have ready access to the independent professional services of a lawyer of integrity and competence.

The legal profession, the collectivity of licensed attorneys, thus does provide a guarantee to the community as a whole that competent and responsible attorneys will be available to those with need for it. Were it the case that large numbers of attorneys publicly disavow these representations made by organizations undertaking to speak on behalf of the profession, then one would have reason to believe that the public commitment expressed by the codes does not represent a public responsibility undertaken by the profession. But in the absence of widespread visible dissociation, one can only suppose that the codes express a commitment that is generally acknowledged. To be sure, the possibility exists, as Tilden foresaw, that the bar associations of today are merely yesterday's trade associations with improved public-relations programs. And it may be that the codes are not intended—perhaps were never intended—to bind lawyers to responsible levels of public service. Perhaps they were enunciated merely to convey the illusion of concerned attention. To the extent that this is so, the liberal profession will have failed, professional responsibility will have failed. Some other mechanism must be instituted to meet the conditions of information and exercise.

Students of contract law may have detected here the equitable doctrine of promissory estoppel. Ordinarily, a gratuitous promise does not create a legal obligation. Not owing the money in any sense, W says to B that he will give B twenty dollars tomorrow. Other things being equal, no legal obligation is created. But if B has made it clear to W that he will be acting to his detriment in reliance upon W's promise, that he will be giving up something of value if W doesn't come through, then a legally binding obligation may be created. Suppose B were to say to W: "Because you will be giving me twenty dollars tomorrow, today I will put down a nonrefundable twenty dollars deposit on a coat I have wanted, and I will promise the merchant to pay the balance tomorrow when I receive the money from you." At that point the law may well acknowledge a contract. When the maker of a promise ought reasonably to expect that the promise will induce a particular kind of action or forbearance on the part of the promisee, and where the promise does induce the action or forbearance, the promise may be held to be legally binding (*Fried* v. *Fisher*, 328 Pa 497, 196 A 39 [1938]).

In granting the legal profession monopoly status, the community relies to its detriment upon the profession's collective representation that it will meet the conditions of information and exercise. The community loses something universally acknowledged to be of inestimable value if the legal profession fails to meet the responsibilities it has assumed in the process of professionalization. Of course, if we assume that the granting of monopoly status to the bar is the "consideration" that the bar receives in return for having agreed to meet the conditions of information and exercise, then the contract is a much more ordinary one. In either event, unlike the free-market pettifogger, professional attorneys have a clear duty to address the legal needs of nonparticipants; indeed, a duty to see to it that there are no nonparticipants. It is not a matter of gratuitous charity "pro bono publico." It is a "basic tenet" of the bar's professional responsibility.

The nature of the bar's obligation here is only one of the two critical issues. The other is whether it is reasonable for the public to rely exclusively upon an unregulated monopoly in legal services; to accede to the professionalization of the bar. It does not appear that the delegation of such responsibility is always unwise. Much would depend upon the political dimensions of the institutional and individual autonomy that the community grants, the soundness of the profession's claim to its distinctive competence, and the degree to which the profession is genuinely committed to public service. A thorough justification of any profession would have to take into account all of these matters. Here, of course, our concern is with the proper scope of the profession's public commitment.[10]

The Public Agency. The community takes the third approach to providing the intermediary between the lay public and the sophisticated adversarial system when it decides to employ attorneys directly, much as it does with fire fighters, judges, and police officers. If the interests that citizens have is important enough (it is difficult to think of a more important interest than civil justice), and if neither the free market nor the liberal profession can be relied upon to do the job, the principal remaining option is directly to employ attorneys in organizations set up to provide legal services to the general public. Though lawyers will *work for* their clients (just as teachers work for their students), they will be *paid by* and will have some of their working conditions set by their employers—in this case, civil government. Where gratuitous charity and professional responsibility have failed, "conditions of employment" that are set by the community can perhaps succeed.

The most serious problem that can emerge within the public agency approach is the compromising of professional autonomy, the damaging erosion of the bar's independence. Even though agency attorneys are nominally employed to provide legal services to the public, government officials may try to discourage these lawyers from bringing certain types of complaint—especially complaints against the government—even when the cases are legitimate. Government, the employer of attorneys, may be able to limit the degree to which citizens can challenge the state for having exceeded its proper authority. As the legal profession's "boss," it will do this by setting conditions of employment that restrict the types of case that can be brought to court. In controlling the legal profession—and thus access to to the judiciary—the state can circumvent all legal limits to its authority. Though in some sense or other citizens may still "enjoy" legal rights against the community, they will not be able to appeal to the courts to obtain that which the law guarantees to them. Their rights will not have been secured.

Autonomy problems within legal-services agencies can be addressed by carefully attending to the structure of the organization. In universities, for example, the problem of unwarranted encroachment upon professional autonomy has been extensively addressed under the general heading of "academic freedom." In practice, this entails a separation of administrative and professional functions within the institution so as to guarantee that academicians have the latitude that is required if they are to do their work. It is a secured limitation on the employer's right to determine the conditions and content of the professional's work. Substantial control is in the hands of members of the affected profession. By far the most important factor in securing professional autonomy within an employing organization is the type of association created by the professionals themselves.

We have seen how trade associations and professional associations are the characteristic organizations with respect to the two approaches discussed earlier. The social organization that can be expected to emerge among publicly employed attorneys is the public sector labor union. Labor unions exist primarily to negotiate with the employer (in this case, the community) the terms and conditions of employment. The distinction drawn earlier between trade associations and professional associations parallels the two distinct sets of interests that can be furthered by a public-sector legal-services labor union. Employed attorneys may identify themselves as employees. They may feel that the work they are doing is not really their work but, rather, the agency's work. If the quality of service provided is low, that is not the employee's responsibility. Think of an assembly-line worker, building a badly engineered product. "I am just doing a job, earning a living." To the extent that attorneys think of themselves in this way, the collective bargaining process will focus upon "bread and butter" issues: wages, hours, and general working conditions. The employee's posture will in essence be "more money for less work," mirroring the employer's posture of "more work for less money."

On the other hand, attorneys may identify themselves as professionals; not being paid for their work, *but in order that they may do their work.*[11] Employed professionals may focus not upon their interests as employees, but upon their interests as professionals with final responsibility for the quality of their work. Decent salaries and appropriate working conditions may be important, not because it is nice to earn more in better circumstances, but because adequate attention must be given to these matters if the agency and its professional staff are to serve their public purpose. Likewise, if professional autonomy is under attack by administrators (or even by fellow professionals), the membership of a public sector labor union has the option of placing those values high upon its agenda in negotiations. Of course, where the community as a whole adequately appreciates the argument for an independent bar, it is unlikely that employer and employee will be at odds on this issue. Still, provided that lawyers have not lost their sense of responsibility in their roles as employees, labor unions can serve to further professsionalism and buttress autonomy should the need arise to protect these critical values.

Notes

1. I have taken the term "convivial" from the chapter entitled "Institutional Spectrum" in Ivan Illich's *Deschooling Society.*

2. For an illuminating description of a legal system that approaches conviviality, see Victor Li's account of the Chinese legal system in *Law Without Lawyers* (Boulder: Westview Press, 1978).

3. It is probably misleading to think that specialists are required because the system is complicated. While this has without doubt become true, a more adequate account would disclose that a system becomes complicated precisely because it is placed wholly in the hands of specialists. This is not to say that complexity or sophistication are bad things; only that they create problems that need to be solved.

4. See Harold Wilensky, "The Professionalization of Everyone," *American Journal of Sociology* 70 (1964): 137. The general view of professional responsibility here has been more fully developed in my paper, "Professional Responsibility and the Responsibility of the Professions," in Wade Robison, Michael Pritchard, and Joseph Ellin, eds., *Profits and Professions* (Clifton, N.J.: Humana Press, 1983).

5. R. Pound, *The Lawyer from Antiquity to Modern Times* 5 (1953), note 7 at p. 249. Pound describes the period between 1836 and 1870 as the "Era of Decadence," pp. 223-49.

6. Quoted in R. F. Marks, K. Leswing, and B. Fortinsky, *The Lawyer, the Public, and Professional Responsibility* (Chicago: The American Bar Foundation, 1972) p. 13.

7. The New Mexico Supreme Court, in *Norvell* v. *Credit Bur. of Albuquerque, Inc.*, 85, N.M. 521, 514 P.2d 40 (1973), has recognized the following "indicia" of the "practice of law":

> (1) representation of parties before judicial or administrative bodies, (2) preparation of pleadings and other papers incident to actions and special proceedings, (3) management of such action and proceeding; and non-court-related activities such as (4) giving legal advice and counsel, (5) rendering a service that requires the use of legal knowledge or skill, (6) preparing instruments and contracts by which legal rights are secured.

These are typical issues for consideration in determining whether an individual is guilty of the unauthorized practice of law.

8. The characterization of the legal profession as a public utility has been developed by Marks, et al. in *The Lawyer, the Public, and Professional Responsibility*, pp. 288-93. Some of the key elements of their general view were developed decades earlier by Karl Llewellyn in "The Bar Specializes—With What Results?" *Annals of the American Academy of Political and Social Science* 167. (May 1933): 177-92; and "The Bar's Troubles and Poultices—and Cures?" 5 *Law and Contemporary Problems* 104 (1938).

9. *New York and Queens Gas Co.* v. *McCall*, 245 U.S. 345, 351. On the ethical responsibility of public utilities, see Kenneth Sayre, ed., *Values in the Electric Power Industry* (Notre Dame: Notre Dame University Press, 1977). See especially Chapter 3, Charles Murdock, "Legal and Economic Aspects of the Electric Utility's 'Mandate to Serve.'"

10. Strong economic arguments against relying upon professions have been leveled by Milton Friedman in "Occupational Licensure" in his *Capitalism and Freedom* (Chicago: University of Chicago Press, 1963). A different type of argument against professionalization is to be found in the writings of Ivan Illich. See, for example, *Deschooling Society* (New York: Harper & Row, 1972); *Tools for Conviviality* (New York: Harper & Row, 1973); and *Medical Nemesis* (New York: Pantheon Books, 1976).

11. This rich conception of professionalism is developed by Lawrence Haworth in his *Decadence and Objectivity* (Toronto: University of Toronto Press, 1978), p. 112.

Bibliography

Auerbach, Jerold S. *Unequal Justice: Lawyers and Social Change in Modern America.* New York: Oxford University Press, 1976.

Li, Victor. *Law without Lawyers.* Boulder: Westview Press, 1978

Marks, F. Raymond, Kirk Leswing and Barbara Fortinsky. *The Lawyer, the Public, and Professional Responsibility.* Chicago: American Bar Foundation, 1972.

Nader, Ralph, and Mark Green. *Verdicts on Lawyers.* New York: Thomas Y. Crowell, 1976.

Smith, Reginald H. *Justice and the Poor.* New York: Scribner's, 1919.

Part III

Human Needs and The Humane Society

At a fundamental level, the problems of economic justice concern the moral relationship between the haves and the have-nots. In Part II we considered the nature of the entitlement that holders of property have to their belongings along with questions about the responsibility of the well-off for the plight of the poor. In Part III we turn our attention to issues concerning various kinds of poverty and economic disenfranchisement.

Why is poverty something we should be concerned about? One answer seems to underlie much of the writing on the topic: The poor suffer. At the least, they are less satisfied than the rest of us. Their plight claims our attention just because the plight of the suffering always does, especially when it can be averted. But the issue may not be as simple as this. Several of the most difficult problems in legal and social philosophy concern duties to render aid. In its legal variant, the issue is strikingly posed by the bystander who encounters an imperiled swimmer drowning in a surging sea. Bystander, with line and life ring in hand, can easily save the swimmer. Most people would acknowledge such an obligation. Nonetheless, the traditional posture of Anglo-American law has been that there is no general legal duty to render aid in such cases. Thus bystanders typically incur no legal liability, criminal or civil, if they ignore pleas for help and let swimmers drown.

But while the laws of most states will not support a finding that unhelpful bystanders are legally at fault (Vermont, imposing a fine of $100, is the best-known exception), conscience and popular moral judgment take quite a different view of the matter. In widely publicized cases in which minimally inconvenient measures would have prevented serious harms from occurring, public outcry and condemnation have been loud and decisive. Few, if any, defended those spectators who simply watched from their windows and did not call the police while Kitty Genovese was being stabbed to death. Few, if any, defended the patrons of the New Bedford bar who did nothing while rape was committed on a pool table nearby. It would appear that prevailing moral judgment confirms that to stand idly by when, with very little effort, a human life can be saved or serious harm averted is at best to display an outrageous and morally culpable disregard for the well-being of others.

How might the discrepancy between the moral and the legal judgments be reconciled? One answer focuses on the practical problem of specifying precisely what aid is legally required. Suppose someone were to appear at your doorstep on a Saturday morning with a picture of a starving peasant from a poor third-world country. The woman will be saved only if you donate ten dollars to the Fund. The money will buy enough food to last until the harvest, and then the famine will be over. The Fund gives each starving peasant only one chance: If you refuse to donate the money, the photograph will be destroyed, and the peasant will probably starve. Ought people to be legally required to donate (donate?) ten dollars to save a peasant? If not ten dollars, what about ten cents? If people ought legally to be required to give up ten cents to save the life of a fellow human being, what if the man at the door then shows you a picture of a second starving peasant? How many starving peasants should one be legally required to save at ten cents per peasant? While there may be ways to specify precisely what a legal duty to render aid would require, the task is probably not an easy one. Rather than embroiling the law in such controversy, it may seem easier and safer to leave questions of samaritanism to private conscience.

What, if anything, do the well-off owe to the poor? There are two basic approaches to this question. One seeks the answer in a specification of the rights of the poor. Do the poor have some warranted claim to the resources of the affluent? Is there some right that the poor have in virtue of their humanity (a human right) that entitles them to some level of assistance? Since rights are characteristically connected to correlative duties, it is not surprising that the second approach seeks the answer in a specification of the duties of the affluent. These duties may be general or special, and they may be of imperfect or of perfect obligation. A general duty will apply to everyone. There may be, for example, a general duty of humanity that obligates everyone who can to alleviate the plight of the needy. On the other hand, a special duty will apply only to certain individuals, typically in virtue of something they have done. Parents, doctors, teachers, paid lifeguards—all have voluntarily undertaken special obligations to help others.

It is sometimes said that duties of charity are of imperfect obligation. By this it is meant that, although one might have an obligation to contribute to some charity or other, no potential recipient of one's charity has an entitlement to it. A perfect obligation, however, must be discharged in a specific way. Suppose Trudy has given as much to help the starving as the imperfect duty of charity obligates her to give. Someone appears at her door, starving and too weak to crawl to the next house. If there is but an imperfect duty of charity, then Trudy can say in good conscience "I gave at the office" and close the door. However, if charity can generate duties of perfect obligation, then she may be required to render assistance.

All of these questions become complicated when they are raised to the level of collectivities. What would be an unfair and unbearable burden for a single individual might be reasonable and tolerable if equitably shared by the community as a whole. While I may have an imperfect obligation to donate to this or that charity, it may be that I have a perfect obligation to donate my fair share. Thus it might not be unreasonable for a national aid fund, paid for by taxes, to be used to help the needy or, what may be a different issue, to help feed starving peasants in other lands. Whether extra risks, expenses, and inconveniences can be reasonably undertaken by individuals can also depend upon whether the community stands ready to indemnify them for their losses. Perhaps Trudy is required to help the starving visitor only if the community stands ready to pay her fairly for her extra trouble. Moreover, it may be that obligations are generated at the level of the collectivity that do not obtain at the level of the individual. If, for example, communities have obligations to make available courts of law, sewers, and public schools—obligations that lone individuals cannot meet—then there may be duties that are generated and met only at the collective level.

One important thing that may or may not be available in the community is work. An important approach to the problems of the poor begins by considering how the community's work is done and in particular, how work is distributed. It is said that the best way to fight poverty is to get a job. While work has always been central in the lives of most people, the concept of work has changed, both our ideas about which activities count as work and our notions about its purpose.* At the most fundamental level, work is the labor necessary for subsistence: the tasks of constructing shelters and providing clothing and food for oneself and one's kin. But as societies initiate diversification and specialization, the concept of work extends beyond the basic chores. There are political, religious, and intellectual institutions to be built as well as shops, trades, and crafts to be staffed. Yet variety in human activity does not necessarily give rise to an equally rich concept of work. Indeed it was the distinction between physical exertion and mental effort that once provided the basis for distinguishing between "work" and other kinds of social activity. Thus while the medieval noble held his distinctive governmental station in service to others and the monk pursued a spiritual calling in service to God, it was the scullery maid and the blacksmith who were condemned to work.

Because the elect pursued higher ends in pristine surroundings while workers toiled to satisfy physical needs and returned home filthy, work came to be associated in some quarters with degradation. But the linkage of work with degradation has not persisted. Any moderately sophisticated economy will now include occupations such as midwifery and architecture and a host of middle-level clerical, managerial, and technical positions that confound the distinction between vocations and work. Democratization and secularization have robbed politics, the clergy, and scholarship of their prestige, while public education and unionization have removed some of the stigma from physical labor.

---

* The discussion of work that follows draws heavily upon writings by Diana T. Meyers.

This enlargement of the concept of work has made it possible to reassess its point. While most people still work to provide for their basic needs, it is clear that few of us subsist in the manner of our ancestors. We now hold jobs as employees to earn our livelihoods. But as public service and personal growth become incorporated into our ideas about work, it begins to appear that a job can be more than just the way we earn the money to buy our daily bread. In our work we can contribute to society and realize our potential. After the traditional demands for higher income, safer working conditions, better hours, and job security, workers have begun to seek concessions aimed at making work more challenging and meaningful. Thus the issue of economic justice in the workplace poses a dual question: What are the goods that workers are entitled to expect from their jobs, and how ought these goods to be distributed?

Still, the issue of economic justice in the workplace is not limited to the proper content of an employment contract. Some kinds of work may be unduly slighted and some kinds of workers may lack credentials as members of the work force. When a market economy replaces a subsistence economy, working can be identified with holding a job. Thus unremunerated domestic labor—what we have thought of as "housewifery"—may not be included in the category of work. If gainful employment is a necessary feature of work, and if work is necessary to self-esteem, then the tasks of homemaking and involved parenthood will be devalued, their importance to the perpetuation of society notwithstanding. Likewise, an economy can operate to sustain "structural" unemployment, excluding whole sectors of the citizenry from the work force. These unemployed persons can be prey to humiliation and destitution. The plights of the uncompensated worker and the unemployable worker invite us to review our convictions about economic justice and work. Only the most abstract principles of justice can remain static while we alter our ideas about the recipients of justice and the benefits that justice secures. The lively controversies addressed in this section lend support to the contention that our notions of economic justice in the workplace are now in flux.

In the first essay in this section, "Vagrancy, Loitering, and Economic Justice," Burton Leiser reminds us that poverty has historically been more than an embarrassing and tragic social status. He recounts how, through laws proscribing vagrancy and loitering, unemployment and poverty can become, in effect, a criminal offense. Though in 1972 the U.S. Supreme Court struck these laws down, Leiser argues that such statutes and ordinances are legitimate when they are intended "to protect communities from invasion by outsiders intent on exploiting facilities for purposes that go beyond those for which they were originally intended." Leiser takes a narrow view of the community's obligation toward its poor. While he agrees that these legal measures will deprive the poor of "privileges they might like to exercise," Leiser holds that such charity is above and beyond the call of duty and that communities have no obligation to provide for the needs of the poor who happen to be among them.

"Any community that recognized such a claim would undoubtedly be inundated by poverty-stricken persons."

Rex Martin, in his essay, "Poverty and Welfare in Rawls's Theory of Justice: On the Just Response to Needs," criticizes the influential views of John Rawls for failing to take into account needy nonworkers: children, the elderly, the unemployed, and the disabled. Rawls recommends organizing the economic system to ensure that inequalities in income and wealth will improve the expectations of the least advantaged members of society. A hasty reading of Rawls might lead one to assume that special needs will be accommodated through his concept of the least advantaged representative individual. But in his review of Rawls's ideas, Martin contends that Rawls is concerned exclusively with supplementing the incomes of the working poor and that his theory is blind to needs as such. Though Martin suggests ways in which Rawls's views could be adjusted to take care of the temporarily unemployed and those who are too young or too old to work, his conclusion is that persons whose physical or mental impairments render them permanently unemployable may find no consolation in Rawlsian liberalism.

While Rawls advocates economic inequalities as a means of drawing out the highest level of performance in socially necessary work, Alistair M. Macleod, in "Economic Inequality: Justice and Incentives," recommends economic equality as a principle of distribution. After reviewing familiar rationales for economic inequality and noting their flaws, Macleod defends economic egalitarianism on two grounds. First, he argues that the same considerations that justify equality under law and equality of opportunity also justify the reduction of economic differentials. Second, he argues that reason can certify only equality as the principle of adjudication between competing interests. Macleod strengthens his case for economic egalitarianism by arguing that incentives to elicit socially necessary work lack a foundation in justice.

In a related discussion of incentives, John J. McCall's "Welfare Reform: Cost Reductions or Increased Work Incentives" explores the moral acceptability of recent proposals to cut welfare expenditures by discouraging welfare dependency. While he begins his treatment by criticizing the view that welfare programs violate the property rights of taxpayers, McCall's primary target is the suggestion that welfare payments be reduced to promote industriousness and self-sufficiency: that benefits be eliminated for persons capable of working or that maximum levels of support be reduced. Both policies provide incentives for parental irresponsibility and fail to secure opportunities for increased work effort. In contrast, McCall finds it effective and permissible—though perhaps also expensive—to require that able welfare recipients work on public projects or to offer financial incentives for obtaining work. Though McCall does not dispute the appropriateness of using incentives, he rejects the exclusive reliance on the market as an arbiter of value and a mechanism for distribution.

Turning from justice in distribution to justice in production, Carol C.

Gould advocates democracy in the workplace. In "Economic Justice, Self-Management, and the Principle of Reciprocity," Gould maintains that equal rights to the conditions of self-development are the core of justice. Applied to lives of involvement in the production process, these rights translate into a right of worker self-management. On the assumption that a social minimum has been secured for everyone, the rights of workers to self-management require that the participants in the production process be accorded the fruits of their collective labor. After highlighting the strengths and weaknesses of the views of John Rawls and Robert Nozick, Gould contends that her own position on economic justice incorporates the advantages evident in these other theories while bypassing their failings. Substituting reciprocity for domination in the workplace, Gould's expanded vision of economic justice implicitly condemns capitalist control over the means of production.

James W. Nickel, in "The Feasibility of Welfare Rights in Less Developed Countries," looks at some of the philosophical issues that arise when the governments of poorer countries attempt to secure welfare rights in the face of profound shortage. Governments of developing nations can legally prohibit actions that deprive people of needed food or the means to obtain it; they can arrange sound systems of production and distribution; and they can ensure that all have adequate ability to draw from the supply. But it can be expensive for a poor country to do these things. Can a less developed nation with liberty rights to secure also afford the welfare right to adequate nutrition? Nickel discusses four tests that can be applied in deciding the affordability of basic rights. A test of consistency would discourage the expenditure of funds to secure one right if it depended for its effective implementation upon the implementation of a second right that was not being secured. A test of importance would favor the implementation of a more valuable right—one that protected "the core of a fundamental freedom or benefit"—over the implementation of less valuable ones. A test of cost would favor less expensive rights (rights having the "highest ratio of importance to costs") over more expensive ones. A test of fruitfulness would favor those that "will lead over time to a greater ability to implement other rights." Nickel applies these tests and concludes that a right to adequate nutrition "belongs on today's lists of human rights."

Commenting on Nickel's essay, Thomas Donaldson claims that it is wrong to suppose, as Nickel does, that limits on resources can require trade-offs between liberty (nonwelfare rights) and welfare. Donaldson's point is that a system designed to protect justice has a *negative cost*. The costs of abandoning it can be higher than the costs of maintaining it. "Even welfare rights probably carry negative economic costs in the long run." The problem, according to Donaldson, is not to make the right trade-offs between welfare rights and nonwelfare rights. It is to make the right trade-offs "among various types of welfare rights in the short term."

Kenneth Kipnis

12
Vagrancy, Loitering, and Economic Justice

Burton M. Leiser
Pace University

I

Philosophical discussions of justice in connection with poverty generally revolve around problems of distributive justice. Since there are no longer many crimes that can be committed by poor people just because they are poor, such discussions seldom deal with justice in its other manifestations. But the "crime" of *being* poor still exists in some forms, and it is appropriate to address ourselves to it.

In 1972 the U.S. Supreme Court unanimously reversed the convictions of eight defendants who had been convicted of violating the vagrancy ordinance of the City of Jacksonville, Florida.[1] Speaking for the Court, Justice Douglas briefly recounted the history of vagrancy statutes. First designed to stabilize the labor force by prohibiting increases in wages and prohibiting the movement of workers from their home areas in search of improved conditions during the breakup of feudal estates in England, they later became criminal adjuncts to the poor laws.[2] But as the Court had observed in *Edwards* v. *California*, the "theory of the Elizabethan poor laws no longer fits the facts."[3]

Early English legislation covered idle and disorderly persons, beggars, tramps, gypsies, fortunetellers, unlicensed peddlers, husbands who had abandoned their families, and persons wandering about who were unable to give a good account of themselves.[4] Officials were permitted to arrest such persons without a warrant and allowed for summary proceedings against them.[5] Penalties for vagrancy in the sixteenth century included branding, slavery, and death,[6] and summary punishment was provided in order to tighten up enforcement as early as the fifteenth century.[7] This was undoubtedly the result of a desire to prevent serfs from abandoning their masters' lands and to concern over the alleged tendencies of vagrants to commit crimes of all sorts.

Eventually, the emphasis shifted from prevention of migration to protection of the countryside against the financial burden and potential criminality of the vagrants. These laws were transported from England to the Colonies and were eventually incorporated into the statutes and ordi-

nances of the various governments of the United States. Paupers and vagabonds were excepted from the privileges and immunities clause of the
Articles of Confederation and from its guarantee of "free ingress and
egress to and from any other state."[8] As early as 1837, the Supreme Court
stated that it is "as competent and as necessary for a state to provide pre-
cautionary measures against the moral pestilence of paupers, vagabonds,
and possible convicts, as it is to guard against the physical pestilence."[9]
Edwards v. *California* [10] declared unconstitutional statutes designed to
keep unwanted migrants out of states—statutes that had been enacted by a
very large number of states during the Depression.[11]

During the periodic depressions of the nineteenth and early twentieth
centuries, thousands of workers who lost their jobs took to the road or
rode the rails in search of better working conditions. In addition, as opportunities shifted westward with the development of industry, mining,
forestry, and the railroads, workers moved wherever they perceived the
opportunities to be. In the early 1890s, tens of thousands of "tramps"
wandered through the Midwest.[12] They were often arrested and placed in
"police lodgings," which in 1893 housed nearly 40,000 persons in Baltimore alone, and more than 1,600 in Buffalo. The public perception of
such persons was well expressed by the chief of police of Lynchburg,
Virginia:

> They are criminals of the lowest type, who use the time while being helped
> by kindly disposed persons to spy into those premises and use the information
> thus acquired to rob those same premises later.
> When a man goes to a freight yard with the intention of riding a freight to the
> next town, he is a thief. He is going to steal a ride, and so even the honest labor-
> er who starts out to "hobo" to the next town in search of work is morally and
> actually a thief, and the transition to the old kind of thief is very easy.[13]

"Industrial armies" occasionally "requisitioned" trains, frequently leading great chases against federal troops. In order to provide housing for 600
workers crowded into Medford, New Jersey, to work on the cranberry
harvest, one group of tramps disconnected the engine from a string of cars
and ran off with it, leaving the cars behind as living quarters for their
comrades.[14] Conductors and engineers were shot when they attempted to
resist the armies of hoboes attempting to commandeer their engines.[15]
There is no doubt that tramps committed a wide variety of crimes, ranging
from petty thefts and burglaries to more serious crimes. By 1898 only four
of the forty-four states had no legislation concerning tramps.[16]

A charitable society formed in Buffalo in 1877 devoted itself to organizing charitable organizations "scientifically" to prevent them from demo-
ralizing the working class and encouraging laziness. It urged its constituent
organizations to distinguish carefully between the worthy poor and the
lazy and improvident, to distribute their assistance in such a way as to put
people back to work as quickly as possible, and to consign tramps and
other "antisocial" elements to workhouses and prison rehabilitation.
Among other things, this charitable society advocated starving the child-

ren of alcoholics in order to reform their parents, and it criticized public-school teachers who fed hungry students.

An economist, Richart T. Ely, expressed the general fear of the crimes that these hungry people might commit when he asserted that a substantial proportion of the unemployed might suffer what he called "social shipwreck" and pose a great danger to the community. "Recent researches in pauperism and crime," he wrote, "make nothing plainer than that there is a section of wage-earning classes comparatively weak, which in times like these tends to yield to the temptation to become beggars and criminals and prey upon society."[17] Thus it was natural that laws would be passed and that the public would demand rigorous enforcement against those who were unfortunate enough to be out of work and moving about, looking for some way to feed themselves and their families. Such laws were intended to prevent "tramps" and "bums" from entering the communities that passed them, and were employed by the officials who enforced them to banish such persons from the areas under their jurisdiction.

II

Vagrancy laws generally permitted arrest without warrant and summary prosecution without a jury before a justice of the peace or magistrate, and the burden of proof was on the defendant to demonstrate that he was innocent. When persons were suspected of involvement with more serious crimes, but the evidence was not sufficient to permit the police to arrest them, they could be arrested and held on a vagrancy charge while the investigation proceeded. Such laws were also useful as a means of banishing or committing unwanted drunks, panhandlers, gamblers, peddlers, and paupers from congested skid-row areas.

In *Edwards* v. *California*, the Court rested its decision (holding that a statute banning the importation of indigent persons into the state was unconstitutional) on the commerce power and the privileges and immunities clause, saying:

> Whatever may have been the notion then prevailing [when the Elizabethan poor laws were passed], we do not think that it will be seriously contended that because a person is without employment and without funds he constitutes a "moral pestilence."[18]

But this did not prevent magistrates from banishing persons who were visiting or passing through a city where poor persons were unwanted or under suspicion.[19] The summary procedure in such cases entailed denial of jury trials to the accused and a studied intention to win convictions without due process and without the necessity of producing competent evidence.[20]

As late as 1953, forty of the forty-eight states defined vagrancy as a crime, which could be "committed" by living in idleness or without employment and having no visible means of support; being a common prostitute; being a common drunkard, a common gambler, a keeper of a house of prostitution, or a keeper of a gambling house or gaming equipment; being a wanton, dissolute, or lascivious person; and being an associate of known thieves.[21] In addition, roaming, wandering, or loitering, especially when one had no visible or lawful purpose in so acting, could give no satisfactory account of his presence, or was wandering at "late or unusual hours," was defined in some states as vagrancy. Many states included begging or being a beggar, at least when one was able to work, as vagrancy. Lodging or sleeping outdoors or in buildings other than residences without the permission of the owner or without being able to give a good account of oneself was punishable in a number of states, and failing to support one's family was vagrancy in about ten states.[22]

The crime or offense of vagrancy was not an act, but a state of being. As a California court put it:

> That which has been done is not to declare that it is unlawful to get drunk, or to prostitute oneself, or to peep in another's building, nor have these acts been declared to be misdemeanors. The punishment provided by section 647 is not for doing, but for being; for being a vagrant.[23]

The precise meaning of the various vagrancy statutes was never clearly spelled out; nor was any serious effort made to enforce constitutional requirements of due process in connection with their enforcement and prosecution.

In an important article published in 1960, Justice William O. Douglas denounced vagrancy statutes and the manner in which they were enforced. "I am sure," he wrote, "that my old friend Carl Sandburg, whom America loves, feels warm inside when I address him as Fellow Hobo. The term implies independence, a restless spirit, the quest for a better life, rebellion against submission to orthodoxy." Justice Douglas went on to quote at length Robert Louis Stevenson's paean to the vagabond, contrasting it with the Tucson police department's "war" on "winter vags." He had known judges and lawyers, he said, who had wandered the streets at night during a bout with insomnia, and recalled the days of his own youth when he had ridden the rods with the casual laborers of the Pacific West, sharing their meals under railroad bridges, sleeping with them in the open air. "I came to know that the 'consumers of injustice' are not the sleepless judges and lawyers," he wrote, "but the wanderers who have no prestige of class or family."[24]

He then proceeded to lay bare what he considered to be the principal defects of such laws: their vagueness; the impact they have on interstate movements of destitute people; whether, when the crime charged under a particular statute is one of status, it may be proved by a single act, or whether one act can constitute several ingredients of the crime; the lack of clarity as to when one ceases to be a vagrant; whether double jeopardy applies; how the vagrancy statute is used in relation to other crimes; whether it is simply an easy device to use in making arrests on suspicion.

Justice Douglas was concerned about what he perceived to be the complete ineffectiveness of penal statutes to cure the problem—which after all is nothing more than poverty.

III

In 1972 the Supreme Court, in *Papachristou* v. *City of Jacksonville*, struck down the Jacksonville vagrancy ordinance and impelled state governments and municipalities to repeal or revise their vagrancy statutes and ordinances. In his opinion for the Court, Justice Douglas argued that loafing and loitering, like walking and strolling and wandering, are "part of the amenities of life as we have known them, amenities that have been in part responsible for giving our people the feeling of independence and self-confidence, the feeling of creativity, . . . [that] have dignified the right of dissent and have honored the right to be nonconformists and the right to defy submissiveness. They have encouraged lives of high spirits rather than hushed, suffocating silence."[25] The presumption that people who walk, loaf, loiter, or stroll, or who frequent liquor stores or taverns, or who are supported by their wives or look suspicious to the police are about to become involved in criminal behavior is "too precarious for a rule of law," he said, an assumption "too extravagant to deserve extended treatment." With that, he dismissed the subject and brought his *Papachristou* opinion to an end.[26]

This decision has considerable appeal. But there is reason to believe that the Supreme Court is modifying the stand that it took in *Papachristou*.[27] A number of statutes and ordinances forbidding loitering or disorderly conduct have been upheld on various grounds, principally the fear that peace, order, or public safety are threatened.[28]

IV

In his *Papachristou* opinion, Justice Douglas left a legacy of doubt and confusion. There is no doubt that the old vagrancy laws and their relatives, the tramp ordinances, the loitering statutes, the disorderly-conduct statutes, and others were vague and left far too much to the discretion of the authorities. Nor is there any doubt that the authorities have been far too readily inclined to arrest "offensive" persons on the basis of subjective feelings of distaste for them, and to throw them into jail on the basis of unproved assumptions and without the controls of due process. The evidence is clear that many thousands of persons have been arrested and incarcerated for greater or lesser periods of time merely because they were poor and unemployed, and therefore, by some standards, unattractive and unappealing.

At the same time, however, it is unreasonable to dismiss out of hand the fact that some poor and unemployed persons do commit substantive criminal offenses. The offenses cited at the beginning of this article were anything but trivial—amusing, perhaps, but not trivial, and potentially extremely dangerous. Running off with a railroad locomotive is scarcely a case of petty theft. From the railroad's point of view, the use of its boxcars as temporary residences for migrant workers must have been serious indeed, since those very cars were probably needed to transport to market the cranberries that those workers were picking. In the literature on the subject, which is almost always sympathetic to the hoboes, it is impossible to find any suggestion that these amateur engineers might not have known what they were doing as they drove their locomotives through the countryside. Nor is there any discussion of the accidents they caused, the injuries attributable to their recklessness, or the loss of property that resulted, or might have resulted, from their romantic adventures.

The joyful vagabonds with whom Justice Douglas associated in his youth undoubtedly provided him with many memories upon which he drew in the nostalgia of later years. But the victims of their crimes—against both persons and property—were simply left to nurse their grievances and their wounds, and to suffer the deprivations imposed upon them by the romantic vagrants without a word of sympathy.

The recent cases lead one to wonder whether, for example, the known pickpocket should be permitted to loiter in a bus terminal when he has no-where to go and is not waiting to meet anyone in particular. Or is it necessary to wait until after he has stolen someone's wallet and been caught and convicted before his thievery can be brought to an end?[29]

Similarly, must the lone wanderer be permitted to hide behind the bushes late at night in a residential area where he has no business and cannot provide a reasonable explanation of his presence?[30] In light of common experience, it is not unreasonable to presume that his motives may not be pure and to insist that he either explain what he is doing there or suffer arrest on some charge designed to protect homeowners and residents against the depredations of burglars, thieves, and muggers. The mere claim that they are innocent nightwalkers who just happen to be fifteen miles from home ought not to be construed to be sufficient to overcome the presumption.

V

Neither poverty nor unemployment entitles a person, or a band of persons, to set up camp wherever they choose to light, intruding upon the peace and harmony of any community that happens to be in their path. When parks, streets, and sidewalks are converted into temporary residences, there can be no doubt of the deleterious impact upon the local community. The stench of human excrement fills the air. Benches intended for the enjoyment of local residents are occupied by sleeping vagabonds. Grounds become littered with the refuse left by persons who use them for purposes for which they were neither intended nor designed. Passersby and householders are intercepted and importuned by beggars and panhandlers, and the peace of the community is disrupted by the influx of strangers, not all of whom are determined to find an honorable way of satisfying their needs.

The fact that a place is not privately owned does not entail its being open to any and all persons for occupation and use for any purpose. Many places are publicly owned, but it is neither unlawful nor immoral to place restrictions upon the persons who may use them and the activities in which they may engage while in those places. A public-school building, for example, is owned by the community; but the school board and its agents are fully justified in demanding that people who are not authorized to be in such buildings because they are not there on business having to do with the public schools must leave the premises or be charged with trespass. The same is true of public hospitals, libraries, courthouses, post offices, and even jails and prisons. If this elementary principle of public ownership were not recognized, it would soon become impossible to carry on the public business for which such structures are erected.

The principle applies to public lands as well as to public buildings. The Supreme Court (though not without some dissent) recognized this point in *Adderley* v. *Florida*, which upheld convictions for conducting a demonstration on the grounds of a county jail. Speaking for the Court, Justice Black said, "The State, no less than a private owner of property, has power to preserve the property under its control for the use to which it is lawfully dedicated. . . . The United States Constitution does not forbid a State to control the use of its own property for its own lawful nondiscriminatory purpose."[31] A year earlier, Justice Black put the matter even more clearly:

> The First and Fourteenth Amendments, I think, take away from government, state and federal, all power to restrict freedom of speech, press, and assembly *where people have a right to be for such purposes*. This does not mean, however, that these amendments also grant a constitutional right to engage in the conduct of picketing or patrolling, whether on publicly owned streets or on privately owned property.[32]

If the Court's most uncompromising proponent of an absolutist reading of the First Amendment could conclude that the liberties guaranteed by that Amendment cannot be exercised without restraint on public grounds dedicated to other purposes, then it is not unreasonable to assume that the Court as a whole would not find that poverty, joblessness, and homelessness do not confer upon a person the unrestrained right to occupy a public place as a temporary or semipermanent residence, or to engage in activities that are incompatible with the uses for which it was intended.

Nor would the Court be morally wrong in arriving at such a conclusion: in concluding, for example, that poor, unemployed, homeless persons could be ejected from a public park; that they could be penalized for hunting without a license; that they could be arrested for camping on a public sidewalk; or that they could be arrested for wandering, in a seemingly aimless fashion, in a neighborhood where they have no lawful business to conduct.

A public park, designed as a place of recreation, may properly be restricted to members of the local community that supports it, and to particular uses. There is no *a priori* reason why residents should feel morally obliged to open their facility to any stranger who happens to pass through town. It could scarcely be argued that they would not be justified in ejecting anyone who attempted to build a campfire in the middle of a tennis court, since it would destroy the surface of the court and render it useless—or at least less useful—for the purposes for which it was intended. By the same reasoning, they might properly eject anyone who erected a squatter's tent on the grounds of the park and attempted to establish a residence there for himself and his family.

Like many so-called human rights, those fundamental "rights" claimed by the poor (including those to food, drink, clothing, and shelter) are of imperfect obligation. They are pleas or requests directed to the good nature, the kindness, the compassion, the charity of those who find themselves in more fortunate circumstances. Thus it does not follow that *this* community, where these poor persons happen to be located, has the obligation to provide them their needs. Nor does it follow that the poor have a special claim upon the members of that community, or that they have a special moral obligation to fill those needs, just because the poor happen to be among *them.* Any community that recognized such a claim would undoubtedly be inundated by poverty-stricken persons. The end would be the impoverishment of the generous citizens of that community and the termination, for lack of resources, of the benefits they might otherwise have extended to the poor among them.

In any event, although one might want to argue that the members of a community in which poor persons happen to be located (whether those impoverished individuals are long-term residents or newly arrived migrants) are morally obliged to assist their less fortunate neighbors by providing them the necessities of life, there is no moral imperative that lays upon anyone in that community or upon the collective whole the duty to make such provisions, when making them would entail sacrificing goods or amenities for which they have worked. Why should *these* individuals or *this* community be saddled with the burden of providing for these impoverished individuals? If such an obligation exists at all, it surely cannot be acquired by mere physical proximity. If a poor person comes uninvited to my door asking for (or demanding) shelter, what moral principle lays the duty of fulfilling his demand upon me rather than upon my neighbor or someone who lives a thousand miles away—or, for that matter, upon the government of China? And if, instead of visiting my home, he visits my city's park, a bus station, or a boxcar and claims the right to camp there on the ground that he will otherwise be denied his fundamental human right to shelter and a place to lay his head, what moral principle obliges the city, the bus company, or the railroad company to allow him to do so? It is evident that they are under no greater obligation to permit him to camp on their grounds than I am to permit him to pitch his tent in my front yard.

Nor is there any moral principle that imposes upon anyone—private individual or public corporation—the duty to permit beggars and panhandlers to solicit donations wherever and however they please. Some principle of charity might be invoked in favor of permitting such activities to be carried on unimpeded by legal restraints. But again, charity is strictly supererogatory. It can scarcely be raised to the status of a constitutional right. In the meantime, beggars disrupt traffic on busy streets and sidewalks; they accost and annoy passersby; and they have been known to engage in trickery and fakery in order to entice open-hearted individuals to part with their money. No community is morally obliged to put up with them. In order to preserve order, for aesthetic reasons, and to expedite the flow of traffic, if for no other reasons, any community may properly prohibit panhandling within its borders.

Similarly, if an impoverished individual claims that his hunger and poverty give him some special entitlement to hunt or to fish out of season, or to hunt game that is completely off-limits to other hunters because there is an imminent possibility that an endangered species might become extinct, the state has the right to disagree, and to enforce its laws—designed, after all, for perfectly legitimate purposes, including the conservation of precious natural resources—even against the worthy poor.

VI

The mere invocation of the expression, "human right," is not sufficient to establish that any particular person is being denied anything to which he has a legitimate claim, or that any particular person or community has failed to meet his or its moral obligations. Even supererogatory duties and duties of imperfect obligation have some meaning. One might ask, then, what moral duties persons and communities have with respect to the poor. I chose *not* to address myself to that question here, where the issue is not what is owed to the poor, but what is *not* owed to them. There are ways of dealing with the problems of poverty, many of them reasonably well known and well tested. People *ought* to be kind and generous, within reasonable limits, both in their private charities and through their governmental institutions. Private institutions exist for dispensing various forms of aid to the needy. Public institutions have fulfilled many of the same functions—in some cases well, and in others not as efficiently as might be desired. Shelters have been erected for the homeless. Clothes have been provided for those who did not have clothes of their own. Food has been dispensed to the hungry. Education and other benefits have been provided for those who could not acquire them with their own resources. All of this and more are highly desirable, and those individuals and communities who have provided them are to be commended for their generosity and their sense of public service.

But none of this has anything to do with the question presently at issue: Does a community have the right to pass ordinances designed to protect communal property and institutions against uses for which they were not intended—in particular, against persons who happen to be poor and destitute? Harsh as it may sound to put it so bluntly, the answer appears to be affirmative. Those who own private property have the right to deny admission to anyone they choose to exclude from their buildings or lands, and to eject them if they trespass. Without such a right, the very notion of real property ceases to have much meaning. Property rights are valuable for a number of excellent utilitarian reasons, not the least of which is the incentive they give individuals to improve the lands they own, both for their own benefit and for the benefit of the wider community. Similarly, states and municipalities provide public facilities for their residents to enhance the quality of life within their borders. In order to guarantee the preservation and improvement of the conditions under which their citizens live, they are entitled to bar nonresidents from the enjoyment of certain amenities, and to restrict the kinds of activities in which residents and nonresidents may engage—despite the claim that some might make that they are entitled to special privileges because they are poor.

Enforcement of such regulations is best accomplished by the enactment of laws and ordinances directed against those who do not qualify as residents and who are not able to establish that they are using the facilities—including such public facilities as streets, sidewalks, and parks—in a lawful way for lawful purposes. This is precisely what the vagrancy statutes were designed to do.

Nothing I have said should be construed as suggesting that such statutes should be allowed to stand if they are worded so vaguely as to allow officials to use them to arrest anyone they choose. Nor do I intend to support the use of vagrancy laws as devices to empower the authorities to punish or banish anyone they find offensive, or as means to evade the requirements of due process. But such laws have legitimate uses. They may properly be employed to protect communities from invasion by outsiders intent on exploiting public facilities for purposes that go beyond those for which they were originally intended. And they are suitable devices for protecting citizens against forms of behavior that amount to public nuisances.

The persons most likely to be affected by vagrancy laws are those who are unfortunate enough to be poor. The laws themselves, however, need not make poverty itself a crime. They may facilitate a legitimate governmental objective. The fact that that objective can be met only by depriving some poor persons of privileges they might like to exercise does not render those objectives or the means employed to meet them illegitimate. Poverty is not in itself an entitlement. Don't poor, destitute persons have a right to a place to lay their heads? Surely one cannot argue that they have no moral right to such an elementary requirement of survival! In the same way, they have the right to air to breathe and water to drink and food to eat.

Even if we grant this proposition, it does not follow that *this* community, where these poor persons happen to be located, has the obligation to provide them their needs, or that the poor have a special claim upon the people of that community, who have a special moral obligation to fill those needs, just because the poor happen to be among *them.* Any community that recognized such a claim would undoubtedly be inundated by poverty-stricken persons. The end would be the impoverishment of the generous citizens of that community and the termination of the benefits they would extend to the poor among them for lack of resources.

Notes

1. *Papachristou* v. *City of Jacksonville*, 405 U.S. 156, 92 S. Ct. 839, 31 L.Ed.2d 110 (1972).

2. See Lacey, "Vagrancy and Other Crimes of Personal Condition," *Harvard Law Review* 66 ( ): 1203 at 1206.

3. 314 U.S. 150, p. 174.

4. See Lacey.

5. Ibid.

6. 1 Edw. 6, c. 3 (1547).

7. 2 Hen. 5, c. 4 (1414).

8. Articles of Confederation, Article IV.

9. *City of New York* v. *Miln*, 36 U.S. (11 Pet.) 102, 143 (1837).

10. 314 U.S. 160 (1941).

11. See Note, "Depression Migrants and the States," *Harvard Law Review* 53 (1940): 1031.

12. See Harring, "Class Conflict and the Suppression of Tramps in Buffalo, 1892-1894," *Law and Society* 11 (1977): p. 876.

13. Cited in Harring, "Class Conflict."

14. *Buffalo Express*, 13 September 1893, cited in Harring, "Class Conflict," p. 877.

15. Harring, "Class Conflict," p. 877.

16. Ibid, p. 879.

17. Ibid, p. 881.

18. 314 U.S. 160 (191), p. 177.

19. Harring, "Class Conflict," *passim.*

20. Ibid.

21. Lacey, "Vagrancy," p. 1207, n. 17, and 1208.

22. Ibid, p. 1209.

23. *People* v. *Allinqton*, 103 Cal. App. 2d 495 (1951).

24. "Vagrancy and Arrest on Suspicion," *Yale Law Journal* 70 1 (1960): 4.

25. 405 U.S. at 153.

26. Ibid, at 171.

27. *Hardie* v. *State*, 333 So.2d 13 (Fla. 1976); *Gordon* v. *State*, 353 So.2d 63g (Fla. App. 1977).

28. *City of Des Moines* v. *Lavigne*, 257 N.W.2d 485 (Iowa, 1977); *State ex rel. Williams* v. *City Court of Tucson*, 21 Ariz. App. 489, 520 P.2d 1166 (1974); *People* v. *Wedlow*, 17 Mich. App. 134, 169 N.W.2d 145 (1969); *People* v. *Taggart*, 66 Misc. 2d 344, 320 N.Y.S.2d 671 (1971); *People* v. *Strauss*, 66 Misc. 2d 268, 320 N.Y.S.2d 628 (1971); *In re Cregler*, 14 Cal. Rptr. 28g, 363 P.2d 305 (1961); *People* v. *Berck*, 32 N.Y.2d 567, 347 N.Y.S.2d 33, 300 N.E.2d 411 (1973), cert. denied, 414 U.S. 1093; *State* v. *Ecker*, 311 So.2d 104 (1975); *People* v. *Solomon*, 33 Cal. App.3d 42g, 108 Cal. Rptr. 867, cert. denied 415 U.S. 951 (1974); *Camarco* v. *City of Orange*, 61 N.J. 463, 295 A.2d 353 (1972); *People of Detroit* v. *Ritchey*, 25 Mich. App. 98, 181 N.E.2d 87 (1970); *State* v. *Jones*, 9 Wash. App. 1, 511 P.2d 74 (1979); *Seattle* v. *Franklin*, 191 Wash. 297, 70 P.2d 1049 (1937); *State* v. *Finrow*, 66 Wash. 2d 818, 405 P.2d 600 (1965); *State* v. *Levin*, 67 Wash. 2d 988, 410 P.2d 901 (1966); *Government of the Canal Zone* v. *Castillo*, 568 F.2d 405 (5th Cir. 1978); *Ellis* v. *Dyson*, 421 U.S. 426 (1975); *Dinitz* v. *Christensen*, 577 P.2d 873 (Nevada, 1978); *State* v. *Maloney*, 78 Wash. 2d 922, 481 P.2d 1 (1971).

29. *Cregler, supra*, p. 306.

30. *Berck, supra*, pp. 416-17.

31. 385 U.S. 39, 47-48 (1966).

32. *Cox* v. *Louisiana*, 379 U.S. 557, 578 (1965).

160 HUMAN NEEDS

Bibliography

Bahr, Howard M. *Skid Row: An Introduction to Disaffilation.* New York: Oxford University Press, 1973.

Baxter, Ellen, and Kim Hopper. *Private Lives/Public Spaces: Homeless Adults on the Streets of New York.* New York: Community Service Society of New York, 1981.

Dubin, Gary V., and Richard H. Robinson. Note: "The Vagrancy Concept Reconsidered—Problems and Abuses of Status Criminality." *New York University Law Review* 37 (1962): 102-36.

Foote, Caleb. "Vagrancy-Type Law and Its Administration." *University of Pennsylvania Law Review* 104 (1956): 603-50.

Harring, Sydney L. "Class Conflict and the Suppression of Tramps in Buffalo, 1892-1894." *Law and Society Review* 11 (1977): 873-911.

Malone, Mark. "Homelessness in a Modern Urban Setting." *Fordham Urban Law Journal* 10 (1982): 749-81.

McSheey, William R. *Skid Row.* Boston: University Books, 1979.

Papachristou v. *Jacksonville.* 405 U.S. 156, 92 S.Ct. 839 (1972).

Perkins, Rollin M. "The Vagrancy Concept." *Hastings Law Journal* 9 (1958): 237-61.

Sherry, Arthur H. "Vagrants, Rogues, and Vagabonds: Old Concepts in Need of Revision." *California Law Review* 48 (1956): 603-50.

13
Poverty and Welfare
In Rawls's Theory of Justice:
On the Just Response to Needs

Rex Martin
Department of Philosophy
University of Kansas

The present paper addresses the issue of distributive shares (received by individuals) by considering the special case of those unable to work, for reasons of age or physical or mental disability. It might seem that such persons are provided for under the Rawlsian difference principle. For that principle stipulates that inequalities, i.e., greater than average returns in income (or greater wealth or special offices) are justified in a given system only if they (1) encourage contributions that (2) result in increased productivity in goods and services; and only if the resultant increase in goods and services is distributed so as (3) continually to improve—ideally, to maximize—the life situation, as measured in income and wealth, of the least advantaged group. But it is by no means clear that this principle can justify benefits to those unable to work if it is interpreted as a covering, perhaps as covering only, those who work. This paper, then, concerns the just response to the needs of those unable to work in a Rawlsian well-ordered society.

The Problem of Needs

The difference principle does not operate alone: It is coordinated with two other considerations of justice: that all individuals have equal basic liberties and have fair equality of opportunity. These points together (and in the right order) make up what Rawls calls the principles of justice.[1] Insofar as individuals can be said to *need* justice—and in a well-ordered society they will need it in order to assure social cooperation along lines of fair and public principles of interaction—then that need is addressed by the two principles. More specifically, individuals need certain goods as a means to or as a part of the actual way of life of each person. People *need* liberties—that is, basic liberties such as liberty of conscience or avoidances of injury such as freedom from torture—just as they need opportunities, positions, capacities and tasks, income and wealth, and withall the bases of self-respect. Such social primary goods, as Rawls calls them, are the primary needs.[2] And the principles of justice address each of these needs in turn. It is the province of the difference principle (once we assume satisfaction of equal basic liberties and fair equality of opportunity) to be concerned with offices (that is, positions and responsibilities) and with attendant income and wealth.

If we simplify this picture somewhat by considering offices or jobs as important because of the income they yield (and this is a valid perspective to take, so long as it is admitted that jobs have other functions as well), then we can say that the difference principle is concerned specifically with the distribution of income and wealth. By income and wealth we intend those "all-purpose means" (things having an exchange value) and we understand that income or wealth can take, besides its principal form as money, the form of various in-kind services or goods.[3] And all people do need income and wealth in this sense. The need that the difference principle addresses in particular is the need for income and wealth so understood.

We often identify the needs of persons in a way different from this. We say the ignorant need to learn, the sick to be well, the blind to be able to see or, failing that, able to get about. Talk of needs in this mode can become very specific, for if a lack can be specified and it can justifiably be filled, then we can speak of a need. If a person is fevered and needs medicine, we can fill that need with aspirin (or an antibiotic) or with money to buy it.

The difference principle, by allowing for the redistribution of money and the provision of in-kind services, can speak to the needs of the poor for particular goods and services (such as medicine), where the poor are defined by the substantial lack of those very things (when measured as income and wealth). But the difference principle does not address specific needs as such; it addresses only the needs of the poor.

Under the difference principle we don't consider *what* people need specifically, but only whether they are poor enough to need income supplementation. Even where the difference principle appears to address a need specifically, by providing an in-kind service, it isn't the need per se that is addressed; instead it is the need of a poor person that is addressed. For, if a person had the same need but wasn't poor, then his need would *not* be addressed by the operation of the difference principle.

Moreover, it should be remembered that the bottom group is still the bottom group, even after redistribution. Thus each of its members will end up with less in total (in dollars or in-kind services) than typical members of the other groups. But we don't assume that the bottom group *needs* less than the others (in fact, we make the opposite assumption); therefore, it follows that need as such is not being addressed. For if it were need as such—specific, identifiable needs—we would see to it that more money went to the poor than does (under the difference principle) and that money (or in-kind services) went to others as well, so long as they had unmet needs.

Rawls says that the common-sense "precept of need is left to the transfer branch";[4] that is, to the governmental branch concerned with redistributions under the difference principle. I have interpreted Rawls's claim here as saying that the difference principle attends only to the needs of the poor for income, and only in a certain amount—specifically, in that amount required to bring the income of a given person up to a certain *level* of income, as set by the difference principle-determined income of the representative person in, say, the bottom quartile. In this way, then, the difference principle attends to the needs of the poor.

But who are the poor? The poor for Rawls are not simply those without sufficient income. Rather, the poor are normal, able-bodied persons who work, who contribute their efforts and the use of their talents toward the production of goods and services, but who do not receive a sufficiently high return in income for their efforts. They receive below-average incomes, indeed so low as to be, let us say, in the bottom quartile. Thus the difference principle addresses the need for income supplementation of those who work but have quite substandard incomes.

There are other kinds of poor people, however. There are those unwilling to work and those unable to work. Let us consider only those unable to work. The difference principle does not address the need for income supplementation (in money or in-kind services) of those *unable* to work; it addresses, rather, the need only of those who work and yet are poor.

It might appear that this problem is easily remedied. We believe that Rawls is as good-hearted and as fair-minded as the next fellow, and we are convinced that the friends of justice would be concerned with the well-being of those unable to work. So we simply interpret the difference principle to include them or put this interpretation in there explicitly. But this ignores the fact that there may be systematic pressures in Rawls's theory which require the very reading of the difference principle that we are here trying to modify.

When we first encountered the difference principle (in Chapter Two of Rawls's book), it was as the second stage of an attempt to deal with the undeserved and morally arbitrary possession by individuals, as their endowment, so to speak, of natural assets and social circumstances and thereby to mitigate the effect of this endowment on the lifelong prospects of those who were adversely affected. The argument whereby the difference principle was justified in this context was the following: Since these starting points are undeserved, and since we cannot fully overcome the differences by assuring absolute equality of opportunity, we fall back on an expedient. We regard the distribution of assets to each as a collective or common asset such that when they *use* that asset it redounds to the benefit of everyone, not simply to the possessor, but to all others as well. We don't require that the effect be equal for all, but merely that it be positive for all, so that no one is hurt by his or her initial endowment and all continue together to improve their lots in life.[5]

We conceive this argument as occurring, of course, in the original position; hence, it is an argument that would be developed by and would appeal to rational persons who, under the rather severe constraints on knowledge characteristic of the original position (behind the "veil of ignorance," in Rawls's phrase), occupy an equal status there. Thus, the idea of collective asset is one that would be agreed on in the original position, and arguments from this idea would lead ultimately to the difference principle.[6]

The difference principle, then, is justified by the collective asset idea.[7] Thus if we regard the collective asset idea as *the* argument for the difference principle, and if the difference principle partakes of the main features of the collective asset idea—as any conclusion should reflect the premisses on which it is based—then the difference principle is properly interpreted as covering within its central scope only those who work but are less fortunate.

The collective asset idea looks at individuals as having *assets*. It contemplates their using those assets and in so doing contributing to the good of each. The whole motif, then, is the contribution each can make to himself and others through the use of his talents and abilities (as mediated through the market and the various background institutions, including ownership, and ultimately the difference principle).[8] Those who receive the redistributive effects of the difference principle are, quite naturally, those who've made their contribution, by using their talents, but who have simply fared, often predictably, much less well than their fellows.

In the collective asset idea, individuals are not contemplated as having defects or extreme liabilities in their natural endowment (or in their social circumstances), as having not assets, but the privation of assets. For critical defects cannot be pooled for the well-being of all and, in fact, are disabling even to their possessors. Because some people have such defects (for example, severe mental retardation or drastically disabling lifelong illness or physical handicap), they cannot contribute to the well-being of either themselves or others. In this way they are outside the scope of the collective asset idea. Thus, those who are unable to work are excluded from this scope or are marginal to it. Their position is precarious on the margin—given, that is, the essential character of the difference principle and the chief argument for it.

There is another consideration as well. Rawls makes it clear at a number of points that the parties in the original position are to be conceived as normal adults with the full range of powers, mental and physical, of such persons. The parties—in representing the normal, adult citizen—do not have some of the defects found among actual people in an ordinary population. Hence the parties do not consider such defects as severe mental retardation or lifelong physical illness or handicap in designing the difference principle. As Rawls says pointedly, we should first construct a principle for the normal range of cases; if we cannot accomplish even this, then there's no reason for considering the special cases at all; only if we are successful in dealing with normal cases do we go on to consider special cases after that.[9] And consistent with this general view, the citizens in a well-ordered society are, all of them then, able-bodied workers, each of whom is regarded as a contributor, through his use of natural assets and the exploitation of his social circumstances, to the production of goods and services in that society. Thus a pervasive heuristic principle—the assumption of normal cases only—attends the development of Rawls's difference principle and must be taken account of in any interpretation of that principle. This heuristic procedure is wholly in accord with the collective asset idea as I have represented it.

Now, the heuristic principle is not decisive by itself. For, we presume, it would always be possible to thicken the veil of ignorance in the original position (leaving people unaware, for example, of whether they were physically normal or not) and thus allow considerations of permanent disability to filter through. Thus, we might include the permanently disabled in the definition of the least well-off group and thereby bring them within the scope of the difference principle.

It is not clear, however, what heuristic principle is to replace the one we are here being asked to discard. We need in any case to keep in mind that there must be a considerable likeness of individuals in the original position in order for an agreement to be struck about the terms of justice. It is difficult to see what likeness there could be among the parties if some were permanently unable to contribute to society. Of course, we are being asked merely to *consider* that some might be. Thus, each must be able to imagine that he or someone is permanently disabled. But people can imagine all sorts of things—that they or others are religious fanatics or scientific geniuses or Nozickean pleasure monsters or platonic dictators or what have you. A line has to be drawn, a thin one really. For the more variety that is introduced, if only in imagination, the more difficult it is to establish as reasonable a preferred theory of justice. Or, to put it differently, the more difficult it is to reach real rather than verbal agreement about binding principles of justice, principles that are going to have significant bite.

Even if the heuristic principle were to be relaxed in the way indicated, it is not likely that Rawls's idea of the mutual disinterest of the parties (in the original position) would allow for a principle of justice in which some were treated specially, in view of their incapacity. For then the distribution of primary goods would be awarded to such persons differently from the way mandated by the principles that governed the normal case. We need not assume hardness of heart here. It might seem to the parties, merely, that such matters were being gathered in under the heading of fundamental justice and that these things might, more appropriately, be dealt with at another point, in the institutional processes of the basic structure or even in another setting altogether (for example, in morality, where considerations of benevolence and charity might be more at home).

But the more significant inhibition occurs in the idea of collective asset—in the notion that people contribute, through the use of their talents and abilities, to the well-being of each and all. It comes, then, in the very notion of mutual benefit. And behind this lies the whole Rawlsian idea of the basic structure of a society as a single schema of interaction, of actions by individuals and with reciprocal effects. Thus, to solve the problem of those permanently unable to work in the way suggested, through a rewriting of the difference principle in the original position, would require a wholesale rearrangement of fundamental features of the entire decision-procedure apparatus.

We are not, accordingly, contemplating minor changes in argumentation and wording. We are not contemplating a mere tinkering with the difference principle. We are talking about far-reaching changes, from the ground up. Most particularly, a radically different master argument from that provided by the idea of collective asset would be required. And any resultant principle, on such a new and different foundation, would have a wholly different meaning and characteristic interpretation from what the difference principle currently has in Rawls's theory. For the difference principle to take on the character we are here considering it would have to become, quite literally, a different principle.

Rawls's theory of justice is a system of justice. The various pieces fit together because they are all of a piece. The main drawback, then, to making the suggested change is that it doesn't fit into the developed system. The two points we have been reviewing (the collective asset idea as the main argument for the difference principle and the heuristic procedure of considering only the case of normal, able-bodied workers) are not isolated, self-standing features in an account of justice. Instead, they have to be taken together as mutually supportive aspects of a single theory.

These two points, then, do count heavily in support of the view I have advanced that, since the difference principle governs the arrangements specifically for those who work and contribute to society through the production of goods and services, the difference principle is not set up to address the needs, even the need for income, of those *unable* to work. The revision of the difference principle in the original position having failed as a proposed remedy, what possible remedies for those unable to work might we find in Rawls's system?

The Welfare of Those Unable to Work

Many problems can be dissipated here if we consider carefully the various classes or types of those unable to work. The main types seem to be: (1) children too young to work; (2) adults beyond retirement age and considered too old to work; (3) people who are temporarily unable to work because of disability (job-related injury, illness, pregnancy);[10] (4) people who are able to work but are temporarily out of work for such reasons as seasonal unemployment or general economic recession; (5) people who are able to work but are unable to work at what they are trained to do because that skill is now obsolete or the demand for it has been radically reduced (such as, old-style linotype operators in the printing industry); and (6) people who are physically or mentally unable to work, either permanently or for very long, indeterminate stretches of time.

Each of these groups represents special problems that call for special remedies. The question is, Where in Rawls's system can we find the appropriate remedies, if at all? One thing noticeable about many of these groups is that, although each person in it is not working *now*, there is a clear sense in which members of that group—for most of their adult, working years—are full contributing members of society. Thus dependent children (and we count as such only those unable to receive adequate support from their families) cannot work now, but they will be workers during their productive adult years. By the same token, old people beyond retirement age cannot work now (we presume this), but they were workers during their productive adult years. And people temporarily disabled cannot work now but can during almost all their productive adult years be presumed to be full contributors in the work force. These groups, then, can be regarded as alike in a significant respect: All can be presumed to be full contributors during all or most of their productive adult years. Thus these groups can be regarded as constituting a single type.

Perhaps the simplest way whereby this composite group could be dealt with, within the Rawlsian system, is to devise an insurance scheme into which all workers would be required to contribute to assure funding for (a) dependent children and perhaps the parent responsible for the care and nurture of such children, (b) retired adults, and (c) people temporarily disabled. Such a scheme would not burden workers for the benefit of nonworkers but, rather, would be a social security insurance plan in which workers are taxed, so to speak, to provide benefits to workers—possibly themselves—when they were unable to work. In short, I am here regarding the provision of such funds as a public good (in the economist's sense) and providing for a standard mechanism (a compulsory payment scheme) to generate the necessary money. Rawls allows for such a provision of public goods in his discussion of a special "branch" of governmental activity, called the Exchange Branch, which would, with full knowledge of the relevant particulars, devise schemes for some public goods and provide for their funding. (It would do so in roughly the way people might pay for clean water through a public utility water company, with everybody paying for sewage and water purification regardless of how much water they use.)

Rawls regards the provision of public goods through this branch as a matter of efficiency rather than justice. Nonetheless, his system does have a place for such a mechanism within the background institutions that superintend and supplement the operations of the market. The only change that my analysis has introduced into the account that Rawls actually gives is that my analysis explicitly identifies social security insurance as a public good; and my analysis would not, incidentally, require that decisions about public goods—even within the Exchange Branch—be made only unanimously by a special representative body of the citizens, as Rawls requires, but instead leaves the decision to the normal legislative channels.[11]

I have, of course, emphasized the proviso that every worker is required to pay and therefore does pay into the master social security fund from which the individual disbursements are made. Thus children pay into the fund once they're grown, and old people, now retired, paid into it when they were working, and so on. The stipulation that everyone is required to pay is a leading feature of the provision of public goods. In the case at hand, the insurance fund is constituted by contributions made by workers during their productive adult years. Workers are paying for something *they* want (that is, social security insurance when they are unable to work).

The case of people who are technologically unemployed is not so easily handled under the social security (or public goods) principle. Such people are not literally *unable* to work; it is simply that they cannot work at what they were trained to do. Their problem is not to find work, but to find work at roughly the skill and income level they previously occupied—or at least to find it at a higher skill and income level than is currently available to them. It is not clear that workers would be willing to pay into a funding scheme specifically designed to provide unemployment benefits (in particular, long-term benefits) for this group. And if people are not willing to pay into such a scheme, let alone willing to see everybody *coerced* to pay in, then we are really out of the province of public goods altogether. Or, to put this point somewhat differently, it seems that the rationale required to cover persons in the technologically unemployed group is significantly different from the one earlier advanced, which concerned the sheer *inability* of people to work. Benefits for this group seem to open up a quite different set of issues from what was posed by social security insurance for those unable to work.

This can be brought out more clearly when we consider that there are actually two quite distinct problems for the technologically unemployed person: (1) the unemployment itself and (2) the cause of that unemployment, that is, the obsolescence of existing skills and the lack of suitable new ones. Now, it would make sense to deal with the fact of unemployment per se through an insurance scheme, but such a remedy, if taken as the *only* one, is unsuited to the problem as a whole and would very likely be resisted. Thus, I am not arguing that society would not cover the technologically unemployed under an insurance scheme, but, rather, that it would probably make something other than insurance funds and unemployment payments its main line of remedy for technological (or "structural") unemployment.

There is a significant ground of remedy for the technologically unemployed remaining in Rawls's theory. We can fall back on the theory of full employment. On the grounds that useful employment is here contemplated and that special job training is sometimes required to provide the opportunity for useful employment, a well-ordered society might be willing to set up, by legislative action, publicly funded job training programs.

Let us consider how the theory of full employment motivates such a solution. If a market system is to be just, constant readjustments by means of so-called background or nonmarket institutions are required in order (a) to supplement market distributions with difference principle-generated redistributions for the least well-off group, even under conditions of perfect competition, and (b) to provide compensations to the

least well off, again under the difference principle rubric, for market im-
perfections that are conceived as putting them at a competitive disadvantage and as further contributing to their disadvantaged status and to the
lowering of their income levels. In case (b) the compensation need not
take the form merely of income supplementation. Rather, part of this
compensation could be provided by full-employment policies
(presumably of the standard Keynesian or fiscal sort).

The maintenance of full employment by governmental policy and
action is conceived here as another governmental device for providing fair
equality of opportunity, which in turn is a *precondition* of a market's being
a fair procedure and, then, of market results being fair results. Thus, on
this reading, even a "perfect" market would not be a fair procedure unless
the full employment condition was met. (We assume, however, that the
condition is met naturally or automatically in a "perfect" market, since a
perfect market is an efficient one.) But in an imperfect market (which is
the normal case, in Rawls's view), we need to assume a governmental full
employment policy and *activity* as a standing background feature designed
to provide fair equality of opportunity and, concurrently, as affording a
form of compensation to the least well off, on the added ground that results in an imperfect market are not *fair* results. And just as the imperfect
market cannot deliver fair results it cannot deliver efficient ones either. A
full employment policy, then, augments efficiency in an *imperfect* market
by providing for the full use of at least one important resource—human
effort.[12]

Clearly, full employment as a necessary precondition of market fairness
and as contributing to the full use of existing resources is an idea that, insofar as it suggests that everyone work, is consistent with Rawls's earlier
use of the notion of collective asset and of his heuristic principle of considering only the normal, able-bodied adult contributor in his argument for
the difference principle. Rawls's commitment to the idea that the well-
ordered society is a society of contributors, of persons who do contribute
to the well-being of one another, requires a parallel commitment to full
employment. No doubt Rawls also believes that gainful or useful employment helps support the bases of self-respect, in that persons have need to
think of themselves as solid contributors to the on-going life of their
society.[13]

Now, let us fit these various parts of our analysis together. The ultimate
rationale of most job retraining programs is economic efficiency—the
rationale that a market system is efficient only when all available
resources are being used at their capacity. Job retraining, then, could be
viewed as the shifting of a complex resource from one use, where it is no
longer needed (because of the obsolescence of the relevant skill), to a
new one where it can be productively employed. (And we presume such
shifting can be done intelligently.) A program of job retraining on this
basis is not, as such, an issue of fairness; a question of fairness (as given in
the notion of fair equality of opportunity) arises only if the individual was
seriously disadvantaged in terms of natural endowment or of initial social

circumstances or was, presumably as a result of those factors, in the lowest income group. The rationale of fairness, then, could cover almost all primary job training (such as, for disadvantaged youth) and some, but not all, *re*training. Nonetheless, a powerful rationale for such retraining is provided by the tie-in between full employment and economic efficiency. Accordingly, a society organized on Rawlsian principles could make legislative provision for publicly funded job training programs (including programs to replace obsolescent skills).

By the same token a society could, in a time of general economic recession, constitute the government as the employer of last resort, thereby creating a corps of people who could perform useful work on public projects at public expense. Thus deep-seated and prolonged unemployment might be dealt with by using both of the remedies identified: an insurance scheme for unemployment payments (under the public goods principle) and a publicly funded job training or work corps program (under the principle of full employment/efficient use of resources).[14]

The matter here is complex for two reasons. First, some of the cases under investigation come under more than one rationale and thus can be handled by more than one of the available strategies. Second, the complexity here reflects in turn the fact that there are different ways or senses in which people can be said to be unable to work. Those who are unable to work by reason of economic recession or of technological unemployment are, strictly speaking, *able* to work; it's simply that there are not enough jobs or that the ones available are not of the right sort. Thus a job training or work corps program (in addition to income supplementation) would make sense for persons in this group.

Now, since we have this variety of rationales and strategies and this complexity in the notion of inability to work, it might be useful to moderate our original argument somewhat. For it could be contended that the difference principle is intended to range over the whole lives of people (over the lifetime expectations of representative persons). Thus, we ought to be able to accommodate the normal incidents of life—old age, illness and injury during working years, and childhood dependence—under it. For these are simply stages that representative working persons go through, or can be expected to. Let us grant this. Accordingly, we acknowledge that the difference principle could probably be designed to cover *some* of those unable to work (specifically, the first three classes mentioned at the beginning of section two); thus, that principle would thereby authorize the appropriate legislative policies for them (including, most likely, a social security insurance fund). However, it is not likely that the difference principle would also cover satisfactorily those unable to work for reasons of technological unemployment or severe recession. For these reasons do not identify incidents in the normal life of persons who work but, rather, incidents of a sophisticated technology for the production of goods and services and incidents of a market economy (especially where the ownership of productive property is in private hands). Or, if the principle did cover them, we assume that more than income maintenance would be involved and that some program of job retraining would be instituted, on independent grounds, as well.

But this leaves one important class as yet uncovered. For, even where we allow the difference principle to cover some or even many of those unable to work, we are still left facing the problem of those *permanently* unable to work (for reasons of severe retardation or of critically disabling illness or physical handicap). The problem here is peculiarly difficult in that neither of the suggested remedies would fit this case.

A social insurance scheme could not apply, for it requires that workers pay into an insurance fund to cover certain foreseeable circumstances; but it is logically impossible that workers could be *permanently* unable to work. Hence, this particular circumstance could not come under such a scheme. (Recall that the provision of public goods, under a coercive, inclusive program of payments by everyone, operates under conditions of full knowledge of particular facts, unlike the case of choosing first principles of justice, which takes place behind a thick veil of ignorance.)

Nor would considerations of full employment policy under either of its guises (as economic efficiency or as fair equality of opportunity) have any weight in the case of those permanently unable to work. For either rationale presupposes ability to work and, hence, is strictly inapplicable in the case at hand. Providing employment opportunities for persons in this group (persons who are completely and permanently unable to perform socially useful work) would be meaningless.

Several possible remedies are present, however, in Rawls's system and I will mention them briefly. We turn, first, to the Rawlsian natural duty of mutual aid.[15] This duty of justice is incumbent on all individuals and requires that they come to the aid of any individual who is in severe difficulty or peril. It is not clear whether this duty assumes reciprocation; for if it did then those permanently unable to work would probably, for the same reason that made them unable to work, be unable to reciprocate the duty. In any event, natural duties hold only between individuals; they are, in this sense, personal duties, that is, duties of persons as individuals. If, however, we are looking for a basic structure or society-wide institutional solution to the problem of dealing with those permanently unable to work, then the doctrine of natural duties would do us no good. For we could not use any such duty to justify legislative policy or coercive governmental activity.

It has been suggested, second, that we turn to Rawls's discussion of paternalism for the outlines of the solution we seek.[16] Rawls introduces his discussion of paternalism with the observation that, in some cases, "we must choose for others as we have reason to believe they would choose for themselves if they were at the age of reason and deciding rationally." As the name implies the theory of paternalism largely concerns the protection of the interests of children by parents, trustees, guardians, and assorted benefactors. Hence, it concerns a condition that is not permanent, that one can grow out of. But Rawls also applies it specifically to those who, "through some misfortune or accident [, are] unable to make decisions for their good, as in the case of those seriously injured or mentally disturbed." Thus, it would cover victims of accident or injury (insofar as they were unconscious) and as well persons who suffered mental disorder (insofar as they were rendered irrational, or nonfunctional).[17]

Even so, we must recognize that this principle, suitably construed, covers only a fraction of those in the class of persons permanently unable to work. We might grant that it covers the severely retarded—though I am uncomfortable with treating an extremely low degree of intellectual capacity as equivalent to irrationality (or even to inability to function). It does not, however, cover the large class of lifelong victims of physical injury or debilitating sickness or handicap who are, at the same time, conscious and able to reason. It is simply presumptuous to treat such persons as if they were children or mentally ill or severely retarded. We cannot presume, then, to act in their interest nor can we confidently predict what their judgments about their own interests will be (as the tragic Bouvia case, in California, shows).[18] Rawls is, of course, guilty of no such presumption. And we are in no position to use the principle of paternalism as a general solution in a well-ordered society to the problem of those permanently unable to work.

We reach, then, the conclusion that the difference principle as formulated in the original position does not cover the class of such persons (as I argued in section one), that the institutional mechanisms of a well-ordered society are not constructed to include them, and that principles of mutual aid and of paternalism are unsuited as well to deal with them. In sum, we have reached an impasse in which the deep moral judgment that society should provide for those permanently unable to work runs afoul of guidelines given in the developed theory of justice. For the guidelines fail to cover, and hence mandate no solution for, a problem which conventional morality demands to be solved, and solved in the right way.

Accordingly, we need to seek out an effective remedy in Rawls's system if we are to deal with the case of those permanently unable to work. And this is a task best left to another day.[19] I mention it now merely to suggest that, contrary to initial appearances, the provision of welfare for persons in this group is, on Rawlsian principles, no straightforward or easy matter. Indeed, I would say that it constitutes a relatively intractable problem for Rawls's theory.[20]

Notes

1. See Rawls, *Theory of Justice*, 60, 83, 250, and especially 302-303 for his various statements of these principles of justice and their proper order. Full references to all things cited in these notes is given in a select bibliography at the end of the paper.

2. "The theory of primary goods is an extension of the notion of needs, which are distinct from aspirations and desires. One might say, then, that as citizens the members of a well-

ordered society collectively take responsibility for dealing justly with one another founded on a public and objective measure of (extended) needs, while as individuals and members of associations they take responsibility for their preferences and devotions" (Rawls, "Kantian Conception of Equality," 204). See also Rawls, "Reply to Alexander and Musgrave," 643, "Basic Structure," 67, "Fairness to Goodness," 554, "Kantian Constructivism," 546, 550, "Basic Liberties," 40, and "Social Unity and Primary Goods," 172-73, 183.

3. The primary characterization of income and wealth as "all-purpose means (having an exchange value)" is from Rawls, "Basic Liberties," 23. See also "Social Unity and Primary Goods," 166. The idea of including in-kind goods and services as a part of income and wealth is a notion I have added.

4. *Theory of Justice*, 309. For Rawls's discussion of the transfer branch, see *Theory of Justice*, 276-77.

5. The idea, then, is to regard "the distribution of natural abilities as a collective asset" (Rawls, *Theory of Justice*, 179). See also Rawls, "Distributive Justice," 68, *Theory of Justice*, 72-74, 101-4, 523, and "Kantian Constructivism in Moral Theory," 551.

6. The principal subject of justice is the basic structure of a society; that is, the arrangement of major social institutions with regard to the way these institutions determine the division of advantages from social cooperation and, in particular, with regard to the distribution of social primary goods.

> For simplicity, [Rawls says, let us] assume that the chief primary goods at the disposition of society are . . . liberties, powers and opportunities, income and wealth. [Later on, he adds the bases of self-respect.] These [Rawls continues] are the social primary goods. Other primary goods such as health and vigor, intelligence and imagination, are natural goods; although their possession is influenced by the basic structure [of society] they are not so directly under its control (*Theory of Justice*, 303).

The Rawlsian problem of justice is to determine a basic structure that leads to a proper or just distribution of *social* primary goods. To do this we need a fair procedure to determine the principles involved, for there are no antecedent or independent standards for such a distribution.

Accordingly, we create a hypothetical bargaining situation (called "the original position" by Rawls) in which certain significant constraints operate: these constraints include those required to discount or bracket off all special, peculiarly personal, or circumstantial fact and biases; those constraints embedded in objective circumstances (such as relative scarcity) or in our psychological orientation (such as mutual disinterest in one another's life plans); and as well a number of other presumed constraints—such as that the principles agreed to are to be public, that they constitute the ultimate or foundational standard, that the principles are to be chosen once and for all, that they are to be chosen unanimously, and so on. (Rawls's own summary is given in *Theory of Justice*, 146-47; see also pp. 126-27, 137.) Then, whatever principles emerge from the original position, they are the preferred principles of justice for the organization of the basic structure of society.

7. See Rawls, "Reply to Alexander and Musgrave," 647-48; see also Rawls, "Distributive Justice: Some Addenda," 59, 67, 71. It is the argument from collective asset that Rawls calls the "compelling" one for the difference principle (see "Some Reasons for the Maximin Criterion," 144-45). For elaboration of the basic contention in the text, see Martin, *Rawls and Rights*, especially chaps. 4 and 5.

8. For an elaboration of the Rawlsian theory of the market, see my article "Rawlsian Economic Justice and the Proper Bounds of Government Regulation," especially sec. 2. (And see sec. 4 of that paper for a discussion of Rawls's position on the ownership of productive property.)

9. Rawls says that his theory, in the original position, starts from "the conception of persons as capable of being normal and fully cooperating members of society . . . over a complete life" ("Basic Liberties," 52; see also pp. 15, 48). Since he assumes normal capacities, Rawls says that he will not consider "special health and medical needs" ("Social Unity and Primary Goods," 168, including n. 8, and 178n). See also Rawls, "Reply to Alexander and Musgrave," 640; "Some Reasons for the Maximin Criterion," 142; "Basic Structure," 57, 70, n. 9; and "Kantian Constructivism," 546).

10. It is, of course, possible that in a well-ordered society pregnancy (and the at-home nurture of very young children by their parents) or the various forms of rehabilitation (including self-rehabilitation) following disabling sickness or injury could be regarded as productive work and be remunerated (though not through market processes). Even so, it is unlikely that people while sick or injured can engage in socially useful work; accordingly, there will probably always be *some* people in this category in a well-ordered society.

11. For Rawls's discussion of the exchange branch, see *Theory of Justice*, 282-84. Rawls says there that the principles of this branch are those of efficiency and general benefit rather than of justice.

I should add that, although Rawls conceives some public goods (e.g., national parks) as coming under this branch, it is unlikely that he would bring them all under it. (For example, national defense would probably not be handled by the exchange branch.) Thus, some public goods are conceived by him as falling, from the beginning, within the province of the legislature (rather than the exchange branch). And it is likely that social security would be of this nature for Rawls. It is likely, too, that the legislature would enact some sort of insurance scheme of the sort I've described. But no fundamental change in my basic argument would be required if these last two points were granted.

12. Over and beyond the exchange branch (mentioned in the previous note), Rawls refers to four basic "branches" or goals of governmental economic policy and activity (*Theory of Justice*, sec. 43). He says, "The stabilization branch . . . strives to bring about reasonably full employment in the sense that those who want work can find it and the free choice of occupation and the deployment of finance are supported by strong effective demand" (*Theory of Justice*, 276). The two main objects of a full employment policy, as mediated through the Rawlsian notion of pure procedural justice (see *Theory of Justice*, 85-87, 89, 274-75, 310), are (a) fair equality of opportunity (see p. 87) and (b) efficiency (see pp. 87, 276).

13. See Rawls, *Theory of Justice*, 303 and sec. 67; also Rawls, "Basic Liberties," 32-34, 52, 85.

14. I realize that full employment, as that idea is conceived in political economy, is compatible with the fact that *some* are unable to work. For full employment is defined by reference to those who are able and willing to work. Moreover, the legislative definition of full employment (in the United States and Britain, at least) allows a margin of some actual unemployment (for it never sets the full employment target amount at exactly 100 percent of those able and willing to work). My use of the notion of full employment has assumed these two definitional constraints throughout; moreover, it is important to recognize that what is contemplated under the heading of full employment is, not make-work, but socially *useful* work. (On this last point, see Rawls, *Theory of Justice*, 290.)

15. The Rawlsian duty of mutual aid is discussed in *Theory of Justice*, secs. 19 and 51 (see especially pp. 338-339).

16. For Rawls's discussion of paternalism, see *Theory of Justice*, sect. 39 (especially pp. 248-250); also pp. 209, 510.

17. For the matter quoted above, see Rawls, *Theory of Justice*, 209 and 249 respectively. Elsewhere Rawls adds, "But those more or less permanently deprived of moral personality may present a difficulty. I cannot examine this problem here..." (*Theory of Justice*, 510). This passage suggests to me that those permanently comatose probably are not intended to be covered by Rawls's principle of paternalism.

18. Elizabeth Bouvia, stricken with cerebral palsy since birth 26 years ago, suffering severe pains from arthritis, confined to a wheelchair and almost wholly dependent on others for care and feeding, has despaired of this lifelong dependency and requested that officials at the Riverside General Hospital desist from force-feeding her and allow her to die. Her lawyer, who is also a medical doctor, has said both that he thinks she is making the wrong decision but that, as regards the control of her own medical treatment, it is her decision to make.

19. See Martin, *Rawls and Rights*, chap. 9, sec. 2, where an attempt at solving this problem is developed using the notion of reflective equilibrium.

20. I want to thank, for helpful comments and suggestions on this section and the previous one, Richard De George, Susan Daniel, Robert Hall, Dan Hausman, Diana Meyers, Jim Nickel, John Rawls, and Alan Fuchs (who suggested, among other things, the turn to paternalism as a possible solution).

Bibliography

Martin, Rex. *Rawls and Rights*. Lawrence: University Press of Kansas, 1985.

———. "Rawlsian Economic Justice and the Proper Bounds of Government Regulation." In *Ethical Issues in Government*, N. Bowie, ed., pp. 114-32. Philadelphia: Temple University Press, 1981.

Rawls, John. "The Basic Liberties and Their Priority." In *The Tanner Lectures on Human Values*, S. M. McMurrin, ed., vol. III, pp. 3-87. Salt Lake City: University of Utah Press, 1982.

———. "The Basic Structure as Subject." *American Philosophical Quarterly* 14 (1977): 159-65.

———. "The Basic Structure as Subject." In *Values and Morals*, Alvin I. Goldman and J. Kim, eds., pp. 47-71. Dordrecht, Holland: Reidel, 1978. (This essay is a considerable revision of the previous entry; selections II and III are new. All my references are to the present entry.)

———. "Distributive Justice." In *Philosophy, Politics and Society*, P. Laslett and W. G. Runciman, eds., 3d series, pp. 58-82. Oxford: B. Blackwell, 1967.

———. "Distributive Justice." In *Economic Justice*, E. S. Phelps, ed., pp. 319-62. Baltimore: Penguin, 1973. (This entry includes all of the previous entry as sections 1-4 and 11-14 and most of the next entry as sections 5-10.)

———. "Distributive Justice: Some Addenda." *Natural Law Forum* 13 (1968): 51-71.

———. "Fairness to Goodness." *Philosophical Review* 84 (1975): 536-54.

———. "A Kantian Conception of Equality." In *Property, Profits, and Economic Justice*, Virginia Held, ed., pp. 198-208. Belmont, Calif.: Wadsworth, 1980. (This essay is reprinted, slightly revised, from an essay of the same name in *Cambridge Review* [February 1975], pp. 94-99; it has also been reprinted under the title "A Well-Ordered Society." In *Philosophy, Politics and Society*, Peter Laslett and James Fishkin, eds., 5th series, pp. 6-20. New Haven: Yale University Press, 1979.)

———. "Kantian Constructivism in Moral Theory." *Journal of Philosophy* 77 (1980): 515-72. (Published version of three lectures given as the John Dewey Lectures, at Columbia University, 14-16 April 1980.)

———. "Reply to Alexander and Musgrave." *Quarterly Journal of Economics* 88 (1974): 633-55.

———. "Social Unity and Primary Goods." In *Utilitarianism and Beyond*, A. Sen and B. Williams, eds., pp. 159-85. Cambridge: Cambridge University Press, 1982.

———. "Some Reasons for the Maximin Criterion." *American Economic Review* 64 (1974): 141-46.

———. *A Theory of Justice*. Cambridge, Mass.: Harvard University Press, Belknap Press, 1971.

Shenoy, Prakash P., and Rex Martin. "Two Interpretations of the Difference Principle in Rawls's Theory of Justice." *Theoria* 49, (1983): (This article is the source for note 6 above.)

14

Economic Inequality: Justice and Incentives

Alistair M. Macleod
Department of Philosophy
Queen's University, Ontario

Schemes that are designed to provide people with economic incentives, whether for the purpose of increasing productivity in the workplace, for example, or (somewhat differently) for the purpose of encouraging investment, typically contribute to economic inequality in society. This is partly because the potential beneficiaries of such schemes generally belong to (often quite small) subclasses of the community and partly because the members of these subclasses will in any case not benefit to the same extent by what they do in response to the offered inducements. The question I want to discuss is whether incentive-providing economic differences can be justified on grounds of justice. Since the assumption is sometimes made that *economic* inequalities—including those associated with the provision of incentives—need occasion no concern from the standpoint of justice, my first task is to try to show that the project of differentiating sharply between economic and noneconomic versions of the ideal of equality is bound to fail.

After a brief exploration of certain common but confused attitudes toward economic inequality, I argue that there is a presumption on fairness grounds in favor of equality in the distribution of economic resources, both because the most persuasive argument for the view that the members of a just society must be assured of equality in legal, political, educational, and employment contexts can be invoked in condemnation of certain common forms of economic inequality, and because it is impossible in any case to provide effective protection for these ostensibly noneconomic equalities without endorsing measures to reduce economic inequality. I will consider the question whether there are broader *rational* grounds too for this presumption in favor of equal distribution of economic resources. Finally, I take up the question whether incentive-providing economic differences can be justified on grounds of justice. I review several commonly touted ways of trying to bring incentive schemes under the 'umbrella' of a theory of distributive justice and conclude that this is a forlorn hope, since it is only *per accidens* that just economic inequalities will coincide with incentive-providing inequalities.

I

I begin with the fact of economic inequality, inequality within and be-tween societies. By economic inequality I understand not only inequality in income or in wealth but also inequality in ease of access to, and in op-portunity for enjoyment of, a wide range of goods and services in both the public and private sectors. In short, I have in mind all those differences among people that show up as differences in their standard of living. It is, of course, a complicated technical question how precisely 'economic ine-quality' is to be defined and how thereafter it is to be measured—if 'measurement' is not too ominously quantitative an expression. For pre-sent purposes, however, these complications do not matter, provided it can be taken for granted both that there is a broadly shared understanding of the kinds of differences among people which go to constitute economic inequality in the sense indicated, and that there is a great deal of economic inequality of this sort both within particular societies (including the most affluent) and between societies.

Is the fact of economic inequality, especially in its more dramatic forms, a disturbing fact? should the fact that some people are well off and others not so well off and yet others are hardly able to eke out a precarious exis-tence occasion concern?

Before identifying a number of distinct grounds, prudential and moral, for an affirmative answer to this question, let me describe briefly three occasionally heard responses on the other side. First, there are people who seem to suppose that economic inequality need not concern us much or at all in practice because by and large we cannot do much about it. The New Testament prediction "The poor ye shall always have with you" has been a perennial source of comfort and reassurance to the rich, offsetting to some extent the unease generated by the pronouncement that "it is easier for a camel to go through the eye of a needle than for a rich man to enter the kingdom of heaven." According to views of this sort, measures to help the poor are bound to be unavailing in the long run, unavailing "because . . ."—with some story supplied after the "because" purporting to show why economic inequality of the sort(s) often thought to be moral-ly troublesome cannot be eliminated in any permanent way.

It is tempting to respond to such defeatist explanations by pointing out that since successful attempts to reduce economic inequality in its more problematic forms have in fact been made, any explanatory story accord-ing to which it is impossible to reduce economic inequality in significant and permanent ways must, on that score alone, be rejected out of hand.

A second argument for the view that economic inequality ought not to occasion serious concern is that the poor are themselves to blame for their poverty and that consequently those who could help them are under no obligation to do so. The obvious rejoinders are two: (1) that no informed explanation of the major differences in standards of living that exist can trace these differences to the laziness or shiftlessness of the poor; and (2) that in any case there may well be an obligation, both prudential and moral, to assist even the so-called "undeserving" poor.

A third reason sometimes heard for not adopting practical measures to reduce economic inequality is that those who are well placed to underwrite such measures are generally not personally responsible for the plight of the poor and therefore have no obligation to enlist as foot soldiers in the war against poverty. Whereas the second argument places responsibility for poverty on the shoulders of the poor, according to this third argument, if the poor are not to blame for their plight, neither are the rich. The short answer to this argument is that even if the rich are not to blame (even indirectly) for the poverty of the poor, they may well have an obligation, both prudential and moral, to play their part in efforts, individual and collective, to diminish economic inequality. By no means all the obligations generated by the fact of injustice in society are obligations that fall upon those who can be reliably identified as having perpetrated the injustices in question: There can, after all, be injustice even when there is no villain in sight.

What, then, is the case for an affirmative answer to the question with which we began: whether the existence of economic inequality is the sort of fact that ought to occasion practical concern?

I have referred more than once to the prudential obligation the rich might be thought to have to help in the battle against economic inequality. What I have in mind is that it is to the advantage of the rich, certainly in the long run and sometimes also in the short run, to take practical steps to remedy the grievances of the economically disadvantaged. One of the clearer lessons of history, confirmed daily by newspaper headlines, is that people with economic grievances are often prepared to resort to socially disruptive measures if they have to. It is a commonplace of criminology, for example, that there is a disturbing correlation between economic deprivation and certain sorts of criminal behavior. Again, the dramatic upheavals associated with war or with civil strife in its various forms or with terrorist activity—all can be seen, at least in part, as attempts to secure economic betterment by violent means. Even from a narrowly prudential standpoint, then, rich nations and individuals have good reason to respond in practical ways to the demands of the poor. When Alexander Haig during his brief tenure at the State Department announced in a U.N. speech that it was "unrealistic" to expect the developed countries to make larger economic transfers to developing countries, he was expressing a profoundly foolish view given the stake the former have in maintaining peaceful relations with the latter.

The moral case for policies aimed at diminishing economic inequality is sometimes thought to require appeal to principles of common humanity. It is immaterial on this view whether the beneficiaries of such policies can be said either to deserve or to have a right to economic assistance. What matters is that they need it and that sympathetic concern for their predicament is often sufficient to motivate people to provide them with assistance. While this sort of benevolently motivated economic aid should not be looked at askance, it provides a very fragile basis for systematic action to eliminate undesirable forms of economic inequality. For one thing there may be too few people with the requisite feelings of sympathy to match the need for assistance. Moreover, it is demeaning to the recipients of such aid to be beholden to their benefactors, especially if the needs to be met are basic economic needs, and if the needy are in need through no fault of their own.

II

The question, then, is whether there are reasons of *justice* for supposing that economic inequality in at least some of its forms is something we ought to seek to diminish. I begin with a view that purports to take justice seriously—and which concedes the closeness of the connection there has traditionally been assumed to be between justice and equality—but which nevertheless contrives to deny that the fact of economic inequality is a source of legitimate concern on grounds of justice. On this view, a sharp distinction is drawn between economic inequality and various other kinds of inequality—inequality under the law, inequality in educational opportunity, inequality in job opportunity, and political inequality: And it is to these noneconomic inequalities alone that there is thought to be any objection from the standpoint of justice.

There are at least two reasons for doubting the feasibility of this kind of surgery on the equality ideal. The first and most obvious is that economic inequality is often itself a serious obstacle to satisfactory implementation of the ideals of equality under the law, equality of opportunity, and political equality. Thus full equality under the law may be unattainable in societies in which there is continuing substantial inequality in income or wealth: The resources of the legal system can be tapped more frequently and effectively by citizens with ample means than by those who cannot afford the best legal advice. Again, it is notoriously difficult to eliminate the many kinds of economic barriers there can be to proper achievement of the ideal of equality of opportunity in education and employment: Children from poor families typically have worse educational and employment prospects than children from more affluent homes even if they are entitled to attend the same schools and apply for the same jobs. And as for political equality, it is something of a commonplace that the right to participate in political decision-making processes cannot be satisfactorily secured for all the members of professedly democratic societies unless fairly far-reaching efforts are made either to eliminate certain kinds of economic inequalities or to neutralize the advantages of wealth in the political marketplace.

There is a second—and perhaps more interesting—reason for the inherent instability of attempts to combine principled commitment to the ideals of equality under the law, equality of opportunity, and political equality with indifference to the question whether economic resources are equally or unequally distributed in society. When it comes to the question *why* we should attach importance to bringing about equality of the favored kinds—and the question cannot be evaded, especially when it is recognized that justice requires equality of certain sorts only—the most plausible answer involves an appeal to the idea that the individual members of a society have an equal stake in being provided with the conditions for the living of a satisfactory life. In the absence of equality under the law, some people will have better prospects than others both of steering clear of the clutches of the law and of availing themselves of the resources of the legal system; and this means that they will be being provided—unfairly—with better general conditions for the living of their lives. Similarly, without equality of educational and employment opportunity, it will be much more difficult for some people than for others—and for reasons outside their control—to give effect over time to the life-plans they favor.

Finally, if political power is unequally distributed, those with little or no political clout run a greater risk of finding that the institutional framework within which they must seek to live out their lives is inimical to the achievement of their most deeply cherished aims. But if the right of the members of society to the conditions for the living of a satisfactory life underlies sponsorship of the ostensibly noneconomic versions of the equality ideal, it provides a plausible basis for concern about the justice of at least certain sorts of economic inequality. When economic resources are unequally distributed among the members of a society, those who are adversely affected by this distribution are arguably at an unfair disadvantage vis-a-vis those who are benefited by it—especially if the individuals in question cannot be said to deserve their good or bad fortune and if there is little they can do as individuals to alter the distribution.

Those who enjoy a larger than average share of economic resources have a much better chance than those with a smaller share of successfully implementing the life-plans they favor. In these circumstances, economic inequality must be seen to be as grave an obstacle to equalization of the conditions for the living of a satisfactory life as legal inequality or inequality of opportunity or political inequality. Would-be defenders of the various noneconomic equality ideals are thus confronted by an awkward dilemma: Either they must jettison the most persuasive defense available for the ideals of which they approve, or they must concede that certain kinds of economic inequality are as objectionable from the standpoint of justice as the inequalities that violate these ideals.

III

If the fundamental requirement of justice is that all the members of a society—and all equally—must be afforded the opportunity to live a satisfactory life, and if this means that there is a presumption on fairness grounds in favor of equal distribution of economic resources no less than of legal protection or of educational and employment opportunity or of political power, it is worth asking whether this presumption can be bolstered by appeal to broader considerations of rationality. Is there a rational presumption in favor of equal distribution of economic resources, or is there apt to be a more or less systematic conflict between the distribution that would be presumptively just and the distribution that would be presumptively rational?

I shall try to sketch an argument for the view that equality has a strong claim to recognition as a principle of rational decision making in situations in which the interests of the members of a society are in potential conflict. The argument is in three parts. In the first, an attempt is made to explain briefly why the principle of self-interest is a nonstarter as a principle for the making of rational allocative decisions when the interests of competing claimants to resources are at odds. In the second, I claim that it is doctrinaire (and question-begging) to assume that there can be no rational solution to the problem of rational allocation once the principle of self-interest peters out. In the final part, I argue that the principle of equality is the natural successor to the principle of self-interest once the latter, despite its appeal as a principle of rational decision making, is seen not to have any interesting application to the problem posed by the conflicting interests of claimants to resources.

(1) The first point to be established, then, is that in situations in which resources are scarce—that is, in situations in which it is impossible to provide all the members of a society with all the resources they would ideally require in order to give full effect to the schemes of life it is in their interest to seek to implement—the rationality of allocative decisions cannot be grounded in the principle of self-interest. The explanation is alarmingly simple. The principle of self-interest can be applied to determine what it would be rational to do only if the individual whose interests are to be promoted is specified, yet there seems to be no nonarbitrary way of providing the requisite specification that will yield a single, consistent answer to the rational distribution question. Let A, B, and C be three typical members of a society in which resources are not plentiful enough to provide all three with all they need for the implementation of the ideally advantageous life-plan. From whose point of view is the principle of self-interest to be applied for the purpose of determining what would constitute a rational distribution of resources among A, B, and C?

One possibility is to adopt A's standpoint as a self-interested agent and to represent as rational the distribution that would be maximally advantageous to A, no matter how disadvantageous it proved to be for B and C. Yet it is entirely arbitrary—and thus in the present context not at all rational—to single out A for specially favored treatment: A solution to the distribution problem just as determinate—and one having the same formal structure, moreover—could have been reached by applying the principle of self-interest from B's point of view as a self-interested agent, or for that matter from C's.

Can we, then, eliminate the taint of arbitrariness from solutions that assign privileged status to the point of view of just one of A, B, and C by applying the principle of self-interest from A's standpoint *and* from B's standpoint *and* from C's and thereafter trying to amalgamate the resulting judgments? The trouble with this strategy, of course, is that it yields either three mutually contradictory judgments about what would constitute a rational distribution or three judgments which, while not mutually contradictory, nevertheless say nothing about what it would be rational to do, all things considered. The latter will be the case if each of the judgments to be amalgamated incorporates a reference to the point of view from which a given distribution would have to be said to be rational. The judgment that distribution D1 is the rational one from A's point of view is clearly quite compatible with the judgment that D2 is the rational distribution from B's point of view (or D3 from C's), yet none of these judgments tells us which of D1, D2, and D3 it would be rational to bring about, *all things considered.*

However, if we eliminate the phrases "from A's point of view," "from B's point of view," and "from C's point of view" from the judgments purporting to tell us what distribution it would be rational to effect, the three judgments are mutually contradictory. While each of them does indeed now identify some determinate distribution of resources among A, B, and C as rational *period*—and not simply as rational *from A's point of view* (or from B's or C's)—it is not the same distribution for all three, yet the rational distribution *period* cannot be the distribution that is maximally advantageous to A (viz. D1) *and* the distribution that is maximally advantageous to B (viz. D2) *and* the distribution that is maximally advantageous to C (viz. D3).

It seems, then, that the attempt to apply the principle of self-interest to our distribution problem by amalgamating into a single comprehensive judgment the judgments made from the standpoints of each of the three members of our hypothetical society cannot give us what we need: Either the component judgments are mutually compatible but unhelpful, or they are judgments that, while individually informative, cancel one another out. Can this stalemate be avoided? Only, it would seem, by transforming the situation in which A, B, and C are at odds with one another about what the answer is to the question what distribution of resources among them it would be *rational* to effect into one in which they are prepared to negotiate a deal with one another that reflects not only their sense of what would be advantageous to them as individuals whose interests conflict but also their sense of their relative power to secure for themselves more than an equal share through issuance of threats and counter threats. Thus if there is a shared recognition of the fact that B and C would be no match for A if it came to a fight for resources, and if it would be advantageous all around for the fight not to take place, there is a clear enough sense in which determinate distribution D4—a distribution of resources markedly more advantageous to A than to B or C—might have to be said to be the distribution required in these circumstances by the principle of self-interest.

It is true that on this reconstruction of the situation—and of what is involved in the application of the principle of self-interest to the resolution of the conflicting claims of A, B, and C—we do not get the kind of stalemate we got earlier. But the price is high. For without acknowledgment, we are now permitting a nonrational criterion—viz., the relative power of the claimants to make a successful grab for more than an equal share—to play a crucial part in determining what distribution of resources it would be rational to try to bring about. The only reason why D4 furnishes the favored solution is that B and C are known to be no match for A in a knock-down fight. That the *rationality* of a judgment about the distribution of resources to be aimed at should be thought to be a function of the relative *power* of the individuals whose interests are in conflict runs counter, however, to the idea that appeals to *reason* must be contrasted in these contexts with appeals (however cunningly veiled or disguised) to *force*.

(2) The failure of the principle of self-interest to provide a rational basis for adjudication of the competing claims to scarce resources of A, B, and C ought not to be taken as evidence that there is *no* rational basis. That would be to assume that the principle of self-interest is the only available principle for the making of rational decisions—which is precisely what is at issue. It is not an a priori truth that self-interest is the only possible principle of practical rationality, and the shape of the resource-allocation problem posed by the fact that the interests of the members of society are often at odds with one another itself strongly suggests that appeal to considerations of self-interest will not suffice: It is, after all, precisely because we know that the shares it would be to the advantage of the competing claimants to receive cannot be made available to them that we face the problem about what distribution of resources it would be rational to aim at.

(3) Is there, then, any rational solution to the problem of conflicting interests if the principle of self-interest provides no satisfactory basis for rational decision making in such contexts? Consider the following argument. Importance attaches from A's point of view to the protection and promotion of A's interests, as the principle of self-interest itself clearly presupposes. Importance must also be held to attach (and for the same reason) to protection and promotion of B's—and indeed of C's—interests. It would be arbitrary (and thus not rational) to give systematic precedence to A's interests when they are in conflict with the interests of B or of C without providing reasons for doing so. But reasons of self-interest (the only reasons so far in sight) cannot be supplied for doing so that could not as easily be offered in support of giving systematic precedence to the interests of B or C. Is it therefore reasonable to conclude that equal importance must be held to attach to protection and promotion of interests of A *and* B *and* C? It is, in short, presumptively rational for the distribution problem posed by the competing claims of A, B, and C to be solved by allocating an equal share of the resources in question to each of A, B, and C.

It should be observed that the principle of equality has a claim to be recognized as the natural successor to the principle of self-interest once the latter is seen to be not even a contender as a principle for the rational adjudication of conflicts of interest. After all, it takes seriously the assumption that importance attaches to protection and promotion of A's interests (which is built into the view that it is rational for A to do what will serve to protect and promote his own interests), and the assumption that importance attaches to protection and promotion of B's interests (which is implicit in the view that B acts rationally when he does what will serve to protect and promote his own interests), and the assumption that importance attaches to protection and promotion of C's interests (which is part and parcel of the view that C acts rationally when he does what is in his own interest). All that the principle of equality as a putative successor principle adds is a recognition that if importance is to be held to attach to the securing of the interests of A *and* B *and* C, then in situations in which these interests are in conflict, the rational assumption for any would-be adjudicator to make is that *equal* importance attaches to protection and promotion of the interests of A and B and C.

IV

Even if there is a presumption in favor of the fairness of equal distribution of resources—a presumption, moreover, which is not at all at odds with the sort of distribution it might be thought to be *rational* to try to effect—it is, of course, a rebuttable presumption. I want to examine briefly the view that the requisite rebuttal can take the form of demonstrating that unequal distribution is sometimes necessary for the provision of incentives.

It should be noted to begin with that incentive arguments are often difficult to get off the ground for reasons unrelated to the question whether incentive-providing economic differentials are *fair*. It is often no small feat to establish that this or that determinate inequality in the distribution of resources is in fact needed in given circumstances for the provision of incentives. Suppose A is an individual who—according to the sponsor of an incentive argument—must be supplied with a larger than equal share of resources to ensure that he engages in activity 'a'. For the argument to be in the running for recognition, three things will have to be established: (1) that A will not in fact engage in activity 'a' if no incentive is offered him to do so; (2) that A will engage in activity 'a' if he is guaranteed extra resources of the sort contemplated in the incentive scheme; and (3) that he cannot be induced to engage in activity 'a' if he is offered any smaller share of the resources available for distribution than that envisaged in the scheme. Where the first condition is not met—because there is good reason to believe that A fully intends to engage in activity 'a' *anyway*—giving additional resources to A cannot even be described without linguistic impropriety as a matter of providing him with an incentive to engage in activity 'a', so the question whether it would be justified on incentive grounds does not arise.

Where (2) is not substantiated, we have no evidence yet that the determinate share of the available resources earmarked for A under the proposed scheme will suffice to induce him to engage in activity 'a'; and we do not even know whether the needed incentive could be supplied by his being offered some larger—perhaps much larger—share. It is simply false that every man has his price: It may be impossible to induce A to engage in activity 'a' no matter how large a share of resources he is promised. Where condition (3) is not satisfied, there is clearly no reason to accept the claim that the sort of unequal allocation of resources envisaged under the scheme is justified on incentive grounds: If a smaller share for A would suffice, what we have is at best an argument for a less dramatic inequality. ("The bigger the bonus, the greater the incentive" is a seductive falsehood.)

At least three additional hurdles must be surmounted if an incentive argument is to be constructed in rebuttal of the presumption in favor of the fairness of equal distribution of resources. First, any doubt there may be about the desirability in principle of activity 'a'—or about the propriety of offering A economic inducements to engage in it—must be laid to rest. Second, the 'payoff' to those who stand to benefit from the doing of 'a' must be examined to determine whether there is a prima facie case for preferring the situation where A is induced to engage in 'a' at the cost to others of the 'extra' resources he needs to motivate him to the situation where others hang on to these resources but lose out on whatever benefit would have come their way had A engaged in activity 'a'. For example, it may cost an employer so much to provide a reluctant employee with the incentive to carry out some workplace task that he may conclude that the bonus would not be worth paying: It might be clearly preferable from the employer's point of view for the task to be left unperformed than for A to be given the kind of extra payment it might take to persuade him to undertake it. While in this case the verdict on the incentive scheme is one the employer reaches on the basis of a review of the benefits and costs *to him* of (a) setting up and (b) not setting up an incentive scheme, it is clear that the 'payoff' issue might call for examination of the benefits and costs associated with incentive schemes for all who are likely to be affected by them, whether favorably or unfavorably. Equally clearly, the broader the investigation, the smaller the likelihood becomes of our being able to plot with any confidence all the advantages and disadvantages associated with an incentive scheme, let alone to determine where the balance of advantage lies.

The final hurdle—and much the most difficult to surmount—has to do with the fairness of the inequalities generated, perpetuated, or accentuated by incentive schemes. If the presumption in favor of the fairness of equal distribution of resources is successfully to be rebutted on the basis of an argument about the need for incentives, it must be shown how incentive-providing differentials are fair, or at any rate not unfair. Can this be shown?

I can only sketch, without much discussion, a number of possible answers. The upshot will be (at best) the highlighting of one part of the problem of trying to give recognition to incentive-providing differentials within the framework of a theory of economic justice. First, a rather bald formulation of the views in question.

(a) According to utilitarians, economic inequalities associated with incentive-providing schemes can be said to be just (or at any rate not unjust) if and only if they serve to maximize the net benefit to society as a whole.

(b) According to Rawls, economic inequalities generated by incentive schemes are just provided they serve to maximize the benefit for the worst-off members of society.

(c) According to one kind of desert theory, incentive-providing differentials are just because and so far as they contribute to a distribution of resources that reflects the deserts or merits of the individual members of society.

(d) According to another sort of desert theory—one that accents the notion of fair compensation—incentive-providing inequalities are just if and so far as they serve to compensate individuals for the unusual burdensomeness (dangerousness, unpleasantness) of the work they do.

What, if anything, is wrong with these arguments?

The first two—that is, the arguments sponsored by utilitarians and by Rawls—reflect a sound grasp of the structure of incentive arguments and attempt to provide "space" for them within the framework of a theory of justice. They do this by imposing a stringent condition on the 'pay-off' associated with incentive schemes. This means that such schemes can be highly beneficial—conferring benefit perhaps on a great many people who were not among their intended beneficiaries—and yet fail to satisfy this condition. Thus the utilitarian is prepared to represent an incentive-providing inequality as just (or not unjust) only if it will serve to maximize the benefit to society as a whole. Tough though this condition is to meet, it is arguably the wrong sort of condition: Even if on some rare occasion the distribution to which an incentive scheme contributed could be said to be both just and benefit-maximizing, it is about as implausible to suppose that a distribution is just *because* it is benefit-maximizing as it would be to claim that conduct is courageous *because* it serves to maximize the benefit for society as a whole.

There is a somewhat similar confusion in Rawls's position when he contrives to represent as just (or not unjust) any incentive-providing inequality that will serve to maximize the benefit to the worst-off. Incentive schemes that measure up to the demanding requirement embedded in Rawls's Difference Principle cannot be said *on that account* to be just. To suppose that they can would be to suppose that we can represent as fair, for example, the exorbitant demands of people who happen to have socially valuable and comparatively rare skills, even where the fact that they press these demands more relentlessly than others with roughly similar competences is principally a reflection of their greater greed or obstinacy in the negotiations that determine the distribution of resources. The lion's share such people are sometimes able to secure for themselves must on Rawls's view be said to be their fair share of the resources at society's disposal—provided, of course, his maximum condition is met—even though their success in securing this share is traceable to their willingness to drive a hard bargain. Yet it offends our sense of what is fair to suppose that ruthless pursuit of one's own interests at the bargaining table can be even a partial determinant of what one's fair share of society's resources is going to have to be said to be.

With the other two views, the trouble is that while the principles to which they appeal are plausibly representable as principles of fair distribution, it is unclear how precisely they serve to constrain acceptance of incentive-providing schemes. Thus it is plausible to argue that it is not unfair to pay A more than B if A has worked longer hours than B. It is only fair, we might say, for A's share of resources (in this case in the form of earnings) to be larger than B's: A, we might say, deserves a larger share. But how does this sort of argument—even if we are disposed to accept it—tell us when we should and when we should not endorse incentive schemes that will contribute to unequal distribution of resources as between A and B? What is at issue is the forging of a connection between desert-reflecting differences in remuneration and incentive-providing differences. These are clearly differences of different kinds. It is one thing to skew rates of pay in A's favor in order to induce him to work longer hours, and quite another to pay him more because he has in fact worked longer hours. Nor are these differences necessarily connected—with the one being a forward-looking and the other a backward-looking version of one and the same position on the question whether A and B should or should not receive the same income. For the evidence may be that A is in fact prepared to work longer hours than B *whether or not* he receives extra pay for doing so. This will be fatal to the incentive argument, yet the desert argument will be unaffected.

Similarly, to turn to the compensation argument, it is plausible to hold that people who work at unusually dangerous or unpleasant or otherwise arduous jobs ought in fairness to be paid more than those who work at safe, pleasant, less arduous jobs, with extra pay being designed to compensate them for the additional burdens they are required to carry. But how does this argument, even if we are disposed to accept it, help us determine when we should and when we should not accept incentive-providing differences in the levels of remuneration proposed for A and B? What is at issue is the forging of a connection between incentive-providing differences in pay and differences in pay designed to provide compensation for unpleasant features of job-related tasks. These are clearly differences of different kinds. It is one thing to pay A more than B in order to induce A to take on the dirty and hazardous job of coal miner; it is quite another to pay him more in order to compensate him for the difficulties and dangers associated with working two miles underground. Moreover, there is a merely contingent connection between remuneration strategies designed to provide employees with incentives and remuneration strategies designed to compensate them for the burdensomeness of the tasks they perform. Thus if it is known to be the case in a remote mining community hard hit by unemployment that local residents are in fact prepared to work underground at rates no higher than those paid workers doing roughly comparable work in a pleasanter and safer environment, the argument that they should be offered extra pay on incentive grounds will be a nonstarter, yet the argument that they ought to be given premium pay to compensate them for the unpleasantness of having to work two miles underground will retain its force.

The general conclusion to be drawn is that the presumption in favor of the fairness of equal distribution of resources cannot easily be rebutted by arguing that economic inequality is necessary for the provision of incentives. There may, of course, be a case for permitting certain inequalities for this purpose. What is questionable is whether the case can be argued on fairness grounds.

There is one obvious enough way in which there may be a direct connection between fair economic differentials and incentive-providing differentials, though it is a connection very different from the sort needed to remedy the deficiencies in incentive arguments noted above. Suppose it would be fair (or at any rate not unfair) for A to receive a larger salary than B, perhaps because this reflects their relative deserts (since A regularly works longer hours than B, say), or because on compensatory grounds it is appropriate for the rate of remuneration for the kind of work A does to be higher than that for the kind of work B does. Suppose too that there is a recognition of this on A's part: Suppose that A firmly believes that he ought in fairness to be paid more than B. And suppose, finally, that A is unprepared to perform job-related tasks—or unprepared to perform them diligently or conscientiously—unless he is fairly remunerated. Under these conditions, arranging fair remuneration for A (paying him more than B) may hold the key to inducing him to continue working, or at any rate to continue working diligently. There would, in short, be a direct connection between giving recognition to principles of fair remuneration in the vetting of income differentials and providing employees like A with an incentive to go on working reasonably diligently.

Two things should be noted, however, about this way of trying to forge a link between incentive-related economic inequalities and just economic inequalities. First, it is a link mediated by the merely contingent fact that people are sometimes motivated to accept or reject proposed remuneration schedules on the basis of the degree to which these conform to their sense of what would be fair in the way of income differentials. It is a nice empirical question as to how far a sense of what is fair in matters of remuneration in fact plays in motivating people. Second, even when the rather special conditions in our example are satisfied, the question of whether economic inequalities are defensible on fairness grounds is clearly logically independent of the question of whether acceptance of such inequalities is defensible on incentive grounds. No matter what the basis of A's belief that it would be fair for him to receive more than an equal share of economic resources, it clearly has nothing to do with his asking himself whether or not he will lack the incentive to undertake job-related tasks if he receives less. The fact that once he has reached the conclusion—on ground quite independent of incentive considerations—that a larger share would be fair, he will be unprepared to undertake job-related tasks unless he receives this share is a contingent fact about him, a fact that does nothing to show that there is any *essential* connection between principles of fair remuneration and principles that accord recognition to incentive-providing economic inequalities.

Notes

Part of the preliminary work on this paper was begun while I was a Visiting Fellow at the Institute for Advanced Studies in the Humanities at the University of Edinburgh. An earlier version was presented at the AMINTAPHIL conference on Economic Justice held in January 1983 at the University of Florida in Gainesville. A travel grant provided by the School of Graduate Studies and Research at Queen's University made it possible for me to take part in the conference.

Bibliography

Amartya, K. Sen. *On Economic Inequality.* Oxford: Oxford University Press, 1973.
Atkinson, A. B. *The Economics of Inequality.* Oxford: Oxford University Press, 1975.
Barry, Brian. *A Liberal Theory of Justice*, chap. 15, "Economics." Oxford: Oxford University Press, 1973.
Clegg, Hugh. *How to Run an Incomes Policy and Why We Made Such a Mess of the Last One.* chaps. IV and V. London: Heinmann, 1971.
Nagel, Thomas. "Equality." In Nagel, *Mortal Questions.* Cambridge: Cambridge University Press, 1979.

15

Welfare Reform: Cost Reductions or Increased Work Incentives

John J. McCall
Department of Philosophy
St. Joseph's University

Since the topic of this essay is about welfare, I suppose it best to provide some rough and ready understanding of what I intend to refer to by the term 'welfare'. I suspect that this understanding is uncontroversial. "Welfare payments are the governmental provision of goods and/or services to individuals who need such provisions despite the fact that those individuals have not earned . . . those payments."[1] Need is, of course, usually determined by income level. The paradigm examples of such welfare payments are Aid to Families with Dependent Children (AFDC), the Unemployed Parent Program (AFDC-U), the Food Stamps Program, Medicaid, and states-sponsored General Assistance (GA). What I have to say applies equally well to any of these programs.

Objections to welfare programs divide into two not quite distinct types of argument: The first argues that welfare payments are violations of the rights of those taxed to pay for the programs; the second claims that welfare programs have undesirable social consequences . I will focus on one particular version of this latter type of argument; namely, the claim that welfare payments provide the recipients of those payments with a substantial disincentive for work or for increased work. In what follows, I propose that particular configurations of claims posing as solutions to the problem of disincentive are neither morally legitimate nor cogent. However, first and briefly, I will discuss the central arguments based on the rights of the taxpaper. Needless to say, I believe that the suggested analyses can be defended. Moreover, these analyses imply that (1) the standard 'rights arguments' are insufficient to stand as in-principle objections to welfare, and (2) we as a society have good presumptive reasons for recognizing some social duty to provide for the welfare of the indigent. These implications strengthen the conclusions I wish to draw concerning solutions offered for the problem of disincentive.

Arguments against welfare programs from the rights of the taxpayer almost universally turn on some claim that the taxpayer has property rights to the income that is confiscated in order to pay for the programs.

Property rights traditionally are troublesome rights for social theorists. There appears no immediately evident reason why society should be organized in a way that includes strong property rights in the list of socially recognized entitlements. Thus, when supporting property rights, theorists present difficult and often obscure arguments. This should be taken as a clear sign that property rights are derivative rights, as are most social or political rights. The usual process of justifying social rights is to argue that such rights are either (1) conceptually required by moral concerns accepted as more fundamental, or (2) practically required as a means for protecting such fundamental values. Historically, this is the case for property rights also. The most forceful derivations of property rights tie such rights to a concern either with fair return on one's effort or with the liberty of the person. These derivations are rhetorically forceful, since fairness and liberty are often taken as fundamental moral values in this society. Unfortunately for objectors to welfare, these traditional justifications of property rights cannot stand as the basis of the principle rejection of welfare payments.

The effort argument in defense of a right to compensation for labor expended is a common and straightforward one. As Studs Terkel has clearly shown, most of us see work as one of life's disagreeable necessities. We would rather exist in some tropical paradise where sustenance fell from trees. (At least I feel that way.) Given that we do not find manna readily available these days, we work in order to provide whatever degree of luxury we choose to seek. Our incomes are the (sometimes meager) compensation for our efforts. So, some argue that welfare is unfair because it deprives a worker of some portion of his income through a coercive tax that is used for the support of others. After all, they would argue, the worker deserves compensation for the pains suffered, and he receives no compensation from this tax. The argument, of course, is a contemporary application of one Locke offered in his *Second Treatise.*

Not everyone, however, finds this Lockean argument convincing. Lawrence Becker, for one, claims that this argument at most justifies some sort of recipient right, but not a strong property right.[2] He means by this that society has good reasons because of the Lockean considerations for allowing a worker to receive and keep earnings. But this socially sanctioned form of ownership exists conditionally and does not lead to the kind of absolute property rights that would conflict under all circumstances with welfare taxes. One major condition upon ownership rights that Becker argues for is that the laborer has a reasonable claim to compensation only if that compensation is for labor beyond what is morally required. Becker argues this since one should not expect reward for the discharge of moral obligations. Thus if we accept an obligation of charity, the Lockean argument will not so easily justify a right to keep income when others are in dire need.

Of course, just what morality requires of us in the way of charity is a large question. The proper answer to that question requires substantiation by a large and comprehensive theory. But we clearly cannot accept without comment the Lockean claim that fairness requires strong property rights to whatever income a worker derives from labor. For further evidence of this, one need only think of Rawls's contrary analysis of fairness and his admonition to investigate the background conditions before asserting that compensation actually received for labor is fair. Or consider another and, I think, reasonable account of the right to earnings that takes such an admonition to heart. Baruch Brody argues that income in part derives from the use of society's resources.[3] If one expects to profit from using these resources under some arrangement, one must also expect to provide for the welfare of those who suffer under that arrangement. The social contract, then, stipulates that benefit from society's resources imposes obligations as well.

Thus there are strong considerations which suggest that the effort argument for property rights is incomplete. The effort argument seems to generate only conditional rights to ownership, rights that are constrained by the need to provide for the welfare of society's less fortunate members. At most, the effort argument could show an unfairness in withholding income from a laborer in order to support the slothful. So while the effort argument might be an argument against welfare support for those who could support themselves, it does not appear to be an argument for the in-principle rejection of all welfare.

The liberty derivations of property rights do not fare much better. Neither the use of liberty to show the conceptual necessity of property rights nor the appeal to property rights as practically necessary for the protection of political liberty can generate rights strong enough to be inconsistent with the existence of all welfare taxes.

Libertarians (Nozick for a prime and familiar example) have frequently defended property as a logical consequence of any social structure that respects individual liberty. For, they argue, individuals should be allowed to make voluntary economic exchanges with one another, since any interference with what an individual freely decides to do, *ceteris paribus*, is a violation of that individual's liberty. Hence, liberty demands that we respect the voluntary contracts individuals make. Since many contracts are made with the expectation of mutual gain, respect for the contract extends to respect for an individual's possession of goods gained as a result of the contract. A government that coercively attempts to seize some of what an individual gains in such contracts is government that violates liberty. Property rights, then, are rights that follow directly upon the supposition that individuals have rights to liberty or noninterference. Obviously, on this analysis, taxes for welfare programs as coercive confiscations of earnings based on voluntary transactions must be rejected in principle.

The cogency of this libertarian defense of property rights and its subsequent rejection of welfare is still hotly debated. I do not intend to or expect to resolve that debate in the next few paragraphs. However, I will sketch what I take to be seriously damaging objections to the libertarian argument. If you accept these objections, then it will appear that a consistent appeal to liberty will generate a defense of welfare.

The first strand of this argument comes from a recent article by Jeffrey Reiman.[4] Reiman argues that Nozick's libertarian defense of absolute property rights is circular. The libertarian first principle is that individuals have a right to absence of force/interference/coercion. This, in turn, is taken to justify strong property rights, as above, to (potentially) unlimited possessions gained through repeated voluntary transactions. However, libertarians assume that the exercise of rights to make voluntary economic transactions and the exercise of powers of ownership thereby gained will not lead to an interference with the lives of others. (Note that the force of the above *ceteris paribus* clause is meant to exclude actions that interfere with others). Thus at first it appears that property rights are to be defined in reference to liberty; later, when it is assumed that strong property rights are legitimate grounds for rejecting welfare, it appears that liberty is defined in terms of some prior commitment to property. Clearly one cannot defend property with a belief in the legitimacy of property itself. Reiman and others point out that this circular reasoning arises because of Nozick's failure to understand that capitalist acquisition can often have coercive effects on others with less market power. Thus interferences in one's life can arise from the activities of private individuals as well as from the activities of government.

Given that the property rights for which Nozick argues can result in interferences with others by effectively preventing them from doing what they might otherwise do, it appears that under any system interferences will abound. What we must decide, then, is which type of interference we wish to avoid as much as possible and which type we will accept. James Sterba argues that (1) the potential for devastating interference with fundamental goods (a life without decent nourishment, for example) exists under a capitalist arrangement where there is no welfare program, and (2) the potential interference under a welfare state amounts only to the confiscation of some portion of our earnings. Since the former interference is the more disagreeable, we ought to choose to guarantee against the interference with our lives that it threatens. That is, we should accept welfare programs that prevent such destitution and hence prevent control over one's life from being a function of one's share of market power.[5]

If these arguments are correct, as I believe they are, then one cannot use the right to liberty as the foundation for property rights that are inconsistent with taxation for welfare. Liberty in this argument cannot justify an in principle rejection of welfare payments.

One could attempt another use of liberty in order to justify property rights that exclude welfare taxes, however. Property is often argued to be a practically necessary instrument for the protection of the individual's ability to exercise control over his or her life. Much of Locke's motivation for introducing property rights was his desire to provide the citizen with a sphere of protection from the arbitrary exercise of the monarch's political power. However, as the above argument reveals, threats to an individual's control over his or her life can come from private individuals as well as from the government. One guarantee against such private interference would be to create a legal protection that allowed the individual some independence from the centers of private economic power, that is, to provide the individual with a guarantee against poverty. That of course is a welfare program. So it is by no means obvious that in order to protect individuals from the exercise of power by others we need to recognize property rights that exclude the possibility of welfare programs.

Thus the suggestion implicit in the foregoing discussions of arguments to justify property rights is that those arguments, rather than providing in-principle objections to welfare, actually provide us with reasons that reveal welfare programs to have presumptive legitimacy. Brody's analysis of property rights from efforts expended, Sterba's and Reiman's claim that guarantees of liberty require guarantees of sustenance, and the recognition that private economic power threatens liberty all lead to the conclusion of a *prima facie* justification for welfare.

The other general category of argument in opposition to welfare must bear the burden, then. That general category claims that welfare programs are productive of socially undesirable consequences. One version of this sort of argument is weakened by the preceding comments. Some have argued that the costs of welfare are enough reason to reject it. If you accept what has gone before, however, negative cost/benefit considerations alone cannot count as a reason for eliminating or reducing welfare payments. For, given the suggestion that welfare has presumptive standing, it is only when the costs are close to catastrophic that we gain good reasons for budget cutting. This seems to eliminate the possibility of a simple utilitarian rejection of welfare on the grounds that its costs in interest satisfaction outweigh its benefits. Without arguing further for this nonutilitarian approach to the justification of welfare, I will only note that acceptance of this approach places a greater burden on other more specific arguments concerning the negative social consequences of welfare programs. I believe that this accords with the manner in which most members of our society, including those who object to welfare, view the matter. For it seems that the chief consequentialist arguments in favor of reducing welfare costs are not of this simple utilitarian form.

Perhaps the most rhetorically effective and politically powerful of these more specific objections is the claim that welfare payments provide a substantial disincentive for work. This disincentive for work supposedly derives from the fact that the life prospects of individuals of low-wage income are not different enough from those of welfare recipients. The effort expended in work, then, seems less than worthwhile. Many might rationally decide not to make the effort.

That this argument is so politically significant underscores the preceding point concerning simple utilitarian objections to welfare. Most people see the absence of industry as a moral failing that would allow us to reduce an individual's benefits when ordinary cost considerations would not. In fact, this argument gains much of its force from its appeal to those moral and/or social virtues (industry, thrift) necessary for the continued functioning of society. Because of the danger to society if these virtues disappear among the citizenry, this objection to welfare gains a seriousness and a righteousness that other objections do not possess. It is interesting to note that even the above implied justifications of welfare stop short of accepting welfare for those who could be self-supporting.

What I now want to investigate is the use of this disincentive effect as a basis for eliminating or reducing total welfare payments. My ultimate thesis is that one cannot claim to have a morally acceptable and efficient policy for reducing disincentive at the same time that one reduces overall costs. If this argument is correct, there is a socially and politically important consequence: Those who wish most to reduce welfare costs cannot parade under the righteous banner of a concern for the moral/social virtue of industry. Let us look at alternative strategies for controlling disincentive and see if any of them are effective, acceptable, and cost-reducing.

There seem to be four basic strategies that have been suggested for reducing the work disincentive effect of welfare: (1) the outright elimination of benefits for those identified as capable of work; (2) a lowering of both the maximum benefits ceiling for the nonworking poor and the (smaller) benefits of the working poor; (3) a work requirement for benefits; and (4) a policy of extending financial incentives for work by easing the benefit-reduction rates for each dollar earned by the working poor. Only the first two strategies are clear cost-cutters; only the second two are both morally acceptable and effective.

What happens if we straightforwardly eliminate benefits for the able-bodied recipients of welfare? Surely the (former) recipients would be forced to enter the labor force to gain sufficiency, to rely on private charity, or to starve. The second alternative, charity, seems a highly unreliable alternative, while the third, starvation, to put it mildly, is a highly undesirable alternative. Thus the elimination of benefits for this group would likely have the direct effect of increasing the work effort by those now on welfare who are able to support themselves. At the same time, this policy would decrease overall welfare costs.

This policy has extreme consequences, however, and those consequences are morally objectionable. First, and perhaps least important, the policy increases the incentive for able-bodied but unemployed parents of dependent children to desert their families so that others in the family could enjoy continued support under AFDC. (Of course, without this potential worker, family members would not be in that class of welfare recipients identified as able to work.) This argument has been advanced against the elimination of AFDC-U payments as a way to reduce welfare costs.

Second, the policy has serious potential for increasing the power of capital to exploit the circumstances of the lower classes by offering wages to which there is no live (in both senses) option. This difficulty is exacerbated by current moves to gain more and more exceptions to the federal minimum wage laws in the unskilled service sector of the economy.

Third, and most important, the elimination of benefits under this strategy occurs whether or not the individual finds employment. Many economists now talk, paradoxically, of full employment circumstances for our economy that include a rate of between four and seven percent unemployment (not counting those currently on welfare). Because the (former) recipients of welfare have less job experience, less training and less positive social status, we could expect that they would be among the least likely to find employment in such circumstances. In a morally important sense, then, they would not be 'able to work.' As such, we cannot reasonably hold them responsible for not working and, hence, we cannot justify morally any punitive actions against them. As some have already indicated, there seems to be no legitimate distinction between such individuals and those without the real physical capacity for work.[6] Thus cost-reduction techniques such as this cannot by themselves, be accepted as a morally legitimate policy for increasing motivation to work.

The second policy strategy for dealing with the work-incentive problem takes its cue from the results of studies concerning the effect of income guarantees on work effort. Not surprisingly, such studies have shown an inverse relationship between work effort and level of welfare support; the higher the level of support available, the lower the total of hours worked.[7] Common sense tells us that if we increased the differential between the maximum level of welfare support and the income level of low-wage workers by lowering the ceiling for welfare aid and by reducing the benefits given to the working poor, the standard of living for the nonworking poor and the part-time working poor (who receive benefits) would be disagreeable enough to encourage them to seek (additional) support through work. Again, we have a strategy for increasing work incentive and decreasing costs; policies similar to this one should be familiar to those aware of the current political climate.

There is a potential ambiguity in this policy, however. A lowering of the ceiling-level benefits (the greatest benefits available to the nonworking poor) could be implemented either across the board for all welfare recipients or only for those who are somehow identified as able to work. The former method for implementing the policy should be morally objectionable to all in the spectrum, from utilitarians to Rawlsians. Because increments in disposable income seem to have diminishing marginal utility (ten dollars is more significant to a starving person than to a wealthy one), across-the-board reductions do not appear to have the possibility of a utilitarian foundation, since the savings to taxpayers on average would be less in amount and/or intensity of interest satisfaction than would be the harm to welfare recipients. But, in fact, No doubt most in our society would reject this approach even if it had a utilitarian justification, for an adequate level of benefits is generally acknowledged to be the right of the aged and the disabled poor. Reduction in benefits to such groups would be acceptable in our society only to avoid catastrophic conditions. These conditions do not appear to be on the contemporary horizon.

This second basic strategy for reducing disincentive has its only chance for acceptability, then, if the benefit reductions apply only to those identified by some criteria as capable of work. (Note that the cost savings here are significantly reduced over those in the former interpretation of the strategy. Note also that if the policy attempts to encourage single-parent families on AFDC to be self-supporting, it ought to expand the child-care coverage under social services. This again would reduce the cost savings, since, in fact, such services are now a shrinking part of the welfare budget.)[8]

But this interpretation of the second basic strategy also fails to meet conditions of moral acceptability, and for reasons similar to the ones for which the first strategy failed. First, it would increase incentive for AFDC-U or CA parents to desert their families. Second, it could also increase the incentive for AFDC mothers to have subsequent children when their current children reached the age at which welfare mothers are expected to work.[9] (Usually, benefit reductions for such mothers on the basis of the ability to work are tied to the age of the youngest child.) This incentive is increased in proportion to the differential between maximal welfare payments to the recipients not expected to work and those recipients expected to find employment. Thus if one accepts that such a plan would be pursued by welfare mothers, one has to accept that this policy for reducing disincentives has an in-built tendency to increase some costs. Third, and again most important, it might not be possible for a welfare recipient to increase work effort. If there are no jobs to be found or no extra hours to be worked, then it seems unreasonable to penalize someone for not working more. This is more unreasonable still when one sees the impossibility of unemployment compensation for such individuals (who have not worked in the recent past). Thus this second policy for reducing work disincentives, when taken alone, must be found wanting, for it decreases costs little and increases incentive only by the institution of morally objectionable policies.

But perhaps we have been too quick to eliminate these first two approaches to increasing incentive to work. For might not they both be amended by a simple jobs-search test similar to that used in determining eligibility for unemployment compensation? These strategies might identify a class of welfare recipients as able to work and then eliminate or reduce benefits only if the person in that category was not actively involved in a job search. Recipients of welfare grants in such a category might be required to present evidence of job applications to their caseworker, for example.

Of course, this addition to these two strategies solves some of the moral difficulties indicated above. However, with such an addition, the strategies would not necessarily increase incentive to work, while they might have the consequence of increasing administrative costs. This additional requirement would be harder to police and hence incur new costs, for instance. More important, the actual incentive for finding work may not be changed; recipients may simply have incentive to apply for jobs in such a way that continued unemployment is assured.[10] (We know enough examples of this from the unemployment program.) This latter possibility becomes more and more probable if the policy allows small differentials between benefits for those unable to work or to find work and the disposable income of low-wage workers. But we have already seen that an adequate level of support for those physically unable to work has moral justification, and I have argued that those unable to find work are, morally, not an importantly different category than those physically unable to work. Thus, since the differential between morally adequate benefit levels for those groups and the current disposable income of low-wage workers is likely to be small, the probability is that rational economic decisions by those required to seek work will be to assure unemployment. Of course, recipients might not act as rational economic agents. However, those who believe that welfare has a serious work disincentive effect do so because they see welfare recipients as rationally self-interested decision makers. Thus those who believe the work disincentive effect of welfare is widespread must also believe that amending the first two reform strategies along the lines of unemployment compensation would be ineffective.

This brings us naturally to the third strategy for increasing work effort—the implementing of a work requirement for benefit recipients identified as able to work. The concept here is the increasingly popular one of workfare. Certainly, however, such a strategy can solve the moral difficulties of the previous strategies only if there is a guarantee of available work.

Workfare, however, solves the problem of work disincentive only by increasing the costs of administering welfare, since additional dollars are needed to create and administer the jobs program for benefit recipients. This cost increases when we recognize that a morally acceptable and non-exploitative use of work requirements demands that workers must be treated humanely and that benefit recipients must get fair value for their labors. For surely it is unacceptable to force a benefit recipient who has no live options to work for an inequitable wage under demeaning or dangerous conditions. However, if we provide acceptable work and fair wages for work done, then either little work is required or welfare/workfare payments increase in total. If we provide only small benefits, then we can require only little work if wages are to be fair. But if the program is meant to encourage self-sufficiency, then providing small benefits and little work will be ineffective. For in order to encourage self-sufficiency the work must either provide extensive training for future private-sector employment or it must provide steady employment at a livable wage on some socially desirable project. Without either of these provisions the goal of self-sufficiency most likely will not be achieved. And only with such a fair jobs program can we judge the work requirement to be a morally acceptable and effective solution to the work-disincentive problem.

However, while such a full-fledged jobs program might reduce the actual payments of welfare to nonworking recipients, it would significantly increase total program costs because jobs are costly to create. Henry Aaron calculates that the creation of one job at minimum-wage levels would cost approximately $10,000 in 1980 funds.[11] Costs of the entire program increase relative to the number of able-bodied individuals one believes are on the welfare roles. Usually, those most concerned with the work disincentive effect see this number as quite large. Thus, to foreshadow my conclusion, those who believe work disincentive is a major problem will have to accept that any effective and morally adequate solution will increase total welfare-related expenditures.

There is one more strategy for increasing work effort among welfare recipients that deserves mention. Some have suggested that the rate of reduction in welfare benefits to the working poor be eased so that for each new dollar earned the working poor lose less in benefits than they now do. As it stands, there are significant disincentives to engage in work or increased work. This is the result of the difference in benefits (cash and services available) for the nonworking poor and the benefits plus disposable income of the working poor. The difference is small in many cases, and sometimes it approaches zero. Reasons for this small difference are numerous; they include the reduction/elimination of Medicaid and food stamp benefits (in terms of the cash value of their replacement) at rates that exceed the increases in disposable income resulting from increased work. In some cases, then, an actual welfare family may face a relative diminishing of benefits and standard of living if it increases its work effort.

In order to eliminate this structural disincentive for increased work, many argue for a reduction in this implicit tax on the working poor.[12] Such a reduction would require a decrease in the rate at which benefits are reduced for each increment in earned income. Of course, this means that more benefits would have to be paid to each working poor person now receiving benefits. It also suggests that the eligibility for benefits be extended beyond the income levels now eligible.[13] For illustration of this point, consider the following example. If benefits were now reduced at a rate of seventy-five cents for each dollar of earned income and a family now making $10,000 received $750 in benefits, then that family would lose all benefits when its income rose to $11,000. Changing the benefit reduction rate to fifty cents on the dollar would mean that the same family would not lose all benefits until its income reached $11,500. Thus easing the benefit-reduction rate means that income-eligibility ceilings for welfare would rise.[14]

In any case, it seems probable that without very sharp decreases in benefit-reduction rates, the marginal utility of increased units of work effort will seem small. This is the case because (1) the low-wage work most likely available would be inherently undesirable, and (2) the current realistic wage expectation of the independent working poor is not that much greater than the benefits (cash and services) available to those not working. Thus the effectiveness of this last policy requires sharp decreases in the benefit-reduction rate, and this would extend the upward limit of eligibility further into the lower-middle class and, by implication, result in a more radical redistribution of wealth in this country. Even with the elimination from the benefit roles of those encouraged to gain self-sufficiency, it appears that this policy would increase total program costs. So this final proposal will have guaranteed effectiveness only with increased welfare expenditures. Thus it would appear that the only two morally acceptable and efficient programs for dealing with the work-disincentive problem are a costly jobs guarantee or a redistributive and costly extension of welfare eligibility.

My conclusion should now be obvious. A sincere and justified belief in the legitimacy of some welfare, when coupled with a moral concern for the virtue of industry, entails greatly increased costs for welfare and/or workfare programs. If social theorists and politicians are able honestly to commit themselves to such concerns, they must no longer present themselves to the public as cost-cutters. Alternatively, if they are predominantly concerned with budget reductions, they ought to openly disavow any real commitment to fostering the morally important value of industry. Such an occurrence would have profound effects on the American political environment, since it requires the unlikely event that those engaged in rhetoric about budget cutting will present themselves honestly.

Notes

1. Joe DesJardins, "The Right to Welfare: A Philosophical and Psychological Examination," *The Social Science Forum* 4 (1981): 16.

2. Lawrence Becker, *Property Rights* (London: Routledge and Kegan Paul, 1977), pp. 40-41.

3. Baruch Brody, "Work Requirements and Welfare Rights," in *Income Support: Conceptual and Policy Issues*, Peter Brown et al., eds. (Totowa, N.J.: Rowman and Littlefield, 1981), pp. 250-57.

4. Jeffrey Reiman, "The Fallacy of Libertarian Capitalism," *Ethics* 92 (1981): 85-95. See also Onora O'Neil, "Nozick's Entitlements," Cheney Ryan, "Yours, Mine and Ours," and Thomas Nagel, "Libertarianism Without Foundations," all in *Reading Nozick*, Jeffrey Paul, ed. (Totowa, N.J.: Rowman and Littlefield, 1981).

5. James Sterba, *The Demands of Justice* (Notre Dame: University of Notre Dame Press, 1980), pp. 118-25.

6. Henry Aaron, "Welfare Reform: What Kind and When?" in *Income Support*, p. 334.

7. Michael Keeley et al., "Labor-Supply Effects and the Cost of Alternative Negative Income Tax Programs," quoted in *Welfare: The Political Economy of Welfare Reform in the United States*, Martin Anderson, ed. (Palo Alto: Hoover Institute Press, 1978), p. 121.

8. Mildred Rein, "Work in Welfare: Past Failures and Future Strategies," *The Social Science Review* 56 (1982): 213-15.

9. Henry Aaron, *Why Is Welfare So Hard to Reform?* (Washington, D.C.: The Brookings Institute, 1973), p. 59.

10. Ibid., p. 48.

11. Aaron, "Welfare Reform" p. 325.

12. Aaron, *Why Is Welfare So Hard to Reform?* pp. 59-68.

13. Gordon L. Weil, *The Welfare Debate of 1978* (White Plains, N.Y.: Institute for Socio-economic Studies, 1978), pp. 47-50.

14. Of course, one could attach a rider to the new benefit-reduction function that required the same income ceilings would remain in effect. This, however, only serves to concentrate the disincentive effect on those workers closest to achieving self-sufficiency.

Bibliography

Aaron, Henry. *Why is Welfare so Hard to Reform?* Washington, D.C.: Brookings Institute, 1973.

Becker, Lawrence. *Property Rights.* London: Routledge and Kegan Paul, 1977.

Brown, Peter et al., eds. *Income Support: Conceptual and Policy Issues.* Totowa, N.J.: Rowman and Littlefield, 1981.

Daniels, Norman. *Reading Rawls.* New York: Basic Books, 1975.

Held, Virginia. *Property, Profits and Economic Justice.* Belmont, Calif.: Wadsworth, 1980.

Nozick, Robert. *Anarchy, State and Utopia.* New York: Basic Books, 1974.

Paul, Jeffrey. *Reading Nozick.* Totowa, N.J.: Rowman and Littlefield, 1981.

Rawls, John. *A Theory of Justice.* Cambridge, Mass.: Harvard University Press, 1971.

Sterba, James. *The Demands of Justice.* Notre Dame: University of Notre Dame Press, 1980.

Weil, Gordon. *The Welfare Debate of 1978.* White Plains, N.Y.: Institute for Socioeconomic Studies, 1978.

16

Economic Justice, Self-Management, and the Principle of Reciprocity

Carol C. Gould
Department of Humanities
Stevens Institute of Technology

Recent theories of economic justice have generally focused on the question of just distribution of goods or wealth.[1] Where they have focused on production and not only on distribution, such theories have generally operated with conception of property and specifically of private property, and of the products of one's labor.[2] Very few, if any, of these theories have given significant attention to the question of justice in the organization of the production process, or to the distribution of powers and rights in this domain. In this essay, I propose a conception of economic justice in which the right to participate in economic decision making in the production process, that is, worker self-management—is understood as a requirement of justice. Although other theorists have argued for such worker self-management, they have not seen it as required by justice, but rather by other values as meaningful work, democracy, or utility.

This requirement for worker participation emerges from a more general framework of a theory of justice, in which justice is understood as fundamentally involving equal positive freedom. By this I mean the equal right to the conditions of self-development, including enabling material and social conditions in addition to civil liberties and political rights. I will develop this framework as it relates to questions of the production and distribution of goods and the allocation of economic rights. In this connection, I will also consider when inequalities may be justified. In my discussion of the principle of equality, which is central to the theory of justice, I will introduce the principle of reciprocity and argue that equality is to be understood not simply as a principle of allocation or distribution, but as involving reciprocal relations among persons. This discussion of reciprocal relations will cast light on the earlier thesis—that worker self-management is a requirement for economic justice.

I begin with a consideration of some themes in two major recent theories of economic justice—those of Rawls and Nozick—focusing on a few leading points from a critical perspective in order to articulate a specific position that contrasts with both of theirs in important respects.

Beyond Rawls and Nozick

We may begin with a consideration of some relevant features of Rawls's conception in *A Theory of Justice*. I shall focus on four points. First, Rawls's difference principle—that social and economic inequalities should be to the greatest benefit of the least advantaged—permits relations of economic exploitation and possibly of social domination, particularly as he represents this principle in various examples. Because the principle focuses only on the relative standing of representative individuals in terms of their advantages and disadvantages, it does not take into account the nonreciprocal social and economic relations that hold between them. This results at least in part from Rawls's interpretation of relative advantage and disadvantage only in terms of how much of the primary goods (such as wealth and income) each possess. However, this leaves out of account the ways in which these primary goods are acquired or used, and it also leaves out of account the internal social relations among the individuals. Thus the principle does not exclude a relation in which some individuals would benefit from the exploitation of the labor of others, so long as their enrichment by this exploitation increases the income or wealth of those exploited.

In economic exploitation, the value produced by wage labor exceeds the rate at which it is compensated, where this difference in value is appropriated by those who own and control the means or conditions of productive activity.[3] This is therefore a nonreciprocal relation, in which one may be said to benefit at the expense of the other, both in the fact that one controls the conditions of labor (and thus the productive activity of the other) and that one appropriates without equivalent return a part of the other's product or contribution. Such exploitation violates the norm of reciprocity that should be a part of justice. It is also not clear that the difference principle would exclude nonreciprocal relations of social or personal domination in which some are able to subordinate the actions or decisions of others to their own, whether through coercion or undue influence over them.

Now it is true that Rawls recognizes the norm of reciprocity as involved in justice. However, in his discussion of it with respect to the second principle, he defines it simply as a requirement for mutual benefit, without regard for the relations in terms of which these benefits are acquired. But I would argue that such relations are crucial to reciprocity in the full sense, for reasons I will give later.

One qualification to this discussion needs to be made, however: Rawls does include self-respect among the primary goods, and it would seem that this requirement might prohibit domination or exploitation in social and economic life. But this is unclear, because Rawls suggests that self-respect would be effected primarily by the requirement of equal liberty in civil and political life. Furthermore, the examples that Rawls offers suggest that the difference principle is not meant to exclude economic exploitation and he regards the principle as compatible with both systems of private property or of socialism.[4]

The second point in Rawls's analysis to be considered concerns the separation which he draws between the two principles of justice, and specifically his restriction of equal liberty to the domain of civil and political affairs. Thus Rawls suggests that there would be rational agreement that justice requires equal basic liberties of citizenship, including the political liberties of the right to vote and to be eligible to hold office, as well as the liberties of freedom of speech, thought, and the right to hold property. However, he does not see a comparable principle of equal liberty as applying to the social and economic domain, where, instead, justice concerns the distribution of social and economic advantages. But one might argue that there are important respects in which the principle of equal liberty pertains to this domain as well, and that the restriction of equal liberty to the political and civil domain alone is arbitrary. Thus I would propose that equal liberty also requires an equal right to participate in decisions concerning the social and economic activities in which one engages, as much as it requires the equal right to participate in political matters. For such participation is just as important a requirement for the expression of one's free agency and for one's self-respect as is participation in political decisions. Thus I will argue that worker self-management and rights to participate in decisions concerning social institutions are required by equal liberty, just as is the equal right of political participation.

A third, and related, point is that Rawls fails to take clearly into account that equality with respect to certain social and economic conditions is necessary for freedom or liberty. This is partly because of the separation that Rawls makes between the first and second principles, assigning equal liberty only to the first, and from the priority that he gives to the first principle, interpreted in this way. This account fails to recognize the way in that certain social and economic inequalities can undermine the equal liberty which Rawls regards as preeminent. This point has been made by Norman Daniels as a criticism of Rawls's distinction between equal liberty and the unequal worth of liberty,[5] where this unequal worth of liberty may arise from "[t]he inability to take advantage of one's rights and opportunities as a result of poverty and ignorance, and a lack of means generally."[6] Thus, for example, as Daniels notes, the wealthy are more capable of influencing the political process or exercising their freedom of speech through the media than are the poor, and this discrepancy undercuts the supposedly equal liberties.

This criticism may be extended further by noting that certain social and economic equalities are necessary conditions not only for liberty, as Rawls treats it, but for freedom in the broader sense of self-development, or what Rawls calls the pursuit of one's plan of life. Such a conception is one of what has been called positive freedom or liberty. On this view, freedom is understood not only as the abstract capacity for choice, provided for in the requirement for equal liberty, but also as a process of self-development, where this requires both the absence of constraining conditions and the presence of enabling conditions, including social and economic ones.[7] Without at least minimal conditions of this sort, and most notably minimal means of subsistence, freedom remains empty. Thus although it is correct to give prime importance to equal liberty, as Rawls does, one should also regard the equal right to minimal means of subsistence as of the same importance.[8] A similar point has been made by Shue, who argues that rational agreement on principles of justice would re_ quire a guarantee of some floor or minimal threshold of the provision of subsistence.[9] Beyond this, there may be other social and economic goods and resources that should be distributed equally as a condition for the full development of freedom. I will consider these later, along with the question of the demarcation between those conditions for self-development that are required to be equal and those where inequalities may be justified.

A final criticism of Rawls's position is that he limits the application of the principle of justice in the economic domain only to distribution and not to production. Thus in the first place, he does not explicitly consider the organization and control of the production process or its relation to economic rights with respect to the requirements of justice. Rawls does include rights, powers, opportunities, and self-respect as among the primary goods to distributed and these might seem to bear on these questions concerning production. However, he does not develop this relation explicitly.

A second aspect of this criticism is that Rawls fails to take into account the relation between the economic products or goods that are to be distributed and those who have produced them. One may argue that the producers of the goods have a claim to some return on the value of what they have produced, or that there is some form of entitlement. Thus it is not the case that economic goods are simply available for some distribution out of a common pool. Rather, those who have produced them have some prior right to control over the product or to recompense for their work in producing it. A similar point is made by Nozick, who argues that "the situation is *not* one of something's getting made, and there being an open question of who is to get it. Things come into the world already attached to people having entitlements over them."[10]

Nozick is right in pointing out that the production of goods implies some form of entitlement on the part of the producers of these goods. However, he is wrong about the nature of this entitlement. Nozick's presupposition is that entitlement is originally based on an act of appropriation by an individual. What this account fails to consider is joint or social labor or acts of appropriation. That is, it is plausible to suppose that some of the earliest forms of property took a tribal or communal form or were regarded as property of some smaller group who originally worked together.[11] Thus Nozick's appeal to an original act of just acquisition in terms of individual appropriation is at the very least one-sided. Moreover, contemporary forms of economic production are most often social or cooperative and thus would seem to give rise to some form of joint or social entitlement to the product.

Nozick does in fact deal with social cooperation in the economy in terms of the question of whether "individual entitlements apply to parts of the cooperatively produced product."[12] Here he translates the question of social entitlement to the social product into a question of individual acquisitions and transfers through market exchange. He does this either through a model of sequential exchanges among individuals, each of whom participates on parts of a sequential production process (with each individual as a "miniature firm"), or, more realistically, through a model of a joint working together in which each is entitled to his or her marginal product. But according to Nozick, in this latter case, a free market approximates to such a distribution of marginal products through voluntary transfers. Thus according to him, the individual entitlements based on socially cooperative production are justly approximated through voluntary exchanges in the free market.

However, contrary to Nozick's view, it can be argued that the exchange between the owners of capital and laborers is not a fully voluntary one, but is rather forced or coerced in fundamental respects. Although the laborer sometimes has a choice among alternative jobs, he or she does not in general have the reasonable option of refusing to work in some job under the conditions set by the owners and managers of capital, since this is the only means available to the wage worker for earning a livelihood. Therefore, Nozick's reliance on the notion of voluntary transfer in a free-market situation as the ground for just distribution of the marginal product does not go through. Nozick offers a counterargument here to the effect that whatever options or restrictions on one's choices result form a sequence of legitimate exchanges cannot be regarded as forces or coerced, even if they are unpalatable. But against this one may argue, as G. A. Cohen has done, that regardless of how a situation has been arrived at, if one has no real choice but to engage in a certain action that is necessary for one's existence or well-being, then one can speak of being forced to act in this way.[13] Thus it seems to be a piece of semantic sleight of hand to define away the notion of force or coercion by appeal to the legitimacy of previous acquisitions or exchanges.

Furthermore, in the case at issue—that of the voluntariness of the exchange between wage labor and capital—one may put in question whether the original acquisition of capital and the ensuing exchanges are in fact legitimate. One may argue that in the market exchange between capital and labor, the laborer does not receive recompense for the value of what he or she has produced, but rather that the capitalist-market form of exchange recompenses only a portion of this. To develop this argument, however, would require a fuller discussion of the economic relation between labor and capital. Furthermore, with respect to the original acquisition, one may note that the historical cases of original acquisition of capital—that is, of so-called primitive accumulation of capital—include so many instances of appropriation by force or stealth that one cannot base a legitimation of subsequent exchanges on such illegitimate original acquisition. Yet in Nozick's argument against the notion that labor is forced to exchange in the market, there is a tacit appeal to just such legitimacy in the initial appropriation and the subsequent exchanges.

I have argued that Nozick fails to take into account adequately the notions of social production of social entitlement. While he is correct in recognizing that there should be some relation between the activity of producers and their entitlement to the products of their labor, he fails to recognize how much productive activity is in fact social, and where he does recognize it, he misinterprets the entitlement that derives from it. I would argue that where labor is social, there is a right to joint control over the process and the product by all those who participate in the production. This amounts to a requirement of worker self-management or worker control in the economy.

Before considering Nozick's objections to worker control, there is a point concerning his objections to any redistribution through taxation, which can be made on the previous argument. Just as I have argued that someone may be forced or coerced in a certain situation apart from the question of the legitimacy of how the situation arose, so too one may speak of the injustice of a situation in which some are able to exert undue power over others or to dominate them, even if there were some sense in which one could speak of the sequence of steps by which they attain to such power as legitimate or just. Thus one of the requirements of justice is freedom from such domination. This becomes a ground for an argument for the legitimacy of the redistribution of resources through taxation, as well as for the redistribution of powers in worker self-management, so as to exclude such domination or exploitation.

Against Nozick's further objection that such a redistribution would require continual interference with individuals' liberties and violations of their entitlements, one may note first of all that his view disregards the liberty of those who are dominated. Second, some justifiable redistribution would be in recognition of social entitlements not presently recompensed in market exchanges and thus would not be a violation of individual entitlements. Third, it is possible to be sensitive to the requirement for not interfering with individuals' liberties by devising social policies or institutions that require minimal intervention. The distribution of rights and powers needs to be structured in such a way as to preserve equal freedom through the working of these institutions. In my view, the form such institutions would take would be that of democracy, not only in politics, but in economic life, where it would more specifically take the form of worker self-management.

Nozick briefly considers the question of worker-controlled firms, which would involve democratic decision making in the firms and would extend to powers of ownership. Nozick suggests that workers' control is less efficient than capitalist forms of enterprise on the grounds that if they were in fact more efficient economically, means would have been found to introduce them on a broad scale, such as by the use of union funds or by attracting private investment. Nozick's argument here is flawed on several grounds. First, there is striking and rapidly growing evidence that worker participation in industry contributes to economic efficiency and to the profitability of the firm. Though the evidence concerns worker participation short of worker control, there is no reason to think that the efficiency would be less if the firms were controlled by the workers. Second, Nozick's supposition that private investors, investment groups, or banks would overlook their class interests in order to get a good return by investing in worker-controlled firms is highly implausible, since such investment would directly undercut the future prospects of the system of private investment itself. A system of widespread worker control would clearly involve a greater degree of public investment.

Third, within the United States at least, in the few cases in which firms are available for purchase or investment by workers or their unions, such firms usually have failed or gone bankrupt within the prevailing capitalist market and are most often technologically inefficient or outmoded. Therefore, such firms are not likely to be purchased by the workers, or where they are, they begin with a severe handicap that hardly makes them models of what would be possible under workers' control. Fourth, contrary to Nozick's assertion, union funds, which are mainly pension funds, are not usually available for this sort of investment because of restrictions on how they may be invested. Finally, in the few cases in the U.S. where it has been possible to implement worker ownership and management, there have been several noteworthy successes.[14]

Economic Justice and the Requirement of Self-Management

Against the background of these criticisms of Rawls and Nozick, I now proceed to consider a general framework of a theory of economic justice which avoids the problems that I have noted in their views. A theory of economic justice concerns the principles that ought to govern the distribution of rights, powers, and goods within the economic domain. The main principle of justice is that of equal positive freedom, defined as equal rights to the conditions of self-development. On this very freedom is understood not merely as the capacity for choice, which characterizes all agents, but beyond this as the exercise of this capacity in the concrete realization of one's own purposes and the development of one's powers. It is therefore characterized as positive freedom from external constraint. In this conception of freedom, the exercise of agency requires both material and social conditions for without these conditions the capacity for choice remains merely formal and cannot be actualized. Thus such conditions are necessary or enabling conditions for action.

Since it is the fundamental capacity to exercise choice that characterizes all human beings as agents, they are all equal in this respect. Although individuals may differ in the degrees of their development, the basic capacity for choice is equally present in each of them. Since in order to realize this capacity or agency in the form of self-development, it is necessary to have access to the conditions necessary for this concrete exercise of their freedom, no agent has prima facie more of a right to the conditions for the exercise of this freedom than any other. This is the principle of equal positive freedom, which defines the basic requirement of economic justice. Such economic justice therefore requires equal rights of access to the economic conditions for one's self-development. It will be seen that this prima facie equality is qualified by some permissible inequalities.

Furthermore, I will propose that economic justice also entails a principle of reciprocity, in addition to the fundamental principle of equal rights.

If economic justice is understood in terms of this principle of equal rights to the conditions of self-development, then it is clear that it pertains not only to the distribution of goods but also to the distribution of rights and powers that are involved in economic production, since these rights and powers are among the social conditions necessary for agency. Central among such rights is the right to participate in decisions or choices concerning the productive activities in which one engages jointly with others. The argument for such a right of participation derives from the characterization of agency as the freedom to choose the purpose or direction of one's actions, a freedom that all agents equally share. Where activity is joint or social, as it is in the economic activity of social production, this equal right of agency implies a right by all who participate in an activity to co-determine it; that is, to participate equally in decisions concerning it. This right to participate in decisions concerning joint activities of production is, in effect, the right to workers' self-management or to the democratic sharing of authority in economic production.

Such workers' self-management is therefore analogous to democracy in political life, in which the equal right to participate in decisions concerning common actions is recognized. The argument is similar in both cases: Free agents have a right of self-determination or self-rule, which therefore implies an equal right of co-determination concerning all social activities in which they engage, whether political or economic. In the case of economic democracy, the locus of participation in decision making is more narrowly defined as the basic unit of production. In most cases this would be the firm. The argument for this restriction is that the right of co-determination belongs to those who are themselves agents in this activity; that is, who are engaged in a common project. I am not proposing that all those who are affected by an economic activity have a right to participate in decisions about production, but rather that it is the producers themselves that principally have this right. This formulation avoids the objection that has been raised against proposals for economic democracy to the effect that there is no way of demarcating who is or who is not affected by economic decisions. Thus it is argued that ultimately everyone is affected and therefore such participation in economic decision making is unworkable and meaningless. On my proposal, the locus of decision making in matters of production is principally defined as the firm, and participation is in the first instance delimited to those who are actively engaged in the firm. Therefore, the firm retains relative autonomy as the principal locus of participation in economic decision making.[15]

Workers' self-management in this model would mean that the workers in a firm would have the right to decide jointly on questions of the planning and organization of production or the provision of services, including what to produce or what services to provide, as well as rates of production, allocation of work, working hours, and work discipline. They would also have the right to determine jointly how the firm's income is to be distributed, how much of it is to be plowed back into the firm itself and how much distributed in wages, and how these wages are to be divided among themselves. They would also control the decisions concerning sales and marketing of the product or service. However, this workers' self-management surely does not require that all the workers participate in every decision concerning all aspects of production and sale of their products. In any large firm, one would expect that they would delegate various functions of the firm's activities to directors and managers whom they appoint. However, in this model, ultimate authority and decision-making power remains with all those who work in the firm.

It is clear, then, that workers' self-management as it is described here involves more than worker participation in the management decisions of privately owned corporations. Rather, it is understood as worker control; that is, as involving property rights of ownership, as well as management rights. In this way, this view introduces a conception of social or cooperative ownership of the means of production by the participating workers in a firm. Although I do not give the argument for this conception of property here, I have given it at some length elsewhere.[16]

However, economic production generally involves more than the single firm as its unit. It typically involves complex interactions among many firms through a market or other means of exchange (such as in the acquisition or sale of raw or processed materials for production, of tools, transportation, warehousing, and credit facilities). In such complex economic interactions, decisions are made through the medium of the market itself, where the joint decisions of the members of each firm come into play with respect to each other. Insofar as the market permits a free agreement based on the decisions of worker-controlled firms, it is compatible with such economic democracy. In the model proposed here, then, firms are free to buy from and sell to other firms, institutions, or individual consumers. The market is the locus for such exchanges and therefore adjusts supply and demand and influences the setting of prices. However, this model would generally exclude the market between capital and labor, since the wages would be determined in the process of self-management by the workers' own allocation of the net revenue of the firms among themselves.

Yet, there is a domain of economic decision making that involves questions of social policy, regional or national economic planning and investment, taxation, and welfare. Since such questions involve the most general conditions for the economic activity of all those who are participants in a common economic life, the right to participate in decison making properly extends to all those who are involved. Such participation should be direct where possible, but it may of course proceed through representation where necessary. Furthermore, it may be part of the political processes of decision making in a democratic government. In the context of such regional or national economic policy, one may propose that there should be market-regulatory and planning or investment commissions that are democratically representative. These would aim at serving general social interests, such as by regulating abuses of the market systems, by some long-range planning to meet social needs, and by fostering innovation.

I have argued that economic justice requires equal rights to participate in decision making by those who are jointly engaged in economic activity. Now let's consider what the implications of the principle of equal positive freedom are for the question of the distribution of economic goods. It is clear in the first instance that this principle requires equal rights to those goods and services that are minimal conditions for any human action whatever. Without such minimal conditions, the very possibility of exercising human agency or of self-development would not exist. Such minimal economic conditions would include means of subsistence, health care, and basic education. Because these are universally necessary conditions for any agent, each human being has an equal right to these minimal conditions by virtue of his or her equal agency.

Beyond these minimal conditions, however, it may be seen to follow from the principle of equal positive freedom that individuals have a right to conditions for their specific and differentiated forms of self-development. Because such self-development is what characterizes human activity, and because different human beings pursue individually differentiated purposes or ends in their self-development, the equal rights to conditions here are not rights to the same conditions in each case, but rather rights to equivalent though differentiated conditions. This right has to be qualified, however, as a right to basic conditions for self-development, rather than to all the conditions that would be necessary for full self-development. This qualification is necessary because it is a practical impossibility to achieve the level of abundance that would be required to meet everyone's needs for the conditions for full self-development without any limits.

In this situation of relative scarcity, the principle should not be interpreted to require an equal distribution of inadequate means at the level of the lowest common denominator, for then no one would achieve freedom. Therefore, some differential criterion for just distribution is required with regard to those conditions beyond the basic ones (which are equally distributed). The introduction of such a principle for differential distribution may be derived not only from this recognition of practical consideration of relative scarcity, but also from consideration of desert or of social value, related to one's effort or contribution. Needless to say, where such differential principles of allocation of goods or resources are applied, there needs to be equality of opportunity with respect to the possibility of gaining them.

The principle for differential distribution of economic goods is based on the right of agents to control the products of their activity. Therefore, it may be characterized as a principle of entitlement to the fruits of one's labor. However, since this labor is most often social, the entitlement in such cases is a social entitlement and is vested in the associated producers in a given firm. They therefore have the right to dispose of the product and to benefit from whatever they receive in exchange for it. The presupposition here is that the products will be sold in a market and that the net income from the sale will be allocated democratically by the workers as reinvestment in the firm or as shared profits. This principle of distribution is to some degree a principle of distribution according to work, but one where the value of the work is measured in economic terms by the social value of its product as it is determined in the market. It is a principle of distribution according to work to the degree that it is by participation in the work process that the individual is entitled to the control over the product of that labor and to a share in the income deriving from its sale.

It is likely that the operation of such a market will lead to inequalities in income among different firms and even to the elimination or bankruptcy of some of them. To counteract the effects of such inequalities without at the same time subsidizing inefficiency, I would propose that there be some means of opening up new opportunities for profitable production. One such means would be by public investment commissions, democratically elected, which would choose to disburse tax monies so as to fund new and promising industries.

Beyond the principle of differential economic distribution according to work, there is a place for reward for those forms of achievement that are not adequately reflected in market response and also for the promotion of activities that are socially needed but may not be adequately supported by the operations of the market. An example of the first case, of achievement, would be that of the arts, in which excellence might be appropriately determined by expert or peer judgments rather than simply by mass popularity as determined by market response. An example of the latter case, of social need, might be theoretical research in the sciences or in medicine, where the market cannot be counted on to support such long-range projects for technological payoffs, or research carried on for its own sake, whose social value consists precisely in this characteristic.

Thus I have proposed a conception of economic justice based on the principle of equal positive freedom, which requires equal rights of participation in economic decision making: worker self-management or worker control. As it applies to the distribution of economic goods, this principle of equal positive freedom requires equality in the minimal conditions necessary for any human action and equal rights to a basic level of equivalent conditions for individuals' self-development. Beyond this, the differential distribution of goods and resources appropriately operates in accordance with a principle of entitlement to the fruits of one's labor, where this entitlement is understood as social. This was analyzed in terms of a principle of distribution according to work. [17]

My conception of economic justice thus differs in crucial ways from those of Rawls and Nozick. It also avoids the difficulties in their views that I noted earlier. Thus where Rawls's difference principle does not exclude relations of exploitation or domination, the right to participate in economic decision making that I have proposed precludes such relations of exploitation. On the one hand, it rules out the control by others over decisions concerning an individual's own economic activity; and on the other hand, it rules out control by another over the products of an individual's labor. Further, whereas Rawls defines equal liberty as pertaining only to the sphere of political and civil rights, I propose that equal liberty extend as well to the domain of economic activity, where it requires equal rights to the basic conditions of human activity, as well as equal rights of participation in economic decision making. In this extension, freedom is defined more inclusively as self-development and not only as political liberty. Democracy is seen to be required in the economy as in the political domain. Further, it may be suggested that if the equal rights in the economic sphere that I proposed were in fact established, then political liberty and political democracy would be more fully realized. Finally, Rawls's emphasis on distribution neglects the question of rights, powers, and entitlements in the domain of economic production. By contrast, on my view, economic justice is seen to apply to both domains.

With respect to Nozick's conception of economic justice, my view stresses the importance of social entitlement in addition to the individual entitlement that is his sole model. Beyond this, I propose an ongoing requirement for equal rights to basic economic conditions and to participate in economic decision making, whereas he denies rights such as these in favor of what he calls a historical account of justice in terms of acquisitions and transfers. Further, Nozick's claim to the contrary notwithstanding, it is possible to arrange economic institutions in such a way that they maintain such equal rights and yet do not require constant interference with individuals' liberties.

Equality and Reciprocity

I want to turn briefly to a consideration of the principle of reciprocity as an aspect of a theory of economic justice, and more specifically as it bears on the argument I have made for self-management as a requirement of justice. Traditional theories of justice have most often seen justice as a matter of treating equals equally and unequals unequally. In modern versions, the relevant equality from the standpoint of justice has been defined in terms of those features of the human that are taken to be universal and these have served as the ground for claims of equal rights in civil and political contexts. What I have proposed in extending this conception of justice beyond the political is the principle of equal rights to the conditions of self-development, understood therefore as applying also to social and economic life. On this view, just social relations among individuals are constituted by the mutual recognition among equals of each other's equal rights. That is, no external authority determines or imposes this equality of rights. Rather, it depends for its realization on this reciprocal recognition. Thus justice in this sense involves reciprocity.

Reciprocity may be defined as a social relation among agents in which each recognizes the other as an agent—that is, as equally free—and each acts with respect to the other on the basis of a shared understanding and a free agreement to the effect that the actions of each with respect to the other are equivalent. Insofar as each requires the other equally as an agent, each takes the other's rights as equal to his or her own. Beyond this, such a reciprocal relation involves the recognition by each of the other's differences. This follows from the acknowledgment of the other as an agent; that is, as having free choice to pursue purposes and projects of his of her own. Therefore, each recognizes the other's equal right to his or her own distinctive development and acts so as to enhance the other's agency. Where such reciprocal relations characterize a group of individuals engaged in a common project, this reciprocity involves a free and joint agreement among all the members on the common purposes and procedures. One may therefore say that as a normative principle for social interaction reciprocity is the requirement to establish social relations of the sort described above, whether between two individuals or among the members of groups.

This principle of reciprocity goes beyond the principle of equality in various ways. The principle of equality may be understood as an abstract standard of comparison by which one can objectively measure whether, in the context of political rights or economic conditions, two cases are the same or different. In a sense, then, equality functions here as an extensional concept. The principle of reciprocity, by contrast, can be realized only in terms of an intentional relation; that is, by the reciprocal recognition by agents of each other's equal agency. In this case, the equivalence of their recognition and of their actions with respect to each other is constituted by their shared understanding and their agreement about this equivalence. A second respect in which reciprocity goes beyond equality is that it requires in principle a recognition of the differences of the other and not only the respects in which they are the same. The principle of reciprocity therefore includes as a value the specific modes of self-development that individuals choose for themselves.

This view of reciprocity may be contrasted with the conception of reciprocity discussed by Rawls. For Rawls, the principle of reciprocity is closely related to the principles of justice. Rawls discusses the principle of reciprocity mainly in connection with moral development, but he also considers it in his discussion of the difference principle.[18] He interprets it as a principle of return for benefit done or as rooted in "a tendency to answer in kind."[19] Alternatively, he characterizes it as a principle of mutual benefit. But in both cases, reciprocity remains a response to a perceived benefit and thus is a principle of tit for tat. It does not yet involve what I have characterized as the recognition of another's distinctiveness as a value to be enhanced by one's own action.

The principle of reciprocity may be interpreted with respect to economic justice as requiring mutual recognition by the members of a society of each other's equal right to the basic economic goods that are necessary conditions for self-development. Further, it requires that each member of an economic group recognize the equal rights of all the others to participate in joint decisions of the group. Thus the principle of reciprocity specifies the procedures for determining the just distribution of goods and the just allocation of rights and powers in economic contexts. It requires that each take into account the needs and interests of the others and their equal rights in making decisions concerning joint actions. In effect, the principle of reciprocity prescribes the operations or actions incumbent upon individuals in a group with respect to each other such that these actions will fulfill the requirements of the principle of equal positive freedom.

Notes

For the presentation to the Ninth Plenary Session of AMINTAPHIL, Gainesville, Florida, 14-15 January 1983.

1. See John Rawls, *A Theory of Justice* (Cambridge, Mass.: Harvard University Press, 1971).

2. See Robert Nozick, *Anarchy, State and Utopia* (New York: Basic Books, 1974).

3. Rawls briefly discusses exploitation in *A Theory of Justice*, pp. 309-10, but he does not interpret it in this sense—but only as a market phenomenon of imperfect competition. His position on the injustice of exploitation in the way I define it here is not pursued.

4. See, for example, *A Theory of Justice*, pp. 78, 309.

5. Norman Daniels, "Equal Liberty and Unequal Worth of Liberty," in Norman Daniels, ed., *Reading Rawls* (New York: Basic Books).

6. Rawls, *A Theory of Justice*, p. 204.

7. I have developed this idea of positive freedom elsewhere. See C. Gould, *Marx's Social Ontology: Individuality and Community in Marx's Theory of Social Reality* (Cambridge, Mass.: MIT Press, 1978), chap. 4; "Contemporary Legal Conceptions of Property and their Implications for Democracy," *Journal of Philosophy*, vol. 77, no. 1 (April 1981). See also the criticism of Rawls on this point in Lawrence Crocker, *Positive Liberty* (The Hague: Martinus Nijhoff, 1980), pp. 87-92.

8. Rawls seems to qualify his view by asserting that the principles of justice are meant to apply only when conditions of no worse than moderate scarcity pertain. But this qualification does not seem adequate to meet the criticism inasmuch as the conditions of moderate scarcity are not defined in such a way as to exclude all instances of life-threatening or debilitating and submarginal poverty. See Rawls, *A Theory of Justice*, pp. 542-43, and "Kantian Constructivism in Moral Theory," *The Journal of Philosophy*, vol. 77, no. 9 (September 1980), p. 536.

9. Henry Shue, *Basic Rights* (Princeton: Princeton University Press, 1980), pp. 127-29.

10. Nozick, *Anarchy, State and Utopia*, p. 160.

11. See Bronislaw Malinowski, *Argonauts of the Western Pacific* (New York: Dutton, 1961), and *Crime and Custom in Savage Society* (Atlantic Highlands, N.J.: Humanities Press, 1970); William H. R. Rivers, *History of Melanesian Society* (Atlantic Highlands, N.J.: Humanities Press, 1968), and *Social Organization* (London, 1924); Marshall Sahlins, *Stone Age Economics* (Hawthorne, N.Y.: De Gruyter, 1972).

12. Nozick, *Anarchy, State and Utopia*, p. 186.

13. G. A. Cohen, "Robert Nozick and Wilt Chamberlain: How Patterns Preserve Liberty," in J. Arthur and W. H. Shaw, eds., *Justice and Economic Distribution* (Englewood Cliffs, N.J.: Prentice-Hall, 1978).

14. See Daniel Zwerdling, *Workplace Democracy* (New York: Harper & Row, 1980).

15. It may be argued that those outside the firm have an indirect voice in production decisions insofar as they constitute the market for the firm's products and thus set the conditions

for the profitability of the firm. However, the market does not make decisions about products; it only provides some of the information on the basis of which those engaged in the firm would make their decisions.

16. C. Gould, "Contemporary Legal Conceptions of Property and Their Implications for Democracy" (cited in note 7 above).

17. It might be argued that the requirements for equal rights to the basic conditions for self-development in fact preempt democratic decision-making procedures in the economy or in the firm in that they establish standards that limit the scope of the decision making. This objection may be addressed in two ways. First, such a limitation on the scope of democratic decision making is in fact intended in my account, since I take these equal rights to be among the human rights which, as such, are rights against majorities. They therefore ought to be inviolable and protected against any incursion or diminution by majority decisions. Second, in a different sense, the equal right to the basic conditions for self-development may itself be seen as a precondition for democracy, since the equal right to participate in decision making is undercut if people lack the resources—subsistence, health, education—that permit them to be agents in such a process. A further discussion of these points is included in my "What are Human Rights?" and "Cosmopolitical Democracy: Moral Principles among Nations" (unpublished manuscripts).

18. Rawls, A Theory of Justice, pp. 462-504; pp. 102ff.

19. Ibid., p. 494.

Bibliography

Crocker, Lawrence. Positive Liberty. The Hague: Martinus Nijhoff, 1980.

Lukes, Steven. "Socialism and Equality." In Essays in Social Theory. London: Macmillan & Co., 1977.

———. Democratic Theory: Essays in Retrieval. Oxford: Oxford University Press, 1973.

———. The Life and Times of Liberal Democracy. Oxford: Oxford University Press, 1977.

Markovic, Mihailo. From Affluence to Praxis. Ann Arbor: University of Michigan Press, 1974.

———. "Philosophical Foundations of the Idea of Self-Management." In Branco Horvat et al., ed., Self-Managing Socialism. New York: International Arts and Sciences Press, 1975.

Pateman, Carole. Participation and Democratic Theory. Cambridge: Cambridge University Press, 1970.

Schwartz, Adina. "Autonomy in the Workplace." In Tom Regan, ed., Just Business: Introductory Essays in Business Ethics. New York: Random House, 1983.

Schweickart, David. Capitalism or Worker Control? An Ethical and Economic Appraisal. New York: Praeger Publishers, 1980.

17

The Feasibility of Welfare Rights In Less Developed Countries

James W. Nickel
Department of Philosophy
University of Colorado

One of the most important ways in which the list of human rights in the Universal Declaration of Human Rights[1] differs from earlier lists is that it includes rights to economic benefits and services. The idea that all people have rights to provision for their physical needs has received widespread acceptance in this century, and after World War II liberals, democratic socialists, and communists all insisted that a concern for economic justice and progress should be part of the agenda of the United Nations Organization. Thus the parties to the U.N. Charter (1945) committed themselves to promoting "higher standards of living, full employment, and conditions of economic and social progress and development." The Universal Declaration and the subsequent International Covenant on Social, Economic and Cultural Rights asserted rights to an adequate standard of living, health services, education, support during disability and old age, employment and protection against unemployment, and limited working hours.

These welfare rights were often rejected by conservatives, who believed that the only economic rights were rights to protections of property and the liberties involved in acquiring, holding, using, and transferring it. Advocates of this view often claimed that it made no sense to speak of rights to supplies of economic goods, and this view prevailed when the European Convention of Human Rights was being formulated. It did not contain economic and social rights, but rather treated these matters as priority goals in a separate document, the European Social Charter (1961). The objections of opponents of welfare rights were also taken into account in the formulation of the International Covenants. These measures to implement the Universal Declaration in international law were separated into two documents so that the countries opposed to recognizing welfare rights as human rights could sign the Covenant on Civil and Political Rights while refusing to sign the Covenant on Economic, Social and Cultural Rights.

This essay deals with one issue about welfare rights: whether they are of high enough priority to merit implementation when resources for implementing rights within a country are very limited. Although the human-rights movement has declared a number of welfare rights, my focus here will mainly be on just one of them—the right to adequate nutrition. I choose this right because it is arguably the most basic welfare right, and because examination of it will raise most of the issues about welfare rights generally.

Reflection on the idea of a right to adequate nutrition leads many people to ask whom it is against and what it requires; they wonder whether it obligates them personally to feed the needy. The answer to this question is that this right, like most rights, has both individuals and governments as its addressees. Individuals have negative duties not to deprive people of needed food or of the liberty and means to grow or buy it. They have positive duties to be productive (so that food and other needed goods will be available), to provide food for their children and other family members, and perhaps to engage in charitable endeavors to help supply food to those in need. Governments have the same negative duties as individuals, but their positive duties are stronger. They must provide protections against violations of the negative duties, arrange a system of food production and distribution that provides an adequate supply of food in all parts of the country, and ensure that all people have the ability to draw from this supply enough food to provide adequate nutrition. This ability can be created by providing remunerative employment, by income grants, or by direct distributions of food. The Covenant on Economic, Social and Cultural Rights recognizes a

> fundamental right of everyone to be free from hunger, and requires its signatories to take steps to "improve methods of production, conservation and distribution of food by making full use of technical and scientific knowledge, by disseminating knowledge of the principles of nutrition and by developing and reforming agrarian systems in such a way as to achieve the most efficient development and utilization of natural resources.

This right does not require that governments nationalize and collectivize agriculture or that they become the main suppliers of food. It does require that governments regulate agricultural and economic systems so that enough food for all is grown or imported and so that all people can get enough food for adequate nutrition. Thus the right to adequate nutrition can serve both as a basis for and as a ground for limits to other economic rights. Where weather is a large variable in a country's ability to feed itself, stored food reserves may be necessary to prevent famine from crop failures or soaring prices. In the area of food distribution, implementation of the right to adequate nutrition will require that food, or the money for its purchase, be distributed in a manner that enables everyone to get the food they need. Most people of course will get their food, or the means to buy it, through work. But programs to provide food to those unable to find or perform remunerative work will also be needed; these might include meals programs for children and the elderly, food stamps, or guarantees of a minimum income.

One might think that the right to adequate nutrition could be rendered unnecessary if a right to employment or a right to a decent income were implemented. But a right to employment would not help people unable to work, and a right to a decent income, while solving the problem of purchasing power, would not necessarily solve problems of food production and distribution. Effective production often needs to be facilitated by land reform, water projects, and programs of agricultural research, development, and education.

One of the largest barriers to the acceptance of welfare rights, such as the right to food, as universal human rights is the belief that these rights are simply too expensive for many countries today to afford. One might try to sidestep this worry by restricting one's list of human rights to rich countries or by allowing that some items on the list are mere "manifesto rights," but the effect of these moves is to make human rights much less useful internationally, and thus we will do better to face directly the problem of affordability.

Suppose that the people of a less developed country have to decide which rights to respect and implement in a time when it is clear that the resources the government has or can acquire without great disruption are insufficient to implement all the rights found in the Universal Declaration. This is the situation, broadly speaking, that many countries are in today. These countries face severe limits not just of financial resources but also of trained personnel and of effective government institutions. And all rights, not just welfare rights, are expensive. What I mean by this is that, in order to respect and implement human rights, governments have to accept substantial restrictions on their resources of power and money. Rights that impose restraints on actions (such as a right against torture) often rule out tactics that are cheap but dirty, and thus they require more costly or difficult tactics to be used. Rights that require the provision of protections will necessitate an expensive police and legal system. And rights that require securing the availability of food or other benefits will obviously necessitate the creation of expensive service agencies and the distribution of scarce commodities.

Deliberation about this problem of implementing rights under scarcity can be thought of as a process of deciding which internationally recognized human rights should be included in a national constitution and implemented through legislation. If we think of the Universal Declaration as providing an international model for a constitutional bill of rights, we can imagine people arguing about which of the rights in the Declaration to include or exclude from their own country's bill of rights. Here are four tests that are helpful in making this sort of decision.

The Consistency Test: Henry Shue has suggested in *Basic Rights* that proposed cuts in rights be subjected to a test of practical consistency.[2] If a right, R1, depends for its effective implementation on the implementation of another right, R2, then a proposed cut that axed R2 but not R1 would be inconsistent as a practical matter, even if there is no logical contradiction involved in endorsing R1 and rejecting R2. This practical inconsistency would come from trying to have one right (R1) without being willing to accept one of its practically necessary conditions (R2).

Shue tries to get a lot of mileage out of the consistency test by trying to identify some rights as *basic* in the sense of being necessary to the effective implementation of all other rights, including all other basic rights. The effect of recognizing a right as basic is to rule out all proposed cuts that ax a basic right while proposing to preserve some other rights. Since the effect of axing any basic right is to make impossible the effective implementation of any other right, basic rights are immune to cuts except when one is willing to ax all rights—or at least to ax all rights for one region of the country. Few, if any, rights are basic in Shue's sense, but this does not rule out more modest uses of the consistency test. Even if there are no rights whose implementation is required for the implementation of *every* other right, there may still be many rights whose implementation is necessary to the implementation of *some* other rights. Even modest relations of dependency between rights may have interesting results for what it is possible to cut.

To officials who want to cut or trim some human rights in order to stay within their resources of power and money, the test of practical consistency is a mixed blessing. On the one hand, it reduces the number of practically possible cuts and thus makes the task of deciding on cuts easier. On the other hand, it may—particularly if interconnections between rights are as extensive as Shue thinks they are—mean that one can't implement any rights at all unless one can implement a large set of them. This sets a high threshold for creating a legal and political system that implements any rights at all. Some countries may therefore find that no system of rights for everyone is affordable—and thus that no rights can be implemented at present, or at least that none can be implemented in all parts of the country. The inequalities involved in excluding some regions or groups from the protections provided by rights may be unavoidable in many poor countries if the interdependencies between rights are extensive. Thus it may be a bad thing if Shue's strong claims about interdependency are true.

The Importance Text: Once we have identified cuts that seem to leave systems of rights that are practically consistent, the next test is to rank the cuts in terms of the importance of the rights they retain. I take it that importance is a matter of how valuable it is, both individually and socially, for people to have secure possession of the freedoms and benefits that their rights are to.

This is obviously a difficult test to apply. First, a right wouldn't be on a list of international human rights unless many people believed that it was important. Second, the rights in the *Universal Declaration* and other contemporary human-rights documents are left largely unranked, although it is suggested in the *European Convention* and the *International Covenant on Civil and Political Rights* that rights to life, freedom from torture, freedom from slavery, and freedom from conviction under retroactive criminal laws should be immune to being set aside, even in emergencies. And third, it is difficult to decide which of the freedoms and benefits that rights secure are most important, and to decide which measures to provide and protect these are most crucial. Hence, in spite of the obvious centrality of the test of importance, alleged results of this test are likely to be highly controversial.

It may be helpful in dealing with such controversies to break down arguments about the importance of rights into several parts. This can be done by asking the following questions:

(1) How important are the freedoms or benefits secured by the right? Perhaps a distinction can be drawn here between freedoms and benefits that are essential parts of a decent life as a person and those that are not. This might allow us to distinguish between, say, the fundamental good of adequate nutrition and the nonfundamental good of having tasty food. But even within fundamental freedoms and benefits we need to distinguish between cores and margins. Movement is a fundamental liberty, but within freedom of movement we need to distinguish the liberty to flee the country, which is at its core, and the liberty to visit wilderness areas, which is typically on its margin.

(2) How vulnerable is this freedom or benefit to the threats to which the right in question responds? A right that responds to a deadly threat, for example, is of higher priority than one that merely responds to a threat to the probability of good health. Also relevant here is whether the damage is reparable or irreparable. This is at least relevant to the justifiability of the short-term suspension of a right, for if the harm done is reparable, suspension of the right so as to accommodate some other important consideration is more easily justified.

(3) How effective is the protection that the right provides against these threats? Here we can distinguish between rights that are very effective as protections and those that are merely useful or sometimes effective. If a right is effective in protecting more than one fundamental freedom or benefit, that too counts in favor of its importance.

Stated broadly as a single standard, these criteria suggest that one right is of greater importance than another if it, to a greater degree, is essential to the protection of the core of a fundamental freedom or benefit against threats that would totally undermine or destroy that core.

Cost Efficiency: This test suggests that in choosing among consistent cuts that save money of the most important rights one should choose to preserve those important rights that have the lowest costs. Thus once we are above a certain threshold of importance, rights should be chosen for retention—assuming consistency—on the grounds of which rights have the highest ratio of importance to cost.

Importance of the secure possession of the freedom or benefit	R1	R3
		R2

high cost   low cost

Cost of securing possession
of the freedom or benefit

Among rights that are above some threshold of importance, this test will have us prefer rights, or packages of rights, that are most to the northeast or north. Thus R3 would be preferable to R2 on grounds of greater importance and preferable to R1 on grounds of lower cost. Since R1 and R2 are on roughly a 45 degree northwest diagonal, they will be ranked equal by this test.

Building a Foundation for Future Rights: This final test asks whether implementing a right will lead over time to a greater ability to implement other rights, and whether cutting a right will undermine over time the ability to implement rights. Creating an effective right to education now, for example, may lead over time to greater productivity and political awareness that will in turn make possible the implementation of other rights.

Before trying to apply these tests to welfare rights, two oversimplifications need to be corrected. One of these is the idea that rights are indivisible and hence either have to be wholly cut or wholly kept. In fact, however, the exact elements that an implemented right involves are appropriately variable in countries with different sorts of problems and different levels of resources. Thus under scarcity, a country has the option not only of axing rights but also of pruning them; that is, removing some of their more expensive elements while trying to retain enough of their substance to make them meaningful. For example, a right against violent crimes might continue to imply duties to refrain from these crimes, and a few measures to punish violations of these duties, while losing some of its more expensive measures that would provide regular police patrols to prevent the occurrence of crimes.

The second way in which our discussion has been oversimplified is that it has ignored the possibility of switching from political to social provision of benefits and protections. Under scarcity, people who are unable to provide for themselves may have to rely on their families and communities for provision of food and other necessities. This doesn't avoid the costs of providing food for these people, since the expense is merely moved from government to families and communities, but it may avoid the overhead costs of the service institutions that systems of government provision require.

Having presented some criteria for deciding which rights to respect and implement when it is impossible to respect and implement them all, I now want to apply these criteria to two possible programs concerning what to do about human rights under scarcity. Both of these strategies are moderate positions; there are other, more extreme positions that I set aside. One of these extreme positions is the Nozickean view that all human rights and economic rights are merely side constraints.[3] This means that their entire role is to identify things that it is never permissible to do. Thus implementation merely requires a commitment to complying with negative duties; not even protection is required. This position would leave people in a Lockean state of nature—or a version of it, involving all sorts of lingering inequalities and injustices—and thus exposed to all the inconveniences of such a state that Locke pointed out. The other extreme position is the view of some communists and authoritarians that it is permissible to sacrifice civil and political rights totally when this is useful in promoting economic rights or goals. I do not take this option seriously because many civil and political rights, particularly those that protect life and security, are just as important as the right to food: thus they are too important to ignore.

The first strategy that I want to discuss proposes to keep a full range of rights but prune the provision of all benefits except the benefit of protection. The only positive legal or political duties that would remain would be duties to provide protection against violations of negative duties. This means that governments should comply with human rights in their actions and policies and provide protections through law for people's liberty and security against the main public and private threats to them. This will require the maintenance of legal and governmental institutions, but the role of these will be restricted to protecting rights and maintaining a structure of liberty in which production and consumption can occur. Welfare rights against government will be effectively axed by this strategy, but rights to acquire, use and consume property can be retained and protected. The axing of all forms of government welfare programs will mean that food programs and educational opportunities will not be available from the government. Education, like other welfare benefits, will have to be paid for by oneself or by one's family.

This strategy strikes me as the most minimal approach that is at all plausible. It says that even under severe scarcity people still owe each other respect for their rights and significant public protections for those rights. It may be that the poorest countries today cannot do any more to implement human rights than this strategy proposes—and they will be lucky if they can do this much effectively. Further, this approach is one that many Americans would advocate as the best strategy for less developed countries to follow. If a government has a good record of not invading people's rights, and if it provides rudimentary protections through law against invasions of rights, it is not likely to come in for much criticism by human-rights organizations, even if many of its people are going uneducated or hungry.

But this strategy has some severe drawbacks, and to see these clearly it will be helpful to apply the tests just described. The first question to ask is whether this proposal results in a system of rights that is practically consistent. Are their items missing whose absence will undermine the effective protection of items that are retained? For example, does the absence of programs to provide food, education, and economic opportunities to people who cannot otherwise get them mean that it will be impossible to protect the other human rights of these people? It is clear that such people can benefit from laws providing protections against crime and violence. Perhaps these protections will not be so valuable to these people as to ones who are better off, but this doesn't mean that such protections will have no value whatever. Even the very poor desire protections for their lives, liberties, and meager possessions, and laws deterring invasions of these can go some distance in satisfying these desires. But the ignorance and incapacities to act that this strategy allows to remain will seriously undermine some people's ability to know what they are permitted to do, to understand when they are entitled to call for protection, and to take steps to protect themselves or flee.

For example, a parent who is malnourished, who has malnourished children, and who is ignorant of legal protections available against unsafe working conditions is unlikely to be able to do anything to protect him or herself against such conditions. This shows how the absence of measures to make food and education available to all will partially undermine the possibility of fully protecting the rights of all. I do not accept Shue's claim that the absence of an effective right to subsistence makes impossible the enjoyment of effective implementation of any rights whatsoever, but I do believe that the absence of an implemented right to subsistence will partially undermine the implementation of a number of other rights. Thus we can say that the strategy under discussion is inconsistent in practice with the *full* protection of the human rights of all people.

The second test is concerned with whether the most important rights have been preserved by this strategy. Here we need to ask whether all protections are more important than all provisions. The answer to this seems to me to be negative; the importance to a decent life of being generally able to find supplies of necessities, and thus avoiding malnutrition and starvation, is surely as great as that of being protected against severe crimes, and surely greater than that of protections against minor crimes.

The third test is that of cost-efficiency, and it may be argued that this test points in a different direction from the other two. One might allow that the availability of food to a person is a matter of the highest importance from a humanitarian and egalitarian point of view, but argue that a right to a supply of food from government is so expensive to implement that there are many other rights that end up having higher priority once cost is factored in. Suppose, for example, that protections of life and health against starvation and malnutrition are of roughly equal importance, but that the former is much less expensive than the latter. This would make the right to protection against violence more cost-efficient than the right to food, and hence of higher priority in situations where a country can't afford both.

Although this argument is logically valid, I doubt that its premise about cost is true; that is, I doubt that it is greatly more expensive to create food programs to prevent starvation and malnutrition than it is to implement effectively protections against violence. In order to do the latter one needs police, lawmakers, judges, lawyers, and prisons. It is expensive to create and staff these institutions. The exact level of expenditure will depend on, among other things, the degree of voluntary compliance with the law. The more crimes there are to block, prosecute, or punish, the higher the costs will be.

The situation in regard to government provision of food is closely analogous. In order to provide food to those unable to get it for themselves or from their families, a welfare bureaucracy will need to be created and staffed. Needy individuals will have to be identified and food delivered to them. As with the case of crime, the exact level of expenditure that this will require will depend on how many people continue to rely on themselves or their families instead of turning to government for assistance.

The personnel costs of a food program of this rudimentary sort may actually be a good deal lower than those of a criminal justice system, since it is far easier and cheaper to give people food than to deal with them in a criminal justice system (such as when the "treatment" required is a fair trial). The cost of supplies, on the other hand, will probably be higher for the food program. But overall, it is far from obvious that a targeted program of nutritional assistance is greatly more expensive than a criminal justice system.

In support of the proposition that a program of food subsidies is affordable for countries that are at the economic level of India or Pakistan, Amartya Sen has noted that Sri Lanka, which is at roughly the same economic level, has long had such programs and that they cost no more than five percent of its GNP.[4]

The final test is that of laying a foundation for implementation of rights in the future. It is clear that a country that allows many of its children to be malnourished, and thus to suffer permanent physical and mental damage, will be handicapped thereby in its efforts to promote productivity and to create effective political and legal institutions. The availability of adequate nutrition is a key factor in health and survival and thus important to the development of a country's human resources.

These criticisms of the first strategy suggest an alternative: a strategy that devotes less to protection and that provides a highly targeted program of nutritional assistance. This will involve provision of food during emergency periods (famines or natural disasters) and to people who are unable to provide for themselves and who have no family to aid them. I have tried to argue that such a right is both affordable and of highest priority. If I am right about this, there is at least one welfare right that belongs on today's lists of human rights.

Notes

1. For the text of the *Universal Declaration* and other human-rights documents mentioned here, see Ian Brownlie, *Basic Documents on Human Rights* (Oxford: Oxford University Press, 1975).

2. Henry Shue, *Basic Rights* (Princeton: Princeton University Press, 1980).

3. Robert Nozick, *Anarchy, State and Utopia* (New York: Basic Books, 1974).

4. Amartya Sen, "How Is India Doing?" *New York Review of Books*, (16 December 1982), p. 43.

18

Trading Justice for Bread: A Reply to James W. Nickel

Thomas Donaldson
Department of Philosophy
Loyola University of Chicago

Professor Nickel has applied his formidable philosophical skills to a pressing human problem: namely, how are countries suffering under the burden of undeveloped technology and inadequate capital to confront the luxuriously lengthy list of demands appearing in documents such as the Universal Declaration of Human Rights? The task of securing not only so-called "negative" rights but also "positive" or "welfare" rights is nearly impossible for wealthy, industrialized countries: How, then, are poverty-trapped third-world countries to manage? Countries confronting a scarcity of resources, coupled with such a bounty of obligations, may well wonder *which* rights to satisfy and which to abandon. Something seemingly must give, and the contribution of Nickel's essay is to provide a decision-making model for choosing among rights under conditions of scarcity.

Nickel uses his four tests—consistency, importance, cost efficiency, and support for future rights—to demonstrate that an underdeveloped country strapped for resources and confronting the difficult decision of which rights to honor, ought not to assume that welfare rights should be abandoned in favor of others. Presumably his principles could also be of use when making specific trade-offs among specific rights, but their application in this essay is limited to a general critique of what might be called a "libertarian" approach to making rights trade-offs under conditions of scarcity.

But although I am wholeheartedly in agreement with Nickel's conclusion, I must take issue with the method he uses to reach it. In particular, I want to deny the legitimacy of the problem that presumably gives rise to the search for a decision-making method; in other words, I want to deny the legitimacy of the problem that the four "tests" or "principles" are designed to solve. The very supposition that a nation might find it necessary to make trade-offs between liberties and welfare on the basis of resources is wrong-headed. In short, nations are never even confronted with the option of choosing between bread and justice in the way Nickel imagines.

The central problem lies with the empirical assumption that under conditions of scarce resources trade-offs may be required between welfare rights and nonwelfare rights. Of course, such an assumption *is* generally satisfied when considering marginal analysis problems in microeconomics. But whereas it makes sense to construct problems in which rational decision makers must make trade-offs between buying books and loaves of bread when constrained by limited incomes, it fails to make sense to construct problems in which nations must make trade-offs between protecting welfare rights and nonwelfare rights. The reason is that the protection of nonwelfare rights—that is, civil and political liberties—is not subject to analysis as a simple "economic commodity." As we shall see, insofar as the protection of civil and political liberties is subject to economic analysis at all, its "cost" is anomalous.

Nickel speaks of the relative costs of a system of justice (of police, law courts, and so forth) compared to those of providing adequate nutrition. The argument has a convincing ring when thinking of countries like El Salvador. Most of us would prefer to see fewer of the blue helmets of the El Salvadorean police and national guard and more peasants tilling their redistributed plots of land. But we must remind ourselves that in El Salvador, as in many poor, authoritarian countries, the costs of maintaining the military police are not the costs of maintaining a system of true justice, but of protecting the special interests of a select group of privileged persons. Indeed, the large expenditures in such countries on police forces are usually counterproductive to the cause of justice.

A proper system designed to protect justice is remarkably inexpensive; indeed, it has a *negative* cost; that is, its costs in terms of overall national economic resources are sufficiently low that the costs of abandoning it are still greater. This should be no surprise. Imagine an underdeveloped country engaged in Nickel's thought experiment. Imagine it finally deciding—no doubt for bad reasons—to withdraw resources from its legitimate institutions used to protect civil liberties and political rights. It decides to shut off funds for trials, for police protection, and for general elections. As a result, disputes between citizens, failing arbitration in courts, would have to be settled by economic power or violence. Robbery, vandalism, and larceny, in the absence of police protection, would escalate even as the class of nonproductively employed thieves, burglars, and con men swelled.

The absence of fair elections would encourage the elite to garner political and economic power disproportionate to their social or economic contributions to the nation, and it would tend to drive others to the destructive alternative of organized revolution. The economic costs alone of abandoning or weakening such civil and political institutions are staggering. Of course, there are exceptions. Unfair elections may not immediately destabilize society, such as in the Soviet Union, and free elections may produce disastrous leaders, such as Hitler in Germany. But history reveals clearly that even in the short term, the protection of basic civil and political rights tends to enhance and sustain a country's gross national product, not retard it.

Hence, the true costs of protecting such rights turn out to be negative—such rights are money savers, not money wasters, and the problem of deciding between using resources to support these rights in contrast to welfare rights, or vice versa, rests upon a false dilemma.

The real problem is not that underdeveloped countries are forced because of scarce resources to choose between bread and justice, but that they find it difficult to protect adequately the specific class of rights known as welfare rights. Whereas the protection of basic liberties and freedoms carries negative short- and long-term economic costs, the same is not necessarily true for welfare rights, whose protection requires considerable initial expenditures for educational institutions, nutritional sustenance, and employment. Even welfare rights probably carry negative economic costs in the long term. But the payoff from such rights is less immediate, and the relatively massive expenditures necessary to secure them in underdeveloped countries are postponable in a way in which expenditures for police protection and law courts are not. One can grant this point while insisting at the same time that welfare rights are worth every penny.

Thus I believe that in the end the set of principles presented by Professor Nickel may contribute to solving a legitimate problem. But that problem is not one of making trade-offs under conditions of economic scarcity between welfare rights and nonwelfare rights, but of making trade-offs among various types of welfare rights in the short term.

Bibliography

Brown, Peter, and Shue, Henry. *Boundaries: National Autonomy and Its Limits.* Totowa, N.J.: Rowman & Littlefield, 1981.

Newberg, Paula R. *The Politics of Human Rights.* New York: New York University Press, 1980.

Okun, Arthur. *Equality and Efficiency: The Big Trade-off.* 1975.

Pettmans, Ralph, ed. *Moral Claims in World Affairs.* New York: St. Martin's Press, 1979. Reviewed in *Ethics* 91 (July 1981).

Shue, Henry. *Basic Rights, Subsistence, Affluence, and U.S. Foreign Policy.* Princeton: Princeton University Press, 1981.

———. "Exporting Hazards," in *Ethics* 91 (July 1981): 579-606.

Sterba, James. "The Welfare Rights of Distant Peoples and Future Generations: Moral Side Constraints on Social Policy." *Social Theory/Practice* 7 (Spring 1981): 99-119.

Thompson, Kenneth W. *Ethics, Functionalism, and Power in International Politics.* Baton Rouge: Louisiana State University Press, 1979.

19

Bibliographic Essay
Welfare Rights

Carl Wellman
Department of Philosophy
Washington University, Saint Louis

Rising unemployment, accelerating medical costs, and the continuing breakdown of the traditional family remind us more painfully than usual of how desperately dependent millions of Americans are upon public welfare programs such as Unemployment Insurance, Medicare and Medicaid, and Aid to Families with Dependent Children. Consequently, there can be no doubt about the practical importance for public policy and individual well-being of the various legal rights to welfare established in the law of the land. Nor can there be much doubt about the significance of moral welfare rights, if there are any, for the moral criticism and political reform of our social institutions. What is in doubt is whether philosophers and jurists have anything of interest to say about welfare rights. Only recently have welfare rights in any strict sense been much discussed in the literature. I propose to review these discussions in order to provide some perspective upon its several aspects and to indicate what progress has been made to date and what crucial philosophical problems remain unresolved. Since this is an impressionistic survey rather than a scholarly article, references will be given simply by author and date of publication.

The Concept of a Welfare Right

The way in which one conceives of a welfare right will obviously depend upon one's more generic conception of a right per se. I shall not pause to discuss the large and rapidly growing literature dealing with the conceptual analysis of the language of rights in general, however, because this task has been completed admirably by Rex Martin and James Nickel (1980). Instead, I shall discuss briefly several recent attempts to define, or at least explain, the notion of one species of right—a welfare right.

One of the first philosophers to address this matter directly was H. J. McCloskey (1965). He asserts that there are at least four distinct concepts of moral rights. The third of these is explained as follows:

> There is a more positive, fuller concept which we may characterize as *the welfare concept* of a right such that a right is not merely a moral entitlement to do or to have, but also an entitlement to the efforts of others or to make demands on others to aid and promote our seeking after or enjoyment of some good.

There are two difficulties with this conception of a welfare right, at least as a conception adequate to define the special sort of right that is the subject of this review essay. First, there is the problem of precisely how this third concept of a right is supposed to relate to McCloskey's fourth concept of a special right, such as the right of a creditor to the repayment of his loan. My right to be paid by Washington University at the end of each month seems to fit the above definition of a welfare right, yet presumably it is a special right to performance of contract rather than a right to welfare. But it will not do to amend the definition to limit it to general rights because under our categorical welfare system in the United States paradigm cases of welfare rights, such as rights to AFDC payments and rights to Medicaid, are special rights possessed by one as a member of some special class. Second, McCloskey's definition fails to define the range or kind of good that is to count as a welfare benefit. Police protection and national defense are goods to the citizen who enjoys them, but our programs of police protection and the armed services are very different from welfare programs such as AFDC or Unemployment Insurance. If a worker does indeed have a moral right to just remuneration, this is primarily a moral claim to earned income holding against one's employer and not a claim to any public or private form of welfare.

A much more widely used concept of a welfare right is that proposed by Martin Golding (1968 and 1978). He explains his conception in these words:

> However, option-rights do not exhaust the entire class of rights. There are rights that are derived from claims to the goods of life which are conferred by the social ideal of a community. These rights cannot be identified with 'a sphere of autonomy' or a 'range of action.' What gives us an edge to think of these rights as option-rights is that they may be claimed (i.e., that which they are rights to may be claimed) on appropriate occasions, or that some of them are subject to waiver.

A weakness in this definition of a welfare right is that it fails to explain fully and clearly enough precisely how welfare rights are supposed to differ from option rights. The context suggests that they might differ as liberty-rights differ from claim-rights, for Golding uses Vinogradoff's phrase "range of action" in explaining his concept of an option-right. But since he also asserts that claimability arises in connection with both types of rights, this reading seems ruled out. Moreover, Golding introduces the concept of a welfare right primarily because he believes that the concept of an option-right is too narrow to cover many claims to the goods of life.

Although I would agree that Hart's option theory of rights is inadequate, I doubt that this is because it fails to apply to paradigm cases of welfare rights. His explanation (1973) of how his model of a legal right can be extended to fit rights to welfare benefits strikes me as sound.

Notice that Golding himself remarks that welfare rights "may be claimed" and often "are subject to waiver," presumably at the option of the possessor. Finally, this definition does not circumscribe the range of "the goods of life" in a way that coincides with welfare in the special sense in which AFDC payments and old-age assistance are welfare, while earned income and birthday presents are not. Indeed, Golding gives the right to compensation for damage inflicted by others as a paradigm of a welfare right.

Rodney Peffer (1978) does what McCloskey and Golding fail to do; he does specify a limited range of goods that can plausibly be taken to constitute welfare benefits.

> On my account, "rights to well-being" is not an all-inclusive category for any right to any benefit we may have (many of these will be social and economic rights which are social contract rights but not rights to well-being as I am using this last term). Rather, it is a category of rights conceptually connected to our basic needs as human organisms. I shall not attempt to characterize this conception, nor the concept of "basic need," nor to give a comprehensive list of these rights. What I have in mind, however, are such rights as the rights to those things which we require if we are to survive and to have any sort of life worth living.

Plausible as this account is, it fails to serve our purposes (although not necessarily Peffer's) in two ways. First, it does not explain properly the way in which human need enters into the conception of a welfare right. The unemployed mother's right to food stamps and the destitute patient's right to Medicaid are clear cases of welfare rights; my right to food I have purchased at the neighborhood grocery and the insured's right to Blue Cross payments are not. Yet all are rights to benefits required to meet our basic human needs. Second, it is not clear that welfare benefits must be limited to things that we require if we are to survive and to have any sort of life worth living.

As the welfare state has developed in Western societies, its activities have often gone beyond human necessities. Imagine our Aid to Families with Dependent Children were to include tickets to symphony concerts or to athletic contests in its benefits or that Medicaid were to cover payments to enable the eligible individual to enroll in a reducing or weight control center. These benefits, although perhaps unwise and extravagant, would still be welfare benefits in the same sense that AFDC payments and Medicaid now are.

James Sterba (1981) advances a related conception of welfare rights:

> the welfare rights of distant peoples and future generations . . . are understood to be rights to receive or to acquire those goods and resources necessary for satisfying the basic needs of distant peoples and future generations.

This explanation suffers from the same defects as the previous one. It fails to explain precisely how need enters into our conception of a welfare benefit, and it fails to allow for welfare benefits that are not really necessary to satisfy our basic needs. What is particularly interesting about this conception, however, is that it includes what Sterba calls "negative" as well as "positive" welfare rights. By the former, he means "a right not to be interfered with in some specific manner," and by the latter, "a right to receive some specific goods or services."

The right of a destitute mother to receive AFDC payments is clearly an example of a positive welfare right. But suppose the mother, although eligible, is unjustly denied such payments. Then her moral right to take (legally speaking, to steal), even without the permission of the owners, those goods and resources necessary for satisfying the basic needs of herself and her child would be a negative welfare right. This strikes me as clearly an extension of our ordinary conception of a welfare right; according to established usage these are limited to claim-rights to be provided with welfare benefits and do not include any liberty-rights to acquire goods, services, or resources by acting in ways with which others are not permitted to interfere. Still, a philosopher need not abide by ordinary usage. I suspect, however, that a proper understanding of just how human need enters into our conception of welfare rights will make it impossible to recognize both positive and negative rights to welfare in any univocal sense.

Carl Wellman (1982) approaches the definition of a welfare right indirectly by first defining a welfare benefit in such a way as to mark off welfare from other sorts of goods, services, or benefits.

> I propose to define a welfare benefit as some form of assistance provided to an individual in need. . . . I define welfare benefits in terms of an individual "in need" in the sense that the individual needs, or is judged to need, assistance in order to achieve an acceptable level of well-being.

The concept of need implicit in this definition is a double one. Not only is the benefit presumed to be a necessary condition for the individual's achieving an acceptable level of well-being, but it is provided because the individual stands in need of assistance of this form to achieve this level. The level need not, however, be the minimal level at which basic needs are satisfied.

> We can now define a primary welfare right as a right to some welfare benefit or benefits. Examples of welfare rights would be the legal right of a mother with one or more dependent children to AFDC payments, or the right of an elderly person entitled to Social Security payments to Medicare as well.

But what of the right to a fair welfare hearing or the right that welfare investigations not invade one's privacy listed in the "Bill of Welfare Rights?" "Accordingly," Wellman states, "I define a secondary welfare right as a right concerning, but not to, some welfare benefit." The task of pointing to the inadequacies in this conception and of proposing a more adequate definition of a welfare right can best be left to others.

Challenges to Welfare Rights

Although secondary welfare rights do not seem problematic in any special way, primary welfare rights do pose a number of philosophical problems that render them particularly suspect. I shall consider here only the most serious and frequently discussed challenges to alleged rights to welfare benefits. (1) So-called rights to welfare cannot be rights in the strict sense because they lack the essential feature of any genuine right. This sort of problem typically arises if one presupposes some version of a will theory of rights and then finds difficulty in applying this conception of a right to rights such as the right to a public education or the right to assistance from one's children or one's society in old age. If a right consists in a legally or morally respected option, then how can a child be said to have any right to a compulsory education? If a right confers some sphere of autonomy upon its possessor, then where is the autonomy of the elderly person who can neither impose nor extinguish the duty of children or society to care for his or her basic human needs? Martin Golding (1968 and 1978) poses this problem clearly, and Hart (1973) recognizes its applicability to his own option theory of rights.

Hart immediately goes on to argue, however, that his legally respected choice model of a legal right can be extended to deal with welfare rights because the state duty to provide welfare benefits is usually contingent upon the application of the eligible individual, and that individual, if denied welfare, frequently has the legal power to bring suit against the welfare agency. Carl Wellman (1982), who defends a more general autonomy model of rights, tries to show in a similar manner that the possessor of a welfare right typically does possess a considerable amount of autonomy concerning its enjoyment. Another way to meet this challenge is either to reject or to extend the presupposed will theory of rights that underlies it.

Neil MacCormick (1976 and 1977) does the former. He rejects Hart's option theory of rights and substitutes a version of the interest theory according to which what is essential to any right is the normative protection of the enjoyment of some good for the individual right-holder. Golding does the latter when he extends the conception of a right to cover welfare rights as well as option-rights. Jeffrie Murphy (1978) makes a similar move when he defends the existence of social-contract rights, in addition to the more traditional autonomy rights recognized by philosophers like Kant. Rodney Peffer (1978) refines this reply further by adding the category of rights to well-being to the previously recognized categories of autonomy rights and social-contract rights.

(2) Another problem, or set of problems, posed by welfare rights is the problem of scarce resources. Maurice Cranston (1967) asserted that the first test of the authenticity or genuineness of any right is practicability. Since a supposed right to a welfare benefit, such as Social Security or an adequate standard of living, is a special sort of claim-right, it implies the existence of a corresponding duty to provide the welfare benefit involved. But today it is impossible to provide full social security or an adequate standard of living for all human beings. Since there can be no duty to do the impossible, there can be no universal claim-right to such welfare benefits. Cranston believes that this difficulty does not undermine the more traditional political and civil human rights because these can be

readily secured by fairly simple legislation, primarily legislation restraining the executive branch of the government from interference with individual liberties.

D. D. Raphael (1967a) questions this belief and suggests that the difference in practicability between civil and political rights on the one hand and social and economic rights on the other is merely one of degree. James Nickel (1978-79 and 1982) has developed this line of argument in detail by showing how the implementation and protection of even the most traditional civil rights, such as the right to life or to a fair trial, require the expenditure of considerable amounts of scarce resources. Henry Shue (1979 and 1980) has gone even farther and questioned the alleged distinction between positive and negative claim-rights, rights to some positive service from a second party and rights that some second party merely refrain from acting in some way, on the grounds that both sorts of rights impose both positive and negative duties. If successful, these responses place anyone worried about the problem of scarce resources between the horns of a dilemma. Either one must deny the existence of all human rights, not merely the newfangled economic rights, or one must somehow show that the scarcity of resources needed to provide welfare benefits does not undermine the individual's right to be provided with them.

One way out is to explain that human welfare rights are not completely impracticable; it is always possible to do something toward fulfilling the duties they impose. Raphael (1967a) points out that even the poorest societies can devise institutions to provide some sort of social security; for example, the Old Testament laws about leaving harvest gleanings for the poor. He adds that we do not deny the existence of the right to life simply because no amount of police protection can prevent all homicides. Thus a right is practicable so long as it is possible to fulfill the corresponding duties at least in part. Another way of defending the practicability of welfare rights is to suggest that when it is impossible to provide the specified welfare benefit, such as an adequate standard of living, it may still be possible to perform some substitute duty. Nickel (1982) suggests that when a government lacks the resources to implement fully some welfare right, it may still have the obligation to take action to increase productivity so that in the future it will be in a position to do so. Finally, one may redefine the content of some welfare right in a way that reduces the welfare benefit to the point where the available resources are sufficient to provide it. Nickel discusses the level of benefits that should be built into human welfare rights and suggests (1982) that perhaps it should be set at that level where most, but not all, countries today have resources adequate to satisfy people's basic human needs. Shue (1980) makes a similar move when he tries to show that the duties imposed by the right to subsistence impose limited, and therefore practicable, duties upon both individuals and states.

Another way to show that human welfare rights are not impracticable might be to locate the duty of providing the benefit claimed upon some relatively affluent second party. The fact that we, as private individuals, lack the resources to feed the millions of starving and undernourished Americans does not undermine their right to be provided with an adequate diet if, as Raphael (1967a) suggests, human welfare rights hold against the government of one's state rather than against individual persons. But what of the starving citizens of India or Bangladesh, whose governments have very limited resources? Shue (1980) tries to solve this problem by arguing in detail and with some sophistication that the right to subsistence imposes duties across national boundaries so that the more affluent states have an obligation to help the less affluent provide for the basic needs of their inhabitants. David Watson (1977) similarly attempts to meet Cranston's challenge of impracticability by spreading the corresponding duties so that the burdens they impose fall upon all living human beings collectively.

Finally, if all else fails, one can deny the correlativity of rights and duties. H. J. McCloskey (1965) argues that rights are entitlements to something rather than claims against some second party. Thus, although rights typically give rise to and ground duties of others, the right itself is prior to and independent of any corresponding duties. Hence, there can be welfare rights even when there is no one in a position to provide the welfare benefit involved. Joel Feinberg (1970 and 1973) articulates a claim theory of legal and moral rights according to which a right is a claim to something holding against some second party. But while he builds the correlativity of rights and duties into his conception of a right in the strict sense, he suggests that there is a manifesto sense of rights according to which every basic human need grounds a right to some good even when there is no second party with any corresponding duty. In this manifesto sense, the test of practicability does not undermine the significance of rights to welfare. Finally, Rodney Peffer (1978) defends welfare rights by holding that the correlativity thesis does not apply to either rights to well-being or social-contract rights.

A very different version of the problem of scarce resources is posed by Charles Fried (1978). It is not merely that no one has any genuine duty to do the impossible; no one has any moral obligation to perform any action that would require morally excessive sacrifices. William Aiken (1977) recognizes this problem and limits the moral obligation of an individual to share his or her resources with those less fortunate to the point where further sharing would reduce that individual to a position of equal or greater hardship than that of the right-holder. Fried thinks that this demands too much and uses Rawls's Difference Principle to limit what is morally required by the welfare rights of the deprived. Henry Shue (1979 and 1980) uses a more complex strategy to deal with this version of the problem of scarce resources. First, he multiplies the correlative duties implied by any right to welfare so that the burdens it imposes are spread over a wider range of duty-bearers. For example, the basic right to subsistence implies (1) duties to avoid depriving anyone of the only available means of subsistence, (2) duties to protect people against such deprivation, and (3) duties to provide the means of subsistence to those unable to provide it on their own. Second, he tries to show that such a constellation of duties does not impose excessive demands upon any duty-bearer. This is not merely because the burdens of these duties fall upon a wide range of individuals and states possessing collectively large amounts of resources. It is partly because fulfillment of duties of the first sort reduces the need to perform duties of the second sort, and performance of duties of the second sort eliminate the need actually to perform duties of the third sort. In addition, these duties are limited in various ways so that under realistic conditions they do not make excessive demands upon any second party. For example, an affluent state has no duty to share its scarce resources with the government of some much poorer state if that state will not use such aid effectively to provide subsistence for its people. In fact, the United States may have a moral obligation to deny aid to any government that systematically violates the basic rights of its own citizens.

Even if one can explain how it is that rights to welfare imply real duties, there is still the problem of identifying the bearer of this duty. How does one know, in other words, against whom some welfare right holds? This problem of identifying the second party of any welfare right is especially acute in the case of human rights to welfare because, as Rex Martin and James Nickel (1980) point out, philosophers disagree about the addressees of human rights. Some assert that they hold against other individuals, others that they hold against the state, and still others that they involve a double-barreled claim against both other individuals and the state. Quite apart from this controversy in the general theory of human rights, there are special problems in identifying the duty-bearers of welfare rights.

D. D. Raphael (1967a and 1967b) maintains that the economic, social and even political rights listed in the Universal Declaration of Human Rights are, strictly speaking, rights of the citizen rather than rights of man, to use the language of the much earlier French declaration. Thus, although fundamental rights to welfare are universal in the sense that they are possessed by all human beings, they are not possessed by individuals *as* human, but *as* members of a society. Accordingly, the responsibility for providing welfare benefits falls upon the members of one's own state, and the duty to carry out this responsibility falls upon the government of this society. Raphael does not explain, however, just why this should be so.

William Nelson (1974) attempts to explain this by determining the scope of Rawls's principles of social justice. He suggests that the principles of distributive justice define a right to a fair share of the advantages of social cooperation. This is a right of the individual as a member of a society because what is to be distributed justly are the benefits arising from *social* cooperation. Since the relatively affluent members of a society have benefited from the cooperation of those who have received less than their fair share, they have a duty to share their economic advantages with the disadvantaged. Although the fundamental right to a fair share is not itself a right to welfare benefits, it is the sort of right upon which both legal and moral welfare rights could be grounded. So is Henry Shue's basic right to subsistence. He refuses to concede, however, that this right imposes duties only upon one's own government or the members of one's own society. He argues (1979 and 1980) that it imposes duties across national boundaries. He also asserts that the duties it imposes fall upon both individual persons and social institutions, including governments.

This multiplication of duty-bearers promises to make it easier to resolve the problem of scarce resources, but Wellman (1982) points out that the number of duty-bearers raises the problem of pointless duplication. Imagine a single individual starving in Chicago or in Calcutta. Who has the duty to provide food, or the money with which to purchase food, for this human being? There are millions of individuals, thousands of private organizatons, and hundreds of states with available resources sufficient to do so. Presumably, if they all can do so and if all have a duty to do so, then all ought morally to provide this welfare benefit to the starving individual. But if all these duty-bearers were to perform their duty, the result would be a vast and wasteful duplication of effort and expenditure. Nor is it any solution to say that each potential duty-bearer has an actual duty provided no other duty-bearer has acted, for this does nothing to locate responsibility upon one or a few second parties before one has acted and while the hapless human individual is starving. Wellman argues (1981 and 1982) that there must be some special relation between the right-holder and the duty-bearer to select from the many potential duty-bearers the one or few who ought to provide welfare benefits for any given individual in need. He suggests that our most fundamental rights to welfare are probably civic rights, rights one has as a citizen, rather than human rights, and that they impose welfare duties upon one's own state. At the same time, other special relations, such as the relation of parent to child, might ground the welfare rights of a child to food and clothing from the parent or the right of a parent to old age assistance from the child.

It is doubtful that this solution is adequate to deal with all situations. Suppose that there are several children. Upon which one does the duty to provide financial assistance to an aged parent fall, or if upon all, precisely how should this burden be shared? And suppose that a parent cannot, or will not, provide for the basic human needs of his or her child. Who then has the obligation to step in and make up for this failure to perform a duty? One needs moral principles to determine both primary duties and duties of last resort and to apportion the burdens imposed by welfare rights. William Aiken (1977) formulates two principles that might do this job. First, among those in a position to do so, the stringency of the duty to help the starving is in inverse proportion to the cost or amount of sacrifice involved in doing so. Thus the greater one's resources, the greater one's duty to provide welfare benefits. Second, among those in a position to help feed the starving, the more effective are one's means of delivering the needed resources to the needy individual, the greater one's duty to provide help to the starving individual. Thus those in the best position to provide welfare benefits have the original duty to do so, and only if they fail to perform their duties do residual duties fall progressively upon those whose available means of delivering the welfare benefits are less effective.

Another challenge to alleged rights to welfare is that these cannot be rights in any strict sense because one does treat a needy individual unjustly by failing to provide him or her with welfare benefits. Thus even granted an imperfect duty to provide welfare falling upon the state and/or upon individuals, the human being in need has no moral claim to or right to welfare. Maurice Cranston (1967) challenged the reality of the human rights to social security or an adequate standard of living on the ground that they fail the test of paramount importance. This way of putting the challenge is misleading, for it fails to capture its full force or its deeper meaning. D. D. Raphael (1967a) is only the first of many to point out that to a desperately impoverished individual the means of subsistence, such as adequate nourishment and simple clothing, are at least as important as liberty or a fair trial. What Cranston really has in mind is brought out more clearly when he writes: "A human right is something of which no one may be deprived without a grave affront to justice." He suggests that the failure to provide welfare benefits is not unjust in the way that racial discrimination or imprisonment without trial are.

There seem to be two ways to meet this challenge. One can argue, as James Nickel (1978-79) does, that the failure to provide welfare is, at least under certain circumstances, gravely unjust. Or with David Lyons (1978), one can deny Cranston's assumption that the violation of a right is always an injustice. To my mind, this challenge to welfare rights has received insufficient attention. It is of considerable importance both because the precise conceptual connection between justice and rights is central to many issues in ethical theory and because of the widespread belief that any duty we may have to provide welfare to the needy is an imperfect duty of charity rather than a perfect duty implied by some moral claim of the needy individual.

A challenge that has received much more attention is the claim that there cannot be any genuine moral rights to welfare because such rights would be inconsistent with other fundamental moral rights. It does not follow, of course, that there cannot be any *legal* rights to welfare benefits, but it would presumably follow that there ought not to be any such rights. Robert Nozick (1974) postulates the existence of certain fundamental rights of the individual that impose side constraints upon morally permissible conduct. He argues that state welfare programs are morally impermissible because they violate the individual's right to property. Such programs can be financed only by compulsory taxation, and such taxation violates the core of the right to property, "the right to determine what shall be done" with one's property. Thus it is unjust to deprive any individual of his or her just holdings, where depriving constitutes a taking without the consent of the right-holder.

Let me mention only the most salient of the items in the vast critical literature. Tony Honore (1977) points out that Nozick's argument against redistribution hinges upon the presupposition that the right to property is absolute, both in the sense that it cannot be overridden by other moral considerations, such as the suffering of the needy individual, and in the sense that it remains unaffected by any changes that may occur between the time of original acquisition and the time of taxation. He articulates a number of conceptions of the right to property that do not embody these presuppositions and argues that some of these seem at least as justified as the conception postulated, but never argued for, by Nozick. Of course, Nozick might try to justify his conception of the right to property. He does suggest that the natural rights of the individual are grounded in what gives meaning to the life of the individual. Samuel Scheffler (1976) has tried to show how this very same ground would justify rights to welfare as readily as it would justify the rights to life, liberty, or property. Theodore Benditt (1982) has discussed with some care the appeal to a state of nature implicit in Nozick's argument. He tries to show that there can be rights of beneficence, rights of a needy individual that some more fortunate individual provide him or her with resources, even in a state of nature. He also argues that when the transition from a state of nature to a state of society brings a collective into existence, the needy dependent individual acquires a right to welfare benefits holding against society. Carl Wellman (1982) notes that to argue that there cannot be any welfare rights because such rights would be inconsistent with the fundamental right to property is to presuppose that genuine rights can never conflict. This assumption seems to be false, and at the very least it stands in need of some justification.

Any detailed critique of these challenges to the reality of rights to welfare would be lengthy and tedious, but perhaps a general retrospective conclusion is in order. Primary welfare rights are subject to several sorts of special challenges, problems they confront as rights to welfare benefits and that many other sorts of rights do not confront. All of the above challenges, and probably some others, are serious; none is either frivolous or easily rebutted. Nevertheless, considerable progress has been made in meeting these challenges. Although the genuineness of welfare rights is not yet thoroughly established, the belief that some such rights exist is philosophically respectable.

Sample Welfare Rights

If there are genuine welfare rights, just what might they be? The least problematic examples are conferred and defined by the law of the land. Their identification and precise definition can on the whole be best left to specialists in welfare law. Carl Wellman (1982) has tried to show how philosophical analysis can be used to clarify the nature and structure of such legal rights. He analyzes the legal right to receive AFDC payments, a primary welfare right, and the legal right to a welfare hearing, a secondary welfare right, in terms of Hohfeld's fundamental legal conceptions.

Our federal-state welfare system is primarily categorical in nature. This is to say that the legal rights to welfare created by the Social Security Act, together with all amendments and relevant court decisions, are all welfare rights possessed by specified categories of individuals, such as members of families with dependent children, the aged, or the permanently disabled. It does not confer any general right to welfare, any right to receive welfare benefits any member of the society possesses simply by virtue of being in need. Frank Michelman (1973) has argued for the existence of just such a general right to welfare on the basis of Rawls's principles of justice. What is philosophically interesting about his argument is that he argues not merely that there ought to be such a welfare right, but that it actually exists implicit in our legal system.

The existence of ethical welfare rights is more controversial and their definition of more obvious philosophical interest. Although many such rights have been asserted or denied in the literature, to my knowledge only a few have received extensive discussion. Let me here merely refer in passing to the right to subsistence analyzed by Henry Shue (1980), the right to beneficence defended by Theodore Benditt (1982), and the right to well-being argued for by Gregory Vlastos (1962) and Alan Gewirth (1981). It is not that I belittle the practical importance or theoretical interest of any of these ethical rights. I pass over them quickly because they seem to be not so much welfare rights in the narrow and strict sense of that term as they are more fundamental rights from which specific rights to welfare benefits might well be derived.

William Aiken (1977) defends the existence of and defines the content of the right to be saved from starvation. This right is possessed by any individual who is in danger of starvation as a result of the deprivation of nourishing food or the resources to obtain such food and who has not voluntarily placed him or herself in the condition of deprivation. It holds against all other persons who are aware of the sufferer's condition of need, have the means to remedy his or her condition, and can do so without reducing themselves to a position of equivalent or greater need. The duty it imposes upon such second parties is to supply goods and services sufficient to save the needy individual from starvation.

James Nickel (1978-79) affirms the existence of a human right to employment. This is a right that every individual possesses just by virtue of being human, and it holds primarily against the government. It imposes upon the government the correlative duty of either being the primary supplier of jobs or of being the employer of last resort supplying jobs to those unable to find employment in the private sector. He raises, but does not answer, the very relevant questions of who is entitled to claim a job, what kinds of jobs must be made available, and where the jobs must be located.

Carl Wellman (1982) analyzes the ethical right to social security in terms of ethical analogues of Hohfeld's fundamental legal conceptions. At its center stands the ethical claim of the individual against his or her state to be provided with a substitute livelihood in the event that he or she lacks the means of sustaining life because of circumstances beyond his or her control. Around this central core stand a number of associated ethical elements that, if respected, confer autonomy concerning the enjoyment of this core claim upon the right-holder. He also advances similar analyses of the right to a fair share and the right to equitable welfare treatment. Obviously much work remains to be done in defining both legal and ethical welfare rights in a philosophically satisfactory manner—that is, in a manner that will reveal their precise content clearly and will display the general nature of such rights perspicuously.

The Justification of Legal Welfare Rights

Although arguments to show that rights to welfare ought or ought not to exist in our legal system abound in the literature, philosophical discussion of the nature of such arguments is rare. This may be because it is generally assumed that such arguments are relatively unproblematic, but this is surely not so. Probably the most systematic treatment of this subject is given by Carl Wellman (1982). He suggests that such rights can be justified in three ways: by appeals to utility, to justice, or to some presupposed ethical right. The most obvious sort of argument tries to show that the legal rules conferring some welfare right are more useful than any available alternative social arrangement. Although Wellman warns of complications in this sort of argument too often ignored, he defends it on principle. David Lyons (1980) argues, however, that contrary to general opinion, no utilitarian justification can explain the moral force of institutional rights, such as the legal rights to welfare benefits. Another sort of justification appeals to justice, either by arguing that welfare rights are an essential means to achieving a just economic distribution in the society or by arguing that legal welfare rights are necessary to prevent the unjust treatment of individuals by state welfare agencies.

Finally, one can justify the creation and maintenance of some legal welfare right by appealing to some ethical right, such as the right to social security or the right to a fair share. It is interesting to notice that one might also justify in these same ways a conclusion that welfare rights ought not to exist in our legal system. Thus Friedrich Hayek (1960) argues that creating rights to welfare benefits has tremendous disutility in various ways, and Robert Nozick argues that legal welfare rights are unjustified because they violate fundamental moral rights to property and freedom. This entire subject deserves much more attention than it has received to date.

The Grounds of Moral Rights to Welfare

Philosophers have spent much more time and energy discussing the possible grounds of moral rights to welfare benefits. William Aiken (1977), for example, has grounded the welfare right to be saved from starvation upon a more general right to be saved from preventable death because of deprivation. This sort of argument—the attempt to ground some specific right to welfare upon some more general fundamental right—is very common. Its main strength and weakness appear clearly in Aiken's version. If one grants the fundamental right presupposed by the argument, then the conclusion follows fairly easily, at least if the content of the presupposed right is as closely related to that of the inferred welfare right as it is in Aiken's argument. But what reason is there to grant the existence of the presupposed right? Aiken suggests that this is a need-right, but he fails to explain precisely how any individual right can be grounded in human need. Thus, this sort of argument seems to do little more than postpone the search for the ultimate grounds of rights.

Still, something may be gained by this, for it may show us how rights to welfare benefits fit into a more general theory of rights. Both Gregory Vlastos (1962) and Alan Gewirth (1981) ground moral rights to specific welfare benefits upon a fundamental human right to well-being. They differ, however, in the way in which they try to establish the existence of this fundamental right. Vlastos argues from the equal worth of well-being to every human being, while Gewirth argues dialectically from the necessary conditions of human action.

Hugo Bedau (1968) hints that some rights to welfare might be based upon the right to life. James Sterba (1981) develops this suggestion. If the right to life is interpreted as a positive right—as a right to receive those goods and resources necessary for sustaining one's life—then it will ground positive welfare rights, moral rights to be provided with welfare benefits adequate to meet one's basic needs. If, on the other hand, the right to life is taken to be merely a negative, a right not to be caused to die, it will imply negative welfare rights, rights not to be interfered with in one's attempt to obtain (even by stealing if necessary) the means to sustain one's own life. Carl Wellman (1982) has tried to show that welfare rights cannot be grounded on the more fundamental right to life.

Wellman appeals to two very different rights to establish the existence of primary moral rights to welfare. He derives a moral right to social security from a more fundamental right to protection by society. Since the right to protection is a civic right, a right one possesses as a member of a society, he concludes that the right to social security is a civic right rather than a human right. He also grounds a civic right to a fair share upon the right of an individual to a remedy by the wrongdoer for any wrongful harm done to him or her. One way he does this is to argue that society has wrongfully harmed the impoverished individual by violating his or her right not to be unjustly impoverished. Another way he does this, in order to avoid the assumption that there is any moral right not to be unjustly impoverished, is to argue that such impoverishment is arbitrary and therefore unjust. The crux of the argument is to show that society owes welfare benefits to the needy individual because society is responsible for his or her plight. Theodore Benditt (1982) develops a similar line of argument, although it is not clear that he takes his argument to hinge on some presupposed right.

Henry Shue (1980) grounds the moral right to subsistence not upon one specific right, but upon moral rights in general. He argues that the right to subsistence is a basic right; that is, a right the enjoyment of which is a necessary condition of the enjoyment of any other right. Therefore, if the individual human being has any moral rights at all, he or she must have a moral right to subsistence.

Although it is often asserted that moral welfare rights are ultimately grounded on something more fundamental than other rights, philosophers have seldom explained in any detail just how this might be so. For example, it is often said that rights to welfare benefits are grounded on basic human needs. But precisely how does the existence of a human need imply any right to that which is needed? James Nickel (1978-79) relates needs to rights *via* a consideration of interests. Since rights have a normative strength, suggested by Ronald Dworkin's slogan that rights are trumps, only the most important interests could ground rights; and since human rights are universal, only interests common to all human beings could ground a human right. The individual's interest in the satisfaction of his or her basic needs meets both tests. Hence it can ground human rights to the satisfaction of these needs. Stanley Benn (1978) denies that one can ground human rights directly upon human needs, even upon basic needs. But once a society adopts some program for the distribution of resources to meet the basic needs of some individuals, one can ground a human right of every member of the society to the satisfaction of his or her basic needs upon those needs together with the moral right to equal consideration. Joel Feinberg (1970 and 1973) holds that human needs ground claims to the resources necessary to fulfill those needs. His argument seems to hinge upon the definition of a need, for to say that S needs X is to say that if S does not have X, then S will be harmed. Assuming that it is morally wrong to harm an individual, then it follows that any second party in a position to meet the need has a moral duty to do so. And correlative to this moral duty to the individual in need is the moral claim-right of the individual. Carl Wellman (1982) has argued that all three lines of argument are inadequate, and Charles Fried (1978) advances more general moral considerations to suggest that needs cannot serve as the grounds of welfare rights.

Jeffrie Murphy (1978) applies the sort of social contract justification John Rawls gives for his two principles of social justice to what he calls "social contract rights." To say that an individual has a social contract right to X is to say that a law guaranteeing X to the individual would be rationally chosen by rational agents in the original position. He then argues that rational agents in the original position would choose laws guaranteeing certain forms of welfare to the individual members of their society. Rodney Peffer (1978) and James Sterba (1981) have also adopted this sort of justification for moral welfare rights.

Retrospective and Prospective Glances

Looking backward over the recent literature dealing with welfare rights, one can discern significant philosophical progress. Philosophers have at last begun to define the specific features of rights to welfare and to mark them off from other species of rights. Although it would be premature to dismiss several of the challenges to welfare rights, considerable progress has been made in meeting these challenges. Some of the considerations central to the justification or counterjustification of legal rights to welfare have been identified, and some plausible grounds for moral welfare rights have been defined.

Looking forward, I would not be audacious enough to predict what will appear in the forthcoming literature. But I will advance a few tentative suggestions as to which lines of investigation seem to me to be most promising. On the whole, new and deeper illumination will result most rapidly by focusing attention not on welfare rights as a class, but on more general or more particular issues. Although the concept of welfare needs to be sharpened, the real difficulties with the concept of a welfare right lie in the obscurity of the more general concept of a right of any kind. Again, fundamental insight into the grounds of welfare rights depends upon a broader understanding of the grounds of rights in general, especially of moral rights. On the other hand, the debate about the existence of welfare rights might profitably move to a more particular level. Instead of trying to prove that there are rights of this sort or that there can be no such rights at all, it would be well to define this or that sample right to welfare with some precision and then consider the reasons for asserting or denying its existence. If grounds for one or two such rights can be identified, then it will be clear that there are welfare rights and the identification of just which alleged rights to welfare are genuine can continue. If none of the more promising candidates turns out to be genuine, there will be solid reason to doubt the existence of any rights of this sort. Moreover, in the process of defining particular welfare rights and seeking their grounds, one will discover a good deal about the nature and grounds of such rights in general. Without an examination of particular instances of such rights, the debate may well prove to be indecisive because neither party really understands fully enough what the debate is all about. So on to the exciting work ahead.

Bibliography

Aiken, William (1977). "The Right to Be Saved from Starvation." In William Aiken and Hugh LaFollette, eds., *World Hunger and Moral Obligation*, pp. 85-102. Englewood Cliffs N.J.: Prentice-Hall.

Bedau, Hugo (1968). "The Right to Life." *The Monist* 52: 550-72.

Benditt, Theodore M. (1982). *Rights*. Totowa, N.J.: Rowman and Littlefield.

Benn, Stanley (1978). "Human Rights—For Whom and For What?" In Eugene Kamenka and Alice Erh-Soon Tay, eds., *Human Rights*, pp. 59-73. London: Edward Arnold:

Cranston, Maurice (1967). "Human Rights, Real and Supposed." In D. D. Raphael, ed., *Political Theory and the Rights of Man*, pp. 43-53. Bloomington and London: Indiana University Press.

Feinberg, Joel (1970). "The Nature and Value of Rights." *Journal of Value Inquiry* 4: 243-57.

Fried, Charles (1978). *Right and Wrong*. Cambridge, Mass. and London: Harvard University Press.

Gewirth, Alan (1981). "The Basis and Content of Human Rights." In J. Roland Pennock and John W. Chapman, eds., *Human Rights* (Nomos XXIII), pp. 119-47. New York and London: New York University Press.

Golding, Martin P. (1978). "The Concept of Rights: A Historical Sketch." In E. and B. Bandman, eds., *Bioethics and Human Rights*, pp. 44-50. Boston: Little Brown & Co.
——— (1968). "Towards a Theory of Human Rights." *The Monist* 52: 521-49.
Hart, H. L. A. (1973). "Bentham on Legal Rights." In A. W. B. Simpson, ed., *Oxford Essays in Jurisprudence*, 2d series, pp. 171-201. Oxford: Clarendon Press.
Hayek, Friedrich (1960). *The Constitution of Liberty.* Chicago: Regnery.
Honor, Tony (1977). "Property, Title and Redistribution." In Carl Wellman, ed., *Equality and Freedom: Past, Present and Future*, pp. 107-15. Wiesbaden: Franz Steiner.
Lyons, David (1978). "Mill's Theory of Justice." in Alvin I. Goldman and Jaegwon Kim, eds., *Values and Morals*, pp. 1-20. Dordrecht, Holland: D. Reidel.
——— (1980). "Utility as a Possible Ground of Rights." *Nous* 14: 17-28.
MacCormick, Neil (1976). "Children's Rights: A Test-Case for Theories of Right." *ARSP* 62: 305-16.
——— (1977). "Rights in Legislation." In P. M. S. Hacker and J. Raz, eds., *Law, Morality and Society*, pp. 189-209. Oxford: Clarendon Press.
Martin, Rex, and Nickel, James W. (1980). "Recent Work on the Concept of Rights." *American Philosophical Quarterly* 17: 165-80.
McCloskey, H. J. (1965). "Rights." *Philosophical Quarterly* 15: 115-27.
Michelman, Frank I. (1973). "Constitutional Welfare Rights and *A Theory of Justice.*" *University of Pennsylvania Law Review* 121: 962-1019.
Murphy, Jeffrie G. (1978). "Rights and Borderline Cases." *Arizona Law Review* 19: 228-41.
Nelson, William N. (1974). "Special Rights, General Rights, and Social Justice." *Philosophy and Public Affairs* 3: 410-30.
Nickel, James W. (1982). "Are Human Rights Utopian?" *Philosophy and Public Affairs* 11: 246-64.
——— (1978-79). "Is There a Human Right to Employment?" *Philosophical Forum* 10: 149-69.
Nozick, Robert (1974). *Anarchy, State and Utopia.* New York: Basic Books.
Peffer, Rodney (1978). "A Defense of Rights to Well-Being." *Philosophy and Public Affairs* 8: 65-87.
Raphael, D. D. (1967a). "Human Rights, Old and New." In D. D. Raphael, ed., *Political Theory and the Rights of Man*, pp. 54-67. Bloomington and London: Indiana University Press.
——— (1967b). "The Rights of Man and the Rights of the Citizen." In D. D. Raphael, ed., *Political Theory and the Rights of Man*, pp. 101-18. Bloomington and London: Indiana University Press.
Scheffler, Samuel (1976). "Natural Rights, Equality, and the Minimal State." *Canadian Journal of Philosophy* 6: 59-76.
Shue, Henry (1980). *Basic Rights.* Princeton: Princeton University Press.
——— ( ). "Rights in the Light of Duties." In Peter G. Brown and Douglas MacLean, eds., *Human Rights and U.S. Foreign Policy*, pp. 65-81. Lexington, Mass.: Lexington Books.
Sterba, James P. (1981). "The Welfare Rights of Distant Peoples and Future Generations: Moral Side-Constraints on Social Policy." *Social Theory and Practice* 7: 99-119.
Vlastos, Gregory (1962). "Justice and Equality." In Richard B. Brandt, ed., *Social Justice*, pp. 31-72. Englewood Cliffs, N.J.: Prentice-Hall.
Watson, David (1977). "Welfare Rights and Human Rights." *Journal of Social Policy* 6: 31-46.
Wellman, Carl (1981). "Taking Economic Rights Seriously." In *Memoria del X Congreso Mundial Ordinario de Filosofia del Derecho y Filosofia Social*, pp. 73-85. Mexico City: Universidad Nacional Autonoma de Mexico.
——— (1982). *Welfare Rights.* Totowa, N.J.: Rowman and Littlefield.

Notes on the Contributors

TIMO AIRAKSINEN received his doctorate from the University of Turku, Finland, in 1975. He is a professor of philosophy (ethics and social theory) at the University of Helsinki; he has held numerous foreign research scholarships. He is writing a book on the moral aspects of coercion and authority. His other research interests include analytic epistemology and idealist metaphysics. Some of his papers have appeared in *American Philosophical Quarterly, Dialectics and Humanism, Philosophia, Philosophy and Phenomenological Research*, and *Synthèse*.

JUNE AXINN is a professor at the University of Pennsylvania School of Social Work and book review editor of the journal *Administration in Social Work*. She is the co-author of *Social Welfare: A History of the American Response to Need* (2d edition, Longman, 1982) and has written on family policy, social security, and a wide variety of other social-welfare topics. Her current research work is in the economics of aging and social policy issues affecting older women.

LAWRENCE BECKER received his Ph.D. from the University of Chicago and is currently a professor of philosophy at Hollins College, where he has taught since 1965. In 1971-72 Becker studied at Oxford University; in 1975-76 he was a Visiting Fellow in Philosophy at Harvard University; and in 1983-84 he was a Fellow at the Center for Advanced Study in the Behavioral Sciences (Stanford). Becker is the author of *On Justifying Moral Judgments* (1973), *Property Rights* (1977), co-editor (with Kenneth Kipnis) of *Property: Cases, Concepts and Critiques* (1983), and the author of numerous journal articles.

THEODORE M. BENDITT is professor and chairman in the Department of Philosophy at the University of Alabama in Birmingham. He has written articles in the areas of moral, social and political, and legal philosophy. Recently he has published two books: *Law as Rule and Principle* (Stanford University Press, 1978) and *Rights* (Rowman and Littlefield, 1982). He is currently working on an article on entrapment and a bibliographical essay on recent literature on rights.

THOMAS DONALDSON is an associate professor of philosophy at Loyola University of Chicago, where he teaches ethics. He has written widely in the area of business and professional ethics. His publications include three books in the area: *Corporations and Morality (1982); Ethical*

Issues in Business (1979), co-edited with Patricia Werhane; and *Case Studies in Business Ethics* (forthcoming). He is a founding member and past president of the Society for Business Ethics and is a member of the editorial board for the *Journal of Business Ethics*.

ALAN GEWIRTH is the Edward Carson Waller Distinguished Service professor of philosophy at the University of Chicago. He is a past president of the American Philosophical Association and current president of the American Society for Political and Legal Philosophy. His books include *Reason and Morality, Human Rights: Essays on Justification and Applications*, and *Marsilius of Padua and Medieval Political Philosophy*. A volume of critical essays on his ethical theory, with his replies (*Gewirth's Ethical Rationalism*, edited Edward Regis, Jr.) was published in 1984.

CAROL GOULD is Associate Professor of Philosophy at Stevens Institute of Technology. She is the author of *Marx's Social Ontology: Individuality and Community in Marx's Theory of Social Reality* (MIT Press, 1978), and the editor of two collections of essays on feminism and philosophy. She has published several articles in political philosophy, including "Contemporary Legal Conceptions of Property and their Implications for Democracy" (*Journal of Philosophy*, 1980) and "Socialism and Democracy" (*Praxis International*, 1981). She is currently completing a book on democratic theory called *The New Democracy: From Politics to Participation*.

MARILYN E. GWALTNEY is an assistant professor of philosophy at the Buffalo Center of Empire State College, the nontraditional college of The State University of New York. She has written study guides for Thiroux's *Ethics: Theory and Practice*, and *Art and Human Values* by Rader and Jessup for her independent-study students. Her most recent focus has been applied ethics and economic justice.

VIRGINIA HELD is a professor of philosophy at the City University of New York, Graduate School and Hunter College. She is the author of *Rights and Goods: Ethical Inquiry and Social Change* (New York: Free Press, forthcoming) and of *The Public Interest and Individual Interests* (1970). She is the editor of *Property, Profits, and Economic Justice* (1980) and co-editor of *Philosophy and Political Action* (1972) and *Philosophy, Morality, and International Affairs* (1974). She has contributed to *Ethics, The Journal of Philosophy, Political Theory, Signs*, and many other journals.

KENNETH KIPNIS is associate professor of philosophy at the University of Hawaii at Manoa. He serves on the Board of Directors of the University of Hawaii Professional Assembly, a public-sector faculty labor union, and chairs the Publications Committee of AMINTAPHIL. He was born in New York City and has received degrees in philosophy from Reed College, the University of Chicago, and Brandeis University. He is editor of *Philosophical Issues in Law: Cases and Materials* (Prentice-Hall, 1977) and co-editor, with Lawrence C. Becker, of *Property: Cases, Concepts, Critiques* (Prentice-Hall, 1984). He has published articles on professional ethics, legal philosophy, and medical ethics and is currently completing a book on legal ethics.

BRUCE M. LANDESMAN is an associate professor of philosophy at the University of Utah. His major interests are political philosophy and professional and business ethics. His publications include "The Obligation to Obey the Law," *Social Theory and Practice* 2(1972); "Egalitarianism", *Canadian Journal of Philosophy* 13 (1983); and "The Lawyer-Client Relationship," in David Luban, ed., *The Good Lawyer* (forthcoming). He is at work on a book on justice and equality.

BURTON LEISER is presently the Edward J. Mortola professor of Philosophy at Pace University in New York City. He holds degrees from the University of Chicago (A.B.), Yeshiva University (M.H.L.), Drake University (J.D.), and Brown University (Ph.D.), and is a member of the Iowa Bar. His publications which range over a wide variety of fields from philosophy and law to religion and archaeology, include *Liberty, Justice, and Morals* (Macmillan, 1972, 1978, 1985), *Values in Conflict* (Macmillan, 1981), and *Custom, Law, and Morality* (Doubleday Anchor, 1969).

REX MARTIN, a professor of philosophy at the University of Kansas in Lawrence, received his Ph.D. in philosophy from Columbia. He also studied at New College and at the University of Edinburgh for a year under a grant from the Society for Religion in Higher Education. He has held a Fulbright Research Fellowship at the University of Helsinki and research fellowships from the National Endowment for the Humanities and the Rockefeller Foundation. He has held visiting appointments at Mount Vernon College (Washington, D.C.) and the University of Auckland (New Zealand) and was a visiting member of the Institute for Advance Study, Princeton (Spring 1984). He serves as Executive Director of the American Section of the International Association for Philosophy of Law and Social Philosophy. Martin's major interests are political and legal philosophy (in particular, rights), philosophy of the social sciences, and philosophy of history. He is the author of *Historical Explanation: Re-enactment and Practical Inference* (Ithaca, New York: Cornell University Press, 1977).

JOHN McCALL is an assistant professor of philosophy at St. Joseph's University in Philadelphia; he taught previously at Iowa State University. Dr. McCall has concentrated his teaching and research on normative ethics, particularly on issues related to social and political philosophy. He has lectured and written papers on abortion, affirmative action, economic justice, and employee rights. He is the co-author and co-editor of a forthcoming anthology of business ethics.

DIANA T. MEYERS received her Ph.D. in philosophy from the City University of New York Graduate Center. She teaches moral and political philosophy and feminist theory at Cornell University. She is the author of *Inalienable Rights: A Defense* (Columbia University Press, Spring 1985), and she is co-editing *Women and Moral Theory* (Rowman and Allenheld, forthcoming). She is currently working on a book about personal autonomy, socialization, and feminist theory.

ALASTAIR M. MACLEOD is a professor of philosophy at Queen's University, Ontario, and is the author of Paul Tillich (London: Allan & Unwin, 1973). His more recent publications include "Rawls's Theory of Justice," "Rule-Utilitarianism in Hume," and "Equality of Opportunity." His two-part contribution to a symposium on Justice and the Market is to appear in a forthcoming issue of the *Canadian Journal of Philosophy*. He is currently writing a book on principles of distributive justice and a collection of papers on ethics and business for Oxford University Press.

WILLIAM NELSON is an associate professor of philosophy at the University of Houston, and he has held a visiting appointment at the University of Illinois, Urbana. His publications include *On Justifying Democracy* (Routledge and Kegan Paul, 1980) and several articles on moral and political philosophy. He is currently working on problems about economic justice and about the nature and foundations of social morality.

JAMES W. NICKEL is director of the Center for the Study of Values and Social Policy and professor of philosophy at the University of Colorado, Boulder. He has taught at Wichita State University and at the University of California, Berkeley. He has held research fellowships from the National Endowment for the Humanities, the American Council of Learned Societies, the National Humanities Center, and the Rockefeller Foundation. Nickel has published essays in philosophy and law journals on issues in ethical theory, philosophy of law, and international human rights. He is currently working on a book entitled *Making Sense of Human Rights*.

CARL WELLMAN is professor of philosophy at Washington University in Saint Louis. His more important publications include *The Language of Ethics, Challenge and Response*, and *Welfare Rights*. This last book is a philosophical examination of the Aid to Families with Dependent Children Program in terms of the nature of the legal rights it incorporates, the arguments for and against institutionalizing such welfare rights, and the moral rights to which one might appeal in criticizing a public welfare program. He is currently working out a model of rights general enough to interpret and illuminate all species of legal rights, nonlegal institutional rights and moral rights.